What people are say

The Creation of Self

Many old-school neuroscientists and philosophers of mind, having retreated to the keep of non-reductive physicalism, seem oblivious to the fact that their materialist position has been overrun both by the evidence, and by panpsychist, dualist, and idealist armies. In this regard, apart from Richard Swinburne, no one has been more vigorous in defending the consistency of emergent-creationist dualism with neuroscience, and the necessity of an immaterial mind to a proper understanding of human personhood, than Joshua Farris. With respect to religious issues, Farris is the leader. Those who think that substance dualism is untenable display their doxastic inertia and ignore Farris's work at their peril.

Bruce Gordon, Associate Professor of History and Philosophy of Science, Houston Baptist University

Farris has established himself as a world leading expert on substance dualism by offering a viable creationist and emergentist view of the soul, which opens up conceptual space for a traditionalist view that is minimally compatible with scientific findings on humans. His work in this area is consistently thorough, innovative, and widely discussed.

Joanna Leidenhag, Lecturer in Theology and the Liberal Arts, University of Leeds

This book is about the Particularity of Persons problem. Sounds sophisticated, right? No doubt, it is. And yet, it's a problem that resonates with our most common intuitions about ourselves. Have you ever thought: *I* am not merely a body. *I* am not merely the properties that describe me. *I* am not repeatable. *I* am not manufacturable. Why is that, you ask? Simply put, *I* am a *soul*.

It is this common intuition that Farris's *The Creation of Self* so sophisticatedly defends.

S. Mark Hamilton, NPI Project Manager, SPM Oil & Gas, A Caterpillar Company

Josh Farris is a leading figure in the field of theological anthropology, and in this volume he has given us a broadly accessible presentation of his academic research on this vital subject. He forthrightly advocates a full-blooded dualist view of human persons while critiquing materialism, and emergentism along the way. More boldly still, he contends that theism is entailed by consciousness, and indeed that souls are created directly by God. This volume is as provocative as it is informative, and represents popular theology at its best.

Jerry L. Walls, Professor of Philosophy, Houston Baptist University

Joshua Farris is a leading defender of a substance dualist account of the human person. In *The Creation of Self*, Farris advances the first full-length defense of a rather unpopular, yet formidable, Cartesian account of the Self that requires an even more unpopular view—that humans are created directly by a supernatural being, someone like the Christian God. He criticizes materialism, emergentisms, and panpsychism in the context of popular scientific discussions. This is an extremely important work for philosophers, theologians, and mainstream intellectuals. Highly recommended!

Benedikt Paul Goecke, Professor of Philosophy, University of Bochum

Joshua Farris's work on personhood is a much-needed contribution to the conversation regarding the uniqueness of individuals. In a world motivated by materialism and naturalism, he proposes a model that shows how each person, as a soul, is more than merely the chemicals in his or her physical body. Taking a neo-Cartesian approach, he uses the resources of modernity but moves beyond the limitations of rationalism to show how the contemporary audience can make space for the spiritual and religious concerning who we are as people. His work will have many implications regarding our understanding of the person in fields such as medicine, technology, and societal justice.

Dr. Page Brooks, Professor of Theology, SUM Bible College and Seminary; Missionary Bishop, Missio Mosaic: A Missional Society

Joshua Farris, one of today's leading thinkers in the philosophy of the mind, has given us a thorough-going rationale for the soul, using the body/soul dualism of René Descartes as a framework. "I am not just my body" is an apologia for the soul, the mind, of man. Matter cannot give rise to consciousness; only God can bestow this. There is an evangelistic aspect to this book, as a witness to the predominantly materialistic community of scholars and the growing trend toward physicalism. These trends are depersonalizing and dehumanizing. Although science can be a tool in the study of the soul, it must take its place in the tool box with theology, philosophy, morality, psychology, the humanities and the tradition of Augustine, Anselm and Aquinas, because matter cannot give rise to consciousness. So the soul is "the carrier of personal identity and particularity," and everything that makes us unique, such that each soul contributes something novel to the world, and survives it after death. Citing his colleagues, Farris examines with them the nature of the soul, its relation to the body, and the question of where souls come from, with the conclusion that souls are the special creation of God. The argument mounted in this thought-provoking book is for what it means to be a self, a subject of conscious experience, possessed of what preserves *personhood*, and the *thisness* that each of us represents. A lyrical metaphor may usefully shed light on the soul: the body is a candle, the brain is a wick, and the flame is the soul, lit by the Holy Spirit. **Rt. Rev. Paul C. Hewett**, Bishop of the Diocese of the Holy Cross

Other titles by this Author

The Soul of Theological Anthropology: A Cartesian Exploration (2016)
ISBN: 978-0367339999

Idealism and Christian Theology: Idealism and Christianity (2016)
ISBN: 978-1501335853

The Ashgate Research Companion to Theological Anthropology (2017)
ISBN: 978-1138051560

Christian Physicalism? Philosophical Theological Criticisms (2018)
ISBN: 978-1498549233

Being Saved (2018) ISBN: 978-0334054955

An Introduction and Transcription, *New England Dogmatics: A Systematic Collection of Questions and Answers by Maltby Gelston* (2019)
ISBN: 978-1610979313

An Introduction to Theological Anthropology: Humans, Both Creaturely and Divine (2020) ISBN: 978-1540962164

Routledge Handbook to Idealism and Immaterialism (2021)
ISBN: 978-1138502819

The Origin of the Soul: A Conversation (forthcoming 2022) ISBN N/A

God and the Soul ISBN N/A

Foundations in Theology & Science ISBN N/A

God and Nature (Natural Theology) ISBN N/A

Science-Engaged Christian Theology ISBN N/A

The Creation
of Self

A Case for the Soul

The Creation of Self

A Case for the Soul

Joshua Farris

**IFF
BOOKS**

Winchester, UK
Washington, USA

JOHN HUNT PUBLISHING

First published by iff Books, 2023
iff Books is an imprint of John Hunt Publishing Ltd., No. 3 East Street, Alresford,
Hampshire SO24 9EE, UK
office@jhpbooks.com
www.johnhuntpublishing.com
www.iff-books.com

For distributor details and how to order please visit the 'Ordering' section on our website.

ISBN: 978 1 80341 086 9
978 1 80341 087 6 (ebook)
Library of Congress Control Number: 2021949891

A CIP catalogue record for this book is available from the British Library.

Design: Stuart Davies

UK: Printed and bound by CPI Group (UK) Ltd, Croydon, CR0 4YY
Printed in North America by CPI GPS partners

We operate a distinctive and ethical publishing philosophy in
all areas of our business, from our global network of authors to
production and worldwide distribution.

Contents

Foreword   1

Preface   4

Introduction: Souls in Contemporary Discourse   7

Part I: Are we souls or bodies?   21

Chapter 1: Initial Reasons favoring the Soul-Concept   23
Chapter 2: Religious and Philosophical Reasons for
    the Soul   44
Chapter 3: Bodies and Souls: Why we matter   53
Chapter 4: Why neo-Cartesian Selves?   61

Part II: Where do selves come from?   85

Chapter 5: Origins of the Self, A Religious and
    Contemporary Problem   87

Part III: Emergent-Selves   103

Chapter 6: A Survey of Materialism, Emergentism, and
    Panpsychism   105
Chapter 7: Emergent-Selves: Created or Magical,
    A Survey of Religious Concerns with Emergentism 115
Chapter 8: Why Selves are Probably Not Generated:
    An Initial Objection to Emergent-Selves (or Mere
    Emergent Dualism)   135
Chapter 9: Do Selves Exist? Perfect Duplicates, A Problem
    for Emergent-Selves and Panpsychism   163
Chapter 10: Why we are Not Animals: Where Aristotle
    and Thomas went Wrong   186

Part IV: Creationist-Selves   **207**

Chapter 11: Why Creation of the Self is a Better Solution?   209
Chapter 12: Constructive Creationist Solutions   223
Conclusions: The Anti-Scientific Worry   230
Afterword   236
Endnotes   241
Index   306

For Matthew Levering, a dedicated and passionate
defender of the soul.

Acknowledgements

I must thank several people who along the way have provided invaluable feedback or invigorating conversations that have aided me in the process of completing my thoughts with respect to *The Creation of Self*. The list of acknowledgements, and thanks, includes: Andrew Hollingsworth, Bruce Gordon, William Hasker, Charles Taliaferro, Jon Loose, Angus Menuge, Benedikt Paul Goecke, Jonathan Chan, Jordan Wessling, J.T. Turner, Aaron Murphy, Christophe Schwoebel, Timothy Kleiser, Sarah Lane Ritchie, Jenna Farris, Jerry L. Walls, and Matthew Levering.

Foreword

Few philosophers are as bold in the same way as Joshua Farris. There are, of course, philosophers like Plotinus or Kant and Hegel or the British Idealists who will boldly develop extraordinarily complex systems which leave behind a common-sense understanding of ourselves and the world. Kant, famously, disparaged common sense, and Bertrand Russell scolded those that adhere to common sense as entrapped in one's current age and its prejudices. Farris, on the other hand, invites us to philosophically investigate our common experience of ourselves. When we do, we discover the (virtually) indisputable realization of our being concrete, particular, mental subjects. Each of us is uniquely who each of us is, not replaceable by some other, particular subject. In a variety of arguments, Farris boldly offers a Cartesian-theistic perspective that makes sense of our origin, our present reality as conscious subjects, and the possibility of there being life after life for human persons. The result involves common sense paired with philosophical acumen. It is refreshing, too, for Farris's being equally at home engaging secular philosophers as well as Christian philosophers who are strident critics of Cartesian philosophical theology.

Farris's project has important repercussions for ethics, political philosophy, and the general topic of the meaning of life. If he is right, you are not an ensemble of social relations (to use Marx's phrase) or a mode of some greater substance; instead, you are the unique, irreducible person you are because of God's creative power. The British poet, novelist, and social critic Robert Graves (1895-1985) once lamented how philosophers, unlike poets, often deny the uniqueness of human persons.

Philosophy is antipoetic. Philosophize about mankind and you brush aside individual uniqueness, which a poet cannot

1

do without self-damage... Poets know that once heads are counted, each owner of a head loses his personal identity and becomes a number in some government scheme.[1]

In Graves's terms, Farris is on the side of the poets; though I should add that, contra Graves, championing the uniqueness of persons makes his work supremely philosophical *qua* the love of wisdom. His philosophy of mind stands in bold terms against philosophies and political institutions that eviscerate the integrity and dignity of persons. In terms of Graves's contemporary, George Orwell (1903-1950), *The Creation of Self* would have strengthened the resistance to the Thought Police and Big Brother in Orwell's classic, dystopian novel *1984*. Its defense of creationism affirms the radical, sacred nature of each person.

When Roderick Chisholm (1916-1999), the great metaphysician, epistemologist, and all-around contributor to some of the great philosophical topics of the last century, was once asked about the evidence he had for one of his positions; he replied: *the other views*.[2] Namely, Chisholm claimed that his position should be preferred because the rival views were comparatively impoverished or otherwise unpromising. Farris positively presents a forceful, clear case for his position, but in a Chisholmian spirit he is also keenly engaged with the critical evaluation of the current alternatives. In this book you will find an abundance of arguments concerning rival accounts of the self and its origin from secular naturalism to emergentism. Farris's work has the virtue of engaging specialists in philosophy, while also providing an excellent entry point for newcomers to the variety of philosophical and theological issues that currently command so much scholarly attention.

I commend *The Creation of Self* to you as one of the best, current works defending the soul. Farris's philosophy of persons as embodied, responsible agents is a bold defense of what is traditionally identified as the soul in Christian Platonic tradition.

Charles Taliaferro
Spring 2022

Notes

1. Robert Graves, "The Case for Xanthippe" in *The Oxford Book of Essays* edited by John Gross (Oxford: Oxford University Press, 1991), 473.
2. In conversation. Chisholm was my dissertation advisor at Brown University.

Preface

We have all had that unwelcome guest who didn't quite fit in. On the surface, he or she comes off as awkward, bombastic, or just a little larger than life. We have also had those cases where, at times, the unwelcome guest positively surprises us. In many ways, the soul is that unwelcome guest. The ancient belief in the soul is now often disregarded in philosophy, ignored by the sciences, mocked in the social sciences, and treated with a hand-wave in theology as no longer necessary and worth taking seriously. However, that same guest who we found a bit off-putting has and is making a comeback as we reconsider what it means to be human. The soul is making a comeback for several reasons.[1]

The impetus for undermining the belief in the soul is that it is not only an unwelcome guest but a spooky, eerie ghost-like figure that no longer has relevance in a scientifically informed view of the world. In fact, it is commonly held by some scientists concerning ultimate reality that souls are not only irrelevant but spooky holdovers from an ancient era that no longer is motivated by what we know from science and has no evidence in its favor. This naturalist frame as I call it here has made its way into many of the 'respectable' disciplines of study all the way into cultural consciousness. Even worse, its creeping influence holds some force in other areas that still desire to retain something of the ancient view of the cosmos as having some relevance to explaining the world and what we hold dear.

Some of the reasons the soul is coming back into mainstream discussions (it never really left) has something to do with ongoing reports of the afterlife, out of body experiences, and near-death experiences that, if true, require, no demand, some explanation beyond the material world to something like a soul. But, it's not just in the contemporary popular consciousness that we find these discussions.

Philosophers have made the soul-concept 'respectable' again as a live view of persons worth taking seriously. This is particularly true of figures like Howard Robinson, Richard Swinburne, John Foster, David Lund, Charles Taliaferro and many others. David Chalmers who famously articulated a not 'new' (it is really only new in an age where materialism permeates) problem and called it the hard problem of consciousness (i.e., the problem of reconciling phenomenal qualitative experience with physics and biology with their explanatory reference being spatially extended objects that are measured by quantities; consciousness just is not the same as the material, nor is it reducible to it) aided in bringing the soul-concept back into discussions about human persons as a respectable option deserving the attention of philosophers.

In these ways, the notion of consciousness, and relatedly personal identity, has and continues to impact how the sciences and the results of the sciences are considered. One of the crucial questions from biological studies is the question of consciousness. Where did it come from? How did it evolve? Was it naturally selected? Does it adapt? And, does consciousness have any place in biological evolution at all? One of the concerns is whether or not the sciences have much of anything at all to say about consciousness or personal identity and the other is whether the sciences have effectively excluded the soul as explanatorily necessary.

Relatedly, the world of religious studies has been influenced by the sciences and some of the dominating patterns from varying scientific communities to rethink this age-old notion of the soul. Some have advanced a complete rejection of the soul as the center of consciousness, the core of personal identity, and the means by which persons will survive this life. Naturally, in an attempt to retrieve these religious ideas, there has been significant pushback to the attempt of a complete revision of the person as a soul.

In *The Creation of Self*, I address these concerns to the soul by energizing the reasons we should not only believe in the soul-concept, but that we must. While there are other competitors worth engaging as respectable options for consideration, I show the link that these have to their naturalist frame and why the soul traditionally construed is a better option. In fact, it might just turn out that what was once conceived as an unwelcome guest turns out to surprise us as a better option to its naturalist competitors.

Joshua R. Farris, September 20, 2021

Introduction

Souls in Contemporary Discourse

Francis Bacon discusses idols of the mind and "empty and idle fancies," which describe ideas that confuse or distract the mind away from things that do exist by disguising them.[2] These are often attempts to bridge the worlds of religion and science of which Bacon concerns himself. Some things haven't changed. With the rise of materialism dominating the minds of scientists in our contemporary world, there is a tendency to eliminate the mind, as an immaterial substance, to replace it, or to affirm ideas that themselves hide or disguise mental reality. In what follows, my objective in *The Creation of Self* is to engage with materialism's progeny and show that they all suffer from an inability to account for the nature of selves as minds. When we think about a loved one, what we want is *that* loved one. We don't want some fictional person artificially designed by technology that acts like them, looks like them, sounds like them, or has the same gestures as them. We want *them*.[3]

This rather obvious truth is so plain that you might think that there's no need to say it. What we long for is the person. Persons are valuable to us. In fact, persons are most cherished above all other things that we regard as valuable. Sure, there are pets that we love and hold as valuable. We value food, our jobs, our homes, and our cars. We like having things, but if we are honest, it's persons that we prize more highly than anything else in the world.

While no one would actually claim that technology or science could get in the way of that which is most highly cherished, we are seeing and hearing of developments that promise the possibility to accommodate all of our needs and wants through artificial means. The prospect of constructing individuals that we can interact with that appear to be flesh and blood persons is certainly something that is not outside the imaginative social consciousness of contemporary society. As artificial intelligence advances, there is a promise made by some explicitly and others implicitly through media and film that we will one day encounter a conscious person created by technological advancement. While this might seem a bit far-fetched to some it hits at the heart of what we care about most and what is at stake in the science-engaged theological conversations today.

However, I contend through *The Creation of Self* that science or technology could never accommodate that which we cherish the most. More than that, I argue that science and technology, no matter what they promise and what contemporaries are primed to believe, is quite limited in what it can tell us about the nature of personhood. Central to our making sense of personhood is the notion of particularity. Particularity of persons, i.e., what it is that makes persons who they are.

This notion of personhood is closely related to the *modern* emphasis on particularity. Just recall contemporary stories like *Ally McBeal* with the fixation on her identity both public and private. While an emphasis on particularity is, arguably, characteristic of modernity, it is modernity that also gave rise to a set of ideas that is now eclipsing the notion of the particularity in persons.[4]

Along with modernity's emphasis on particularity, there was and is an emphasis on objectivity, control, and certainty through scientific means. We've seen the fruit of this in and through film and classical literature like *Dr. Jekyll and Mr. Hyde* and *Frankenstein*. Just recall their stories of scientists desiring to control the making of humans and become something of God-like figures. It is this overemphasis on the values of objectivity and certainty through the means of science that now characterizes much that occupies not only the minds of contemporary scientists but the social consciousness of contemporary man.

The exacerbated notion of scientific objectivity has spread its tentacles through every domain of academic study and every aspect of our lives. So, what's at stake is the subjectivity of persons. In order to regain the sense of what matters most to us, we need to do a bit of rethinking about what it means to be human not just in the sciences but in the areas of philosophy, theology, and the humanities generally.

It is the objective in what follows to show how it is that we begin to reclaim this important truth about the particularity of persons. In order to preserve this notion of the person, we need to rethink all the disciplines of study, and by extension contemporary culture, in light of the facts that make us who we are.

It is my contention in what follows that we can do this by subverting the narrative that dominates much of the scientific consensus, and which has crept into the humanities. That narrative is one dominated by naturalism (i.e., the view that the world is explained by a closed system of causes; and knowledge is known only through a narrow understanding of empirical science) and materialism (i.e., the view that the world is comprised fundamentally of material particles alone and spirits, ghosts are excluded from the picture of reality).

In brevity, naturalism is the view of the world that finds an explanation for all things in a closed system of causes and effects, triggers and pulleys. Exaggerating these notions has effectively severed the sciences from what is fundamental to the world, namely minds. Minds are central to the explanation of the world. You might know it by another name. The ancients often referred to it as the soul or the spirit.

Souls and spirits point us to realities that transcend nature. They point us, in religious contexts, to a supernatural being— what some call God or the gods. The contention of many

9

throughout history is that minds and their ideas are what explain the world rather than what many today take to be mere meat machines.

In an attempt not only to retrieve this ancient insight and to preserve it from the decaying effects in scientific naturalism, I advance a position that preserves personhood via the soul. A soul as I am using it here is nearly synonymous with a mind or a spirit, but more on that later.

If history and religion have any validity in the conversation at all, then it is clear that most people throughout history have believed in the notion of a soul-concept. In fact, the soul-concept stands at the center of religious belief. And, you might say that it is essential to religious thought. Stewart Goetz and Mark Baker affirm that, "Most people, at most times, in most places, at most ages have believed that human beings have some kind of soul."[5] There is clearly some staying power compelling ongoing belief in the soul.

But if you are paying attention, there is and has been a recent and vocal minority report that prompts a complete revision of the notion that persons are souls. With a near complete trust in what has been given to a deity, some are now placing that same trust in the successes of the sciences. And, there are a select few championing that we, the common man, should be doing just that precisely because of all its success. Francis Crick states: "You, your joys and your sorrows, your memories and your ambitions, your sense of personal identity and free will, are in fact no more than the behavior of a vast assembly of nerve cells and their associated molecules."[6] The philosopher Owen Flanagan in his discussion about the image of persons argues that given the role of science in reconstructing an image "desouling is the primary operation of the scientific image."[7]

While these may represent some of the starkest and most dogmatic strands of thought, there is a common belief that scientists proceed as if the mind is just the brain or a function of the brain or some additional capacity of the brain or something similar. There is the further belief that science aids us in the process of becoming more "objective" in our reasoning about the nature of the mind, and that eventually as our culture evolves and we are conditioned by what the sciences clearly show, we too will become more enlightened about our*selves*. *Salon* writer and cognitive scientist Julien Musolino considers some of the evidence from what he takes to be the scientific consensus and concludes with the following: "The current scientific consensus isn't simply a fad, nor is it fueled by antireligious sentiment (as Baker and Goetz suggest in their book). Instead, scientists have abandoned the soul because reason and evidence—the tools of their trade—compelled them to do so."[8]

However, this is not just the belief of neuroscientists, biologists, and cognitive scientists, but this growing trend away from the belief in the soul made its way into philosophy and theology—domains commonly committed to the validity of the soul-concept. Religious philosopher Nancey Murphy makes the case in *Bodies and Souls or Spirited Bodies* that there is a growing number of correlational data between the brain and mental states that have no need of the soul, as a unique substantial entity with novel powers and properties because the brain accommodates what was once perceived to be powers of the soul.[9] Religious scholar Joel Green has in numerous places argued that neuroscience has shown the irrelevance of the soul, which has forced religious scholars to rethink the soul's significance. Green's most important claim is that historic religious texts (specifically the Christian Bible) have no need for the soul-concept.[10]

What the careful reader will notice is that the growing trend to offload the subjects originally in the provenance of philosophy and religion to science is that there's the perceived belief that there's no longer a need for the soul, and there is a

11

slow and steady erosion of what was once firmly held by all—or, at least, a majority.

There is a burgeoning set of literature within science, psychology, and by extension in philosophy and theology that has pushed back on these trends. The famous psychologist Paul Bloom has argued in numerous places that the belief in the soul (and its attending package belief in the afterlife, God, and morality) is a common-sense belief that finds its initial footing in cognitive science and developmental psychology, at least initially he later disregards this rather common-sense belief.[11] Neuroscientist Mario Beauregard and Denyse O'Leary make several arguments from neuroscience that favor a need for the soul.[12] Notably, there have been several recent philosophical defenses of the soul.[13]

In contemporary culture, while there is evidence that trends away from believing in the spiritual world, the soul-concept still, arguably, has impressive resilience as a belief held by the common man. There are certainly studies that shore up reasons to secure ongoing belief in the soul from out of body experiences, near death experiences, as well as religious experiences of the divine.

With all that is said here, this serves as a context and a background to what I aim to defend. There is a growing, and unhealthy, trend to grant pride of place to a specific and narrowly defined conception of science that has inevitably gone some way in eroding belief in the soul, the spiritual world, and, worse, a cluster of important related values that are central to personhood.

It is this trend toward naturalism, physicalism, and the popularity of emergentism, that I intend to show has less footing than many suppose. I show that personhood via the soul has significant difficulty when we attempt to reconcile it with naturalism, physicalism, and emergentism.

For these reasons and others that I will advance in what

follows, I contend for a version of the soul codified in the philosophy of Descartes and carried along in what is oft called the Cartesian tradition.[14] The core idea advanced by Descartes that seems unavoidable is the notion that what is at the core of personhood is this notion of the soul.[15] The soul is the carrier of personal identity, not the body and not even the body-soul strictly speaking.[16] It is this notion of the soul that I argue we cannot ignore because of the nature of consciousness and the fundamental nature of the subject of *that* consciousness. I take this further by developing a more refined conception of the soul that preserves this notion of particularity—call this a kind of neo-Cartesianism. Neo-Cartesianism retains the core conception developed by Descartes, but I take it a step further in that I argue that there is not simply a soul that we can say little about (beyond saying that it is a thinking, experiencing thing), but that we can supply a sufficient designation to the soul that carries a primitive particularity central to what it means to be a person. Finally, I argue that not only is this notion not preserved in materialism or emergentism, but that it seems to demand a form of theism where souls are direct creations of God.

The basic objection to emergentism that opens up space for creationism is actually quite simple really. Persons are singularities. Biological products are regular, generalizable, and universalizable. Hence, persons are not biological products. But, this shouldn't really surprise us as we think about the utter uniqueness of consciousness in the natural world. Consciousness is unaccounted for by biological processes or merely physical processes. So it is with personal identity. This opens the door for creationism because in the same way that we intuitively, and rightly, assume that some events are brought about by persons (i.e., person-causes), it follows that it is natural for us to assume that persons too are brought about by a person, or persons (i.e., person-causes) rather than products of natural events.

Sounds simple right? Intuitive, even. But, there are some who are calling into question all of our basic intuitions about selves, values, morality, and the world around us. This same group is calling us not only to a healthy skepticism of what some of our intuitions and experiences teach us, but, more extravagant still, to call into question the very nature of intuition and conscious experience altogether. In what follows, I advance reasons why we can't do this and reasons to reject the variant options in favor of the soul. Here's a summary of the argument in *The Creation of Self*.

Part I: Are we souls or bodies?

Part I provides an initial defense of the soul and, specifically, the argument that persons are souls. The following chapters comprise an initial defense for the soul and why the concept still matters today, addressing initial objections/defeaters to the soul-concept (e.g., of a religious, philosophical, and scientific sort), and a more specific case for my brand of neo-Cartesianism. These chapters set the groundwork for a defense of creationist-souls and a critique of the dominating paradigm(s) in science and philosophy — materialism and emergentism.

Chapter 1: Initial Reasons favoring the Soul-Concept

In chapter 1, I set out initial reasons that not only favor the fact that we are souls, but why the concept is at the heart of what we cherish most. Souls, minds, and personhood are central to what we value and they are what some philosophers call 'phenomenological givens.' In other words, the *prima facie* belief is that we are not our bodies, the parts of our bodies, but that we are minds, souls and that which is not strictly speaking quantifiable.

Chapter 2: Religious and Philosophical Reasons for the Soul

Due to influences from naturalism, generally, and emergentism, specifically, there are a growing number of objections of a philosophical and religious sort to the soul. I advance some of the reasons favoring the soul and proceed to address religious considerations that have been laid at the feet of traditionalist defenders of the soul by considering Joel Green's objections from a biblical perspective. Green presumes that the sciences have no need of the soul, but, more provocative still, that religion (through the lens of Judeo-Christianity) has no need of the soul. I assess his argument and show why the soul-concept still holds religious promise and, more, why it has been central to religious thought.

Chapter 3: Bodies and Souls: Why we matter

I expand on some of the considerations in the last two chapters by considering some of recent scientific objections to the soul-concept. By specifically engaging with philosopher and science-engaged theologian Nancey Murphy, I show why her concerns are not only faulty but fallacious and re-engage the soul on the basis of qualitative experience, subjectivity, and first-person perspective as lines that are more hospitably accommodated in the belief that we are souls rather than material beings.

Chapter 4: Why neo-Cartesian Selves?

In the final chapter to part I, I defend a neo-Cartesian view of human persons based on development of the knowledge argument and cognitive access argument. I offer more specific analysis to the relation of soul to body and advance initial reasons for a neo-Cartesian understanding of persons. Toward the end, I advance a more specific analytic analysis of my conception of neo-Cartesianism within a broader psychological tradition that respects what many have called the 'transparency thesis.'

Part II: Where do selves come from?
I survey the relationship between the philosophy of mind and the views on the self's origin.

Chapter 5: Origins of the Self, A Religious and Contemporary Problem
By exploring the varying relationships between the mind and the body, I show the relationship contemporary developments in the philosophy of mind have to an ancient debate on the origin of the soul. Through this exploration, I note some of the challenges and implications for a broader view of reality, and lay the groundwork for more explicit critique to materialism and emergentism.

Part III: Emergent-Selves
Transitioning from a general case for the soul to an exploration of mental/soulish origins, the third part specifically treats the emergentist paradigm by showing its relation to naturalism, physicalism, and advancing a critique of it. The heart problem with emergentism, as it is normally conceived, is its inability to supply a sufficient reason for the existence and origination of persons.

Chapter 6: A Survey of Materialism, Emergentism, and Panpsychism
Thus far some initial definition has been given to materialism and emergentism. Chapter 6 gives a more specific description of materialism and emergentism (i.e., non-reductive physicalism) noting its merits, lineage, and its initial conceptual challenge. Through a conceptual tracing of emergentist options and challenges raised, the present chapter notes the historical

relevance of panpsychism and why it too confronts a similar challenge as emergentism—all of which center around objectivity and subjectivity as well as the problem of generating a person from law-like, generalizable events.

Chapter 7: Emergent-Selves: Created or Magical, A Survey of Religious Concerns with Emergentism

Building on the survey of chapter 6 for emergentism, I explore two of the most sophisticated emergentist options in the philosophical literature (e.g., Timothy O'Connor and William Hasker), and note some of their philosophical and religious problems as a pointer to more specific objections that will follow. One of the highlights of the chapter is that if one assumes a hierarchical ontology of the world, then it is not only odd but explanatorily lacking to suggest that a higher-order local ontological event would come from that which it is not (hence the original problem of creation ex-nihilo). In keeping with Timothy O'Connor's concern, emergent dualism requires a form of creationism (unless of course some version of panpsychism is the underlying ontology), but even then I suggest it still presumes a form of creationism, i.e., material creation out of nothing. The advantage to emergent dualism over O'Connor's emergent individualism, or emergent materialism as I call it, is that emergent dualism supplies a thisness to the respective mental items, properties, and powers. Unfortunately, emergent dualism demands more than this type of thisness to explain mental reality.

Chapter 8: Why Selves are Probably Not Generated: An Initial Objection to Emergent-Selves (or Mere Emergent Dualism)

Expanding on the problem from generalizable events to actual persons that require a unique kind of thisness, I develop an initial objection to emergent dualism and show that the generalizable process within biological evolution is insufficient to supply a rationale for persons as souls. In other words, a broadly naturalist frame (or neo-Darwinian frame) or what I call a kind of pseudo-naturalism is the problem. This is suggestive that something like creationism is a better option.

Chapter 9: Do Selves Exist? Perfect Duplicates, A Problem for Emergent-Selves and Panpsychism

Drawing on some of the insights of chapter 8, the present chapter expands the argument more clearly by arguing for two claims. First, a specific kind of thisness underlies and explains our first-person consciousness without which we would have an insufficient designator for persons. Second, without this sufficient designator that is rooted in a subject primitive particularity, we run into the problem of perfect duplicates. The obvious ensuing challenge is that there would be no explanation for distinguishing duplicate persons with all the same properties of the body, memory etc. And, however un-intuitive it may be, the possibility for bringing about perfect duplicates in a science lab (using preexisting material of course) would be the result if something like emergentism with its naturalist frame. Most provocatively, this argument leads to the conclusion that emergentism simply lacks any reason to believe that there are persons ontologically grounded or to the possible elimination of persons without a ground in something like a Divine creationism of souls.

Chapter 10: Why we are Not Animals: Where Aristotle and Thomas went Wrong

Coming back around to a couple of retooled ancient views that have similarities to emergentism, I articulate problems for them that are similar to their emergentism cousins. Call these ancient views Aristotelian and Thomist. However, they have been retooled or updated with contemporary considerations in philosophy and science, so it is best to refer to these as neo-Aristotelian and neo-Thomist in that they preserve the essential ideas from Aristotle and Thomas Aquinas. However, they are also versions of emergentism and it is through the lens of personal origination and personal survival that we can see more clearly why they are problematic.

Part IV: Creationist-Selves

The final part of *The Creation of Self* advances a specific case for Divine creationism of souls or selves.

Chapter 11: Why Creation of the Self is a Better Solution?

I show that Divine creationism is a better solution to its emergentist alternatives. Furthermore, I show that the event of personal origination is crucial to arriving at this claim. Using abductive logic, I show that Divine creationism is a natural (i.e., a common-sense product) explanation. By developing an argument for a strong principle of sufficient reason, I show that something like the neo-Cartesianism I advance is true as an explanation of the person and gesture to a stronger claim of necessity for a kind of agent-creationism (where a supernatural agent is the direct, even immediate, cause of persons coming into existence).

Chapter 12: Constructive Creationist Solutions

By laying out different creationist-soul options, the present chapter shows the plausibility and diversity of the view. More specifically, the chapter lays out what some have called theistic dualism and theistic idealism as macro-frameworks for understanding the Divine creation of souls. While both are minimally idealist in that it is the Divine mind and its ideas, ultimately, that explains reality, there are different conceptions of construing bodies and how they relate to created minds.

It is here that we begin to see some of the implications for reality, especially as this pluralist option is contrasted with a provocative and compelling monist alternative.

Conclusions: The Anti-Scientific Worry

Coming back around to the original problem of naturalism, materialism, and scientism, the conclusion explores what is ultimately at stake from this paradigm concerning persons and whether or not *The Creation of Self* is ultimately anti-scientific. The claim of being anti-science certainly has some cultural weight at the moment—who really wants to be anti-science?!, but it is met with significant confusion, some poorly defined concepts, and arbitrary line-drawing. In attempt to lay out some different ways of understanding 'science,' the present chapter criticizes the defenders of what is called 'scientism' and suggests some ways in which the proposal is consistent with different definitions of science.

Part I

Are we souls or bodies?

Chapter 1

Initial Reasons favoring the Soul-Concept

(Drawn, adapted and substantially rewritten from: Joshua R. Farris, "The Soul-Concept: Meaningfully Disregard or Meaningfully Embrace," *Annales Philosophici*, issue 5 (2012): 59-68)

As I reflect on the question, 'The soul—can the concept of the soul still have meaning?' I am baffled that it has even come to a point where such a question might be posed.[17] The notion of the soul may be questionable or even fuzzy in the minds of many today, but if one were to attend more closely to his/her own mental life then he/she could see that the soul is the clearest concept of all. The metaphysical notion of the soul reduces to a question of substance dualism or immaterialism.[18] This is the notion that persons are strictly identified with the soul or the immaterial part in contrast to the material part—e.g., the body. While I am not concerned, in this chapter, with the variations of each metaphysical position, I am concerned with whether or not the concept of a soul has meaning. By considering more closely the nature of consciousness, I argue that our consciousness entails a specific kind of knowledge about persons (consciousness, knowledge, and the nature of personhood are all intimately related). It is my contention that upon reflection of our own mental lives we can have a clear and robust concept of the soul. The reason for this is that the concept of the soul is rooted in common sense and basic knowledge through direct acquaintance with the self. And, it is important to set out from the beginning the distinct features of the self as an individually conscious being from machine learning and artificial intelligence. Machine learning functions according to a program, an algorithm designed by conscious individuals, and, as a result, is theoretically reproducible. It is a complex entity that itself we have no reason to believe actually bears the hallmarks of consciousness (not to be conflated with intelligence simpliciter) as a qualitative, unified field, which provides the basis for creative thinking.

I argue for the meaningful concept of the soul in three parts. First, I argue that the soul has meaning based on our first-person perspective. Second, I argue based on the knowledge argument and the access argument that we have direct acquaintance with the soul for which all other knowledge is predicable. Third, I argue for the meaningful concept of the soul through discussing recent work in personal identity. All three arguments comprise a robust concept of the soul with meaning.

The first-person perspective and the Concept of Souls

To begin, I discuss the first-person perspective or first-person knowledge; this I believe offers some support and semblance of meaning as to what the soul actually is by nature. The first-person perspective is characteristic of persons that is, arguably, not shareable with other distinct individual objects. In fact, no two persons share the exact same conscious perspectives. The first-person perspective is irreducible to scientific knowledge, material objects or material processes. The first-person perspective is characterized by deep subjectivity, internal knowledge, introspection, and qualitative feel. Opposite of this is third-person knowledge, the notion that knowledge is public, passively received, external, and observable. When contrasting these two kinds of knowledge, there is a massive dissimilarity whereby both are distinct. One is describable or reducible to scientific processes and the other is describable only in terms of something contrary to scientific processes. The first-person perspective is not reducible to or describable in terms of material events or that which is scientifically accessible. The argument is that physicality does not capture the first-person perspective. If in fact this is true, then it seems that the first-person perspective must be reducible to or describable in terms of something different than material objects or material processes. It is describable in terms of something that is substantial, yet not material but immaterial—call this the particularity of consciousness problem for materialism. This one might call the soul; hence, a concept of the soul includes the notion of first-person perspectives rooted in a soul as substance. Connected to this notion of first-person knowledge and particular conscious, I argue for an individual immaterial thing as the suitable ground for knowledge and conscious access.

When we consider the appearance/reality distinction there is a tendency amongst physicalists to one of several options. One is to take the appearance I have of my own phenomenal states of awareness seriously as real in some sense. This can be done by way of trying to account for the identity of phenomenal experience with some neural event or by providing a reductive explanation of the phenomenal experience. But, the divide between neural and physical events compared to phenomenal consciousness events is a difficult, nigh impossible, one to reconcile. And, there are some reasons to believe that identity and reductive solutions really just amount to an elimination of phenomenal experience because of how wide the chasm is between the two. The elimination of conscious experience, along with intuition as an accurate guide to knowledge is another option. And, this isn't to be confused with the position that we should have a healthy skepticism about the items within our experience about the external world, which can at times trick us to believe something is there when it may not be (e.g., the mirage in the desert that appears to be water), but to eliminate experience at its most base level. This is far more extravagant, but the road often taken by honest materialists. In any rate, there is a motivation to the elimination of phenomenal experience as a real feature of the world and of minds in favor of a fiction.

When we consider one of the more acute events revealing the distinction between phenomenal consciousness and physical or neural events, the state of pain focuses the hard problem of consciousness. This is why some philosophers who are often called eliminativists, i.e., the view that consciousness is non-existent or not real, (or reductivists, it's not always easy to discern the difference) wish to have their cake in purporting that consciousness is real just not phenomenal consciousness, which they would call a "fiction written by our brains."[19]

A common-sense set of data regarding pain includes the phenomenal and, arguably, private state of pain that is only accessible by the subject of experience and on the other hand the neural event or physical locatedness of *that* pain (of course there are cases of mental or emotional pain that are just hard to reconcile with physicalism at all because there is a private experience that while it might have some physical cause it not always has a physical cause or a physical correlate of which physicalists might attempt to use as the basis for explaining it) Christopher Hill offers up a helpful explanation for the motivation to elimination of pain. He states:

> We started with the observation that there is no substantive distinction between the appearance of pain and the corresponding reality. We then observed that there is evidence from phenomenology, cognitive psychology, and cognitive neuroscience which appears to mandate the view that awareness of pain is fully perceptual in character. When we combined these observations we arrived at a paradox, for it is of the very essence of perception that there be a distinction between its seeming to a perceiver that such and such is the case and its being true that such and such is the case.
>
> We then saw that it is possible to explain why there is no

substantive appearance/reality distinction in the case of pain in terms of features of the cognitive role of the concept of pain. It follows that there are no empirical or metaphysical facts that preclude a perceptual model of awareness of pain. It is possible to make the world safe for a perceptual model by making appropriate revisions in our conceptual scheme.

After considering these issues, we went on to notice that there is good reason to believe that the concept of pain refers to bodily disturbances that involve actual or potential damage. Evidently, then, it is true to say that pains are bodily disturbances.

But bodily disturbances are empirical phenomena, and therefore admit of an appearance/reality distinction. Because of this, there is considerable tension between two aspects of the concept of pain. Those features of its cognitive role that preclude a substantive distinction between appearance and reality are at variance with its referential dimension. This fact provides additional motivation for revising or eliminating the concept of pain.[20]

There is no surprise that a physicalist will find the temptation toward the elimination of phenomenal consciousness when she considers pain. The reality of phenomenal experience as a given in reality or as a piece of common sense that we cannot deny is a significant problem for the physicalist wishing to sustain the plausibility of her own physicalist view of the world. Any ontology of the person must take seriously the reality of pain as exemplifying something that is real, private, and experiential in nature (along with it having some spatial location in the case of physical pain). What is interesting is how Hill describes the phenomena above as the distinction between the phenomenal seeming and the truth of the case, but this is precisely the problem for physicalists that is not a concern for other respective ontologies (i.e., idealism or dualism that have a place for the substantive reality of minds and souls).

Some physicalists are inclined toward some version of mental (i.e., phenomenal) reduction or identity theory that attempts to preserve the reality of it. However, this is unsatisfactory and cannot do so without eliminating that which is basic to the subject of consciousness, namely the fact of its phenomenal character, which is by nature not physical, but something else. John Foster summarizes it well:

> The token-identity thesis claims that each mental item is identical with a neural item. The prima facie objection to this, as we have seen, is that we simply cannot understand how things of such seemingly different types can be identical—an objection which gets reinforced by Kripke's modal argument, to the effect that the psychological character of a mental item is essential to it, but not to its neural correlate. First, he might adopt some form of analytical reductionism, claiming that the psychological concepts applicable to mental items are to be analysed in wholly nonmentalistic terms. The main option here would be that of analytical functionalism. Secondly, he might endorse the type identity thesis, claiming that the psychological character of a mental item is to be empirically identified with some aspect of its physical character. Thirdly, he might embrace the view of the metaphysical reductionist—conceding that the psychological character of a mental item cannot be specified in any but psychological terms, but insisting that the item's possession of this character is derivative from, and nothing over and above, certain non-mental facts about it. I have tried to show that none of these approaches is successful and that the objection to token-identity stands.[21]

As Foster forcefully argues in his academic treatment, *The Immaterial Self*, there is no way to make sense, epistemically or linguistically, of phenomenal qualia in terms of some neural item. Kripke's use of the terms rigid designator as applied to phenomenal states of consciousness would be simply insufficient to identify with neural states of the brain. Additional thought experiments have been deployed by academic philosophers to show that the mind is not identical to the brain, or the neural correlates of a conscious thinking self. One of those thought experiments using zombies. Zombies are described by philosophers as those physical animals that are like us in all the ways we can observe physically, but they are not conscious like you or I (i.e., they do not know what it is like to be the person that you or I am). They cannot know. They simply function according to built-in survival mechanisms. If one can show a possible distinction (even if not an actual distinction) between the neural correlates of consciousness and conscious thinking selves exemplified in the possibility of zombies contrasted with humans, then it demonstrates the reality expressed in this thought experiment that the neurons are not identical to consciousness. Recent neuroscientific supports the notion of zombies with the recent development of brain organoids that are derived from human embryonic stem cells and serve as duplicates of human brains, but there is reason to believe that these duplicate brains are not conscious and cannot perform all the cognitive operations of humans, assuming they were full-size brains. This takes us some way to showing that conscious minds or selves are not identical to their brains or the neurons comprising brains, but rather it is something else. Furthermore, if physicalism were true then the reality of zombies would not be imaginable, possible, or actual. While there may not exist zombies in the way described the fact that there are these souls or minds as distinct from brains supports the possibility of zombies. Relatedly, the physicalist is unable to reduce phenomenal consciousness with neural states because the character of mental items from non-mental items is something distinct altogether. There is no conceivable way to derive the phenomenal character of consciousness from its neural correlate (even if there is some causal relation between a neuron firing in the brain that brings about the effect of a felt experience). In these ways, the nature of consciousness entails a certain kind of knowledge that is available only to persons that demands we take it seriously.

The Concept of the Soul: The Knowledge Argument and the Access Argument

The argument I propose concludes with the notion of self as a simple immaterial thinking thing.[22] To this end, here I consider Frank Jackson's knowledge argument and whether or not the self with knowledge is an immaterial thing—a soul. My argument is such that we have an I or soul-concept that implicitly entails an immaterial thinking thing that is not material, a bundle of things, nor a compound of the material and immaterial. The basis of my concluding in favor of a soul as a concept is contained in the following.

(1) If the Knowledge Argument necessarily entails property dualism and that is co-joined with self-presenting properties, then we either have a bundle thing of material and/or immaterial properties or we have an immaterial substance.

(2) A material thing alone is excluded because we have property dualism.[23]

(3) We do not have a bundle-thing.[24]

(4) Therefore, we have an immaterial substance.

(5) A Soul is a better alternative with respect to the I-concept and its relation to our mental states/concepts.

I will lay this out and offer evidential support in favor of the premises, then lay out what I take to be the I-concept or soul-concept (hereafter the soul-concept).[25]

Mary is a brilliant scientist living in a black and white room who has studied color, the physics of light, its relation to color, and neurophysiology. Yet she has never experienced the color red. When she steps out of her black and white room, she experiences the color red. At this point, she exclaims, "I see red." At the point that she sees red it is argued that she gains a new concept/mental item of knowledge that is distinct from her knowledge of red prior to seeing red. Accordingly, we know that there is a duality in Mary's knowledge: one that derives from the physical sciences and one that is subject-grounded.[26] We also know that concepts are distinct from propositions.[27] While propositions can exist on their own, mind-independent or mind-extrinsic concepts seem to be mind-dependent and internal to the knower. It is also arguable that the nature of the self can be naturally inferred from this. If there is a duality of knowledge/concepts, then one might say there is a duality of things that these concepts are conferred upon or dependent upon. Moreover, if this is a natural inference to draw, then we do know at least one thing about the nature of the thing having knowledge/concepts, namely, that it is the kind of thing that is able to know and think. Chisholm has argued for the mode or presentation of mental properties. He says that there are two properties distinct with every piece of knowledge or concept. Those properties include the thing directly in the purview of one's perceptual states and the self as presented with the perceptual state. The property of presentation or consciousness he calls "self-presenting properties."[28] I shall call the concept that follows from this the soul-concept. This is the concept that we have of ourselves directly, and immediately attending all other concepts and properties in light of the property of the object presenting itself to the self. When Mary sees red, she knows not only red, but also that *she* sees red or at least upon reflection she can know that *she* sees red. Knowledge and subject-hood seem to be foundational to the knowledge of red and everything else. Thus, knowledge and self-consciousness is co-terminus.[29] From this, it seems not only to support the inextricable connection between mental items and minds, but also the duality of the body/brain with persons who think and have characteristics of persons. I argue for the concept of a soul by arguing the 'I' as coextensive with knowledge/mental items.

If I coexist with my thoughts then that reveals my nature as an enduring continuant.[30] In fact, I must be a simple enduring continuant if I am to make sense of the fact of my mental items.[31] My mental items of seeing red are just that, *my* mental items of seeing red. This is similarly applicable with desires, sensations, ideas and the point is still the same that 'I' endure with these desires, sensations, ideas and other mental items. This is rather unlike propositions. There may be such a thing as propositions that are objective, non-subjective and not dependent on the mind—it seems in fact that there are. Mental items are different. Propositions can be shared among individuals, while concepts cannot—in some significant sense. First-person observers can verify propositions, yet concepts are internally knowable by individual first-person knowers. Although having mental items correlate, at times, with neural activity concepts are not empirically known through some third-person manner of inquiry at least of the awareness of the perceptual state of seeing red. Thus, it seems that material things do not know red, but I do. It seems upon reflection that concepts are this way and are intimately related to the 'I' having them. In part, the soul-concept includes the notion of endurance. The concept also includes the notion of simplicity. To this we turn.

Potentially, the concepts themselves tell us something about the thing having them. Concepts are dependent on the first-person conceiver conceiving the concepts. It also appears that concepts are simple, intrinsic and subjective. It is this 'I' that has first-person awareness and a unified presentation of his

32

concepts that actually is best accounted for by a simple enduring thing with persistence conditions uncharacteristic of material things. Both material things and property-bundle things do not have the persistence conditions to account for my having the property of coexisting with all my concepts/mental items. Pace Hume, there has been this notion that there is no subject present, but this defies common sense, introspection, and the fact that sensations are bound and unified by something. Thus, if I am to be of the sort to have these kinds of mental items/ concepts, then I am probably a simple thing and not a material thing nor composed of a material thing. It might be that the body helps in my perceptual intake of information, but that is not the same as saying the body/soul composing me is the ground for my knowing some object or having a mental item. The soul-concept excludes the notion of a complex person, and is best accounted for by a simple (and, possibly a phenomenal unified presentation—more on that later).

The evidence against a property-bundle view is great. First, if one considers the unity-of-consciousness argument the notion that a person's conscious field of awareness is unified and singular, then we have reason to think that a bundle view cannot account for this. For bundles do not have the tight unity reflective of our conscious mental states. Bundles of properties lack the internal depth characteristic of a conscious field. Bundles of properties lack the intrinsic relation between things and properties that are reflective of the conscious field. Second, as demonstrated above concepts and conscious states are had by some*thing* and accessible by some*thing*—this might be called the privileged access argument, argued by Richard Swinburne.[32] He says that mental events, like in the cases above when Mary sees red, are mental properties that are accessible only by substances. Material things do not have access to certain facets of the world like qualia-red.[33] According to Swinburne, the notion that I am a conscious being is known immediately upon reflection. If I am conscious, what that means is that there is something of what it is like to be conscious, hence phenomenal consciousness for minds, as we know it, just is consciousness. What is important is that there is this feature of privacy that is predicable of minds— unlike that of bodies or physical things. I have privileged access to my own perceptual and phenomenal states of consciousness. I know this is something I have access to by virtue of attending to the ideas, feelings, dispositions that are present to me when having an experience—say the experience of the color red. I can think about the red color as it is exemplified before me in the flower in a field of green. I can further assess the depth of the color and its shade as the light shines upon it.

Yet, more important to privacy of my conscious experience of which another person has no access (at least not in any direct sense) is the fact that it is exemplified by a pure property of mental things—not to be confused with mixed properties, properties that are partly physical and partly mental. When I introspect about the red flower, I know that I have privileged access because of what Swinburne refers to as an informative designator—i.e., a designator that actually refers and by way of content that successfully informs the individual that this is the person. So, when I access my thoughts by intellectually attending to the red flower, I do so with the fact that it is I that is accessing and attending to my own thoughts. By way of the informative designator, I accurately refer in an informed way to the red flower and to my*self* as the possessor of the item of knowledge, which justifies the fact that I am a pure property of a mind, my mind.

But coming back around to the knowledge argument, we see that it reveals property dualism, but there is also something deeper in keeping with the notion of privileged access, which is that the self as substance that has access to that which is not physical. Third, a bundle of material and/or immaterial properties will not do because of the close relation between concepts and conceivers, as discussed briefly above. Bundles do not have ownership of things the way a mental thing has ownership of a concept. Bundles may have relational connections or causal connections, but they seem to lack internal and intrinsic depth. Mental substances seem to have an intimate and internal relation to concepts/mental items. If it is not a property-bundle thing, then I suggest it is unlikely that a compound (and/or a pure immaterial/mental substance) is the kind of thing to have access to mental items/concepts.

One argument in favor of a soul is based on the reality that knowledge/mental items are simple, irreducible to the physical, and intrinsically nonphysical in conjunction with self-presenting properties. It goes something like this, given the previous premises, it seems natural to infer as one did above that persons are simple because of a singular binding thing that unifies the experienceables in a mental state/concept. As shown above, it seems that 'I' attend every mental item/concept and I unify these states.[34] What might be the lines of evidence for such a conclusion? One might argue that the nature of mental items/concepts is an alteration or mode of the mind, thus not a *part* of the mind. If this is the case that concepts are non-composed and simple then it, also, makes sense to think that there is a simple non-composed 'I' that has those thoughts, assuming self-presenting properties and the 'I' that attends the mental items. This 'I' generates the simple thoughts that are *sui generis* in nature. It is not that when new concepts come into the mind that I am somehow added to or subtracted from in the sense of adding or subtracting from material things. When I have a new concept in mind, it is not like that of an organism that might take on the addition of a limb or the subtraction of a limb. Mental items do not seem to work that way. Considering the difference between propositions and concepts, it is not as if I am adding a proposition from the abstract realm to my mind. Concepts do not have the *feel* that a material thing has when we add material to it. Concepts do not come from anywhere else but my mind.[35] *Sui generis* things are deeply foundational, new, and simple in nature. The phenomenology of my mental items is deeply dependent on me not anything else, and if there is a pure mental property to be had it seems it is had by a pure immaterial thing because the pure property is had by a thing and the characteristics of that thing resemble a simple immaterial thing dissimilar from material things—hence a soul.

From the conclusion of the knowledge argument one should infer a metaphysical substance—soul. In fact, it seems to me, that in order to ground the notion that Mary has knowledge of red through acquaintance with the color implies a substance that is not material nor is a bundle of nonmaterial properties but is more likely an immaterial substance or soul. The access argument in conjunction with the knowledge argument demonstrates that it is not simply a material substance or a proper-bundle thing that has a concept, but it is a substance of a different kind that is able to access mental items or concepts. At every moment that a mental item presents itself there is an attending mental item that presupposes the self in question. From this, the individual person is able to think, reflect, and investigate further in a first-person manner. Thus, scientific knowledge and third-person knowledge is grounded in a first-person perspective. This appears to require a soul that is enduring, simple, has the power of self-reflexive thinking, is properly epistemically foundational in some sense, and unifying. Call this the soul-concept. I turn to one final argument based on personal identity in conjunction with what precedes.

When we consider the knowledge argument and its yielding of (a) property dualism taken together with the mode of presentation laid out for us by Roderick Chisholm, as (b) self-presentation, plus the fact that it is 'I' that both persists in time, space, and as the item that (c) unifies the concepts in my visual field of consciousness (whether I am aware of it and point to it or not it is somewhat distinct) buttresses a distinct argument from private (i.e., privileged according to Swinburne's terminology) access as an immaterial power of a substance. And, it is important not to confuse the power of binding these concepts in one unified field according to the materialist theory called the attention schema theory, which effectively makes the mind as an independent substance an illusion, i.e., the view that there is some module processor of information that does the work of storing and focusing that information of an object in the purview of a person. Rather, what is intrinsic to the binding process is the qualitative fact of which only a subject of that consciousness has that fails to map on to what we observe in the physical world. Moving from this ground to conceive of an immaterial substance or a something other than the body occurs, in another way, when we utilize a conceivability framework that takes our modal ideas seriously as presenting us with something actual in the world. If I can conceive of having the power of accessing the items in my field of consciousness apart from the body or the parts of the body accessing these items, then I have justified grounds for believing that I am not the body or the parts of the body doing the work of conscious access of the items in my field of consciousness. I can conceive of it, especially given (a), (b), and (c) presented above, hence… I am not my body or the parts of my body, but a mind that has a pure property and the power of private access to my phenomenal states of consciousness.

Personal Identity and the Concept of a Soul

In connection to the above, I argue positively that we can have a meaningful concept of the soul through interaction with the literature on personal identity—specifically, individuation of individual persons through a rational soulish act. When considering common-sense data, intuitive data, and other thought experiments it appears that the soul-view—often referred to as the simple-view—best accounts for our understanding of persons. Hence, the results comprise a particular understanding of the soul as a meaningful concept.

a. The 'Body View'

The first position is known as the 'body view.'[36] The body view has traditionally come from Aristotle and has some present-day proponents. The bodily criterion for personal identity is the view that persons are identifiable by virtue of the body or the biological organism. The body view identifies persons with their bodies or with a bodily constitutional relation. Broadly speaking the view does not say that I identify with one aspect of my body nor one physical part connected with my body. In fact, the 'I' is a linguistic reference for the body or biological organism. Alternatively, related to this one could say that the body constitutes me.[37] It treats the person as identical to the relationship to the body. Thus, I am my body. This is one popular view held by philosophical and theological physicalists, respectively.

The recent *Harry Potter* films have illustrated the body view. In book two *The Chamber of Secrets* and book seven *Deathly Hallows* J.K. Rowling introduces the reader to the polyjuice potion. This potion can turn one's body into the body of another by simply dropping the hair of the person's body for the purposes of transformation. In book two Hermione transforms herself into a cat by accident. In book seven, there is an attempt from Harry's friends to protect Harry from Voldemort's followers by transforming into Harry's body to transport Harry from one place to another. Both of these illustrations reveal the problem with the body view. We know intuitively that a person is not strictly identical with his body, bodily constitution, or his own biological organism.

I wish to mention one problem. The problem is one of persistence of identity. It is difficult to see how persistence in and through time works on a bodily/bodily constitution view.

The body changes every day and takes on new cells; it seems that it is not the same body. The idea of personal identity with the body rubs against some basic intuitions about personal identity. Is it appropriate to identify persons with their bodies? It seems, intuitively, that the person is something more fixed, stable, unified, and enduring. For these reasons, I believe another view is a more satisfactory depiction of persons.[38]

b. The 'Brain View'

A second view that is another popular physicalist or materialist view is the view often termed the 'brain view' of personal identity. The brain view is similar to the bodily criterion view because thinkers from both vantage points identify the 'I' with some physical or biological thing. It seems very natural indeed for proponents of materialism to link the self or the linguistic 'I' with the brain considering the brain is responsible for much of the 'goings-on' in the biological organism, e.g., body.[39] The 'brain view' is the view that the person identifies with the brain in a holistic sense or identifies with some aspect of the brain, say, the cerebral cortex, wherein the brain controls the functioning of the rest of the body. Call this the 'control center.' Here again philosophers seem to assume a linguistic reference 'I' as identical with the brain controlling the body. This, as well, seems to have problems. Let me ask a couple of questions and explicitly draw out the implicit answers of those questions. Am I a brain? Do brains think? At first glance, these two questions seem very odd. The question "Am I a brain?" seems to imply a response of "no"; but I do have a brain. The second question seems very odd as well, "Do brains think?" Normally, this is not how humans talk or think assuming language is a reflection of how we think. A brain does not seem to think. Usually, when speaking of thinking we implicitly speak of the person doing the thinking, not a faculty of the person. The brain seems to be a faculty or part of the person. We could say it this way, "I use my brain to think." This seems much more natural. I can hardly imagine what it means for a brain to think. It is similar to someone saying, "Hand picks up the cup." A hand may pick up a cup, but it is someone's hand picking up the cup. I use my hand to pick up the cup. As a result, the brain view will not work as a satisfactory view of personal identity, either.[40]

c. The 'Character/Memory Continuity View'

The memory or character theory of personal identity is a third and prominent view. Historically, Locke adheres to this view or something like it, or at least this view is attributed to him.[41] Ultimately, I think these two views are one view but could be distinguished one from the other. Proponents of this theory might come from the camp of materialism/physicalism or from the position that persons are immaterial kinds of things. A noticeable difference between this view and the previous two views is that personal identity, according to the memory-character theory, is not, and cannot be reducible to some physical thing. This requires a materialism of a non-reductive sort. The memory or character view of personal identity associates the person with his memories or character. The assumption is that the person cannot be strictly identified with a physical thing or a physical part, but personhood itself must be more than a physical kind of thing. Personhood must be something of a nonphysical kind. Naturally then some other thing must account for personal identity. That other thing on this view is thoughts, generally, and memories specifically. The thoughts or mental items in the brain make up personhood. Personhood is a bundle of properties instantiated in a nonphysical thing or a physical thing with epiphenomenal or emergent properties. The issue is that something must link these properties of the mental together. The mental properties are causally connected. Here we have a causal link making continuous **thoughts** united, thus resulting in personhood. This too seems an inadequate

40

accounting of human persons as a ground for personal identity.[42]

d. The 'Simple View'

Fourth, the defender of the simple or 'soul' view identifies persons with souls.[43] The simple view is distinguishable from various materialist constructions of human persons and the memory-character view of human persons. Persons identify with souls or an immaterial mental thing.[44] This view of the person is that the person is not identified with any biological organism, physical part, the brain, or the body. It is also distinct from a memory-character view in that the person must exist for mental items to exist, memories, and states of character. The simple view of persons says that persons are not reducible to matter and are not a bundle with properties of both material and nonmaterial qualities. Persons are irreducibly simple, as argued above from first-person knowledge, particular consciousness, the nature of human knowledge, and a pure mental property that requires a pure immaterial soul.[45] The advantages of this view are clear.[46]

The distinct features of the simple view of personhood include independence and the endurance of the substantial soul. The soul is independent with respect to non-dependence for the soul's identity on anything else. The soul has a kind of identity not dependent on or reducible to other properties or substances. The soul precedes its properties in some sense, thus having a kind of independence from them. Next, the soul is an enduring kind of thing. It endures through time. If the soul were a bundle of properties that fluctuates identity would fluctuate, or so it seems. On a simple view, predicating properties and identity of the *thing* is possible. It has a stable kind of identity that does not fluctuate according to the various sortal-phases it encounters. Sortal-phases are nonessential properties wherein a substance exists in and through various moments of existence.

Given the preceding, it is unlikely that persons are material, a continuity of memories, a property, property-bundle or a complex thing. In fact, for a substance to have cognitive access to its own mental states, to endure through time, to lose physical parts and remain, to have a first-person knowledge a soul is presupposed.

In what follows, we will see that this simple view yields a metaphysical simple that provides the individuation (i.e., that which makes you *you*) to persons without which we would lack a sufficient designation for the soul.

Conclusion

The concept of a soul has been assumed throughout history and is the common-sense position concerning the nature of persons. Whilst a common-sense view of the world may not be sufficient or persuasive evidence in favor of a metaphysical position, it certainly does provide reason for thinking that the soul is a meaningful concept. Additionally, I argued above from intuition, conceivability, and from the nature of our human knowledge that the concept of the soul is meaningful in terms of that, which is distinct from material things, material events, and property-bundles. The soul, as I have defined it, is that which we have direct and immediate knowledge and is meaningful in terms of our belief-desire structures that are deeply subjective. If anything has a concept of anything else, it must be a soul as substance. Otherwise, how would I know? However, I do. To answer the question that started the discussion, I must answer by asking a question: "How could the concept of the soul not have meaning?" If the soul does not, then does anything? I am unsure. Thus, even the practice of science is predicable upon this foundation of a soul as substance that has internal access, first-person knowledge, particular consciousness, the ability to introspect and think about what is publicly observable through a third-person manner, and the necessity for rational/soulish individuation of persons. Thus, I encourage the meaningful embrace of the soul as concept.

To this point, what I have argued for positively is something like a soul not only as meaningful but a justified true belief that presumes our cognitive apparatus is functioning properly in holding to that belief. What is shown, or strongly suggested, is that physicalism is false and that we have something other than the physical that accounts for consciousness in relation to personal identity. What this amounts to, at a minimum, if we take seriously our consciousness with its characterizing properties of what it is like to be consciousness (i.e., what philosophers call 'qualia') and the powers that are ancillary to it is that our consciousness points to novelties that are characteristic of persons, which likely entail an immaterial substance or a novel substance that, minimally, unifies the items of which our consciousness holds together (hence it is not simply the brain with its collected neurons firing bound together to present something of a loose bundle). In what follows, I address additional reasons to reject physicalist alternatives, defeaters to the soul, and more finely-grained reasons to accept a particular version that preserves personhood.

Chapter 2

Religious and Philosophical Reasons for the Soul

(Drawn and adapted from, "Aren't Souls Passé: Biblical Reflections on Human Nature," *The Table, shortreads*, August 5, 2015)

The question of what it means to be human is a question we've been attending too thus far in scientific and philosophical contexts. This question too finds its place in contemporary and religious reflections. In what follows, I address a recent set of religious objections to the soul and reasons why the soul-concept still compels belief.

What does it mean to be a human?

Such a question evokes several answers. Recent answers suggest that we are no more than complex machines manageable by science. The film *Ex Machina* depicts such a state of affairs—where artificial intelligence develops to such an extent that a female robot seems to exhibit comparable human intelligence, emotions, and the ability to manipulate others. On the other hand, older Greek views portray humans as something in between God and animal—as similarly depicted in the recent *Hercules* film.

Here, I wish to raise a related but different question: Do humans have souls? By answering this question, we move some direction toward the bigger question about what it means to be human.

In what follows, I consider some reasons to support the soul, but I examine in some detail the claims of religious scholar Joel Green who advances the thesis that religious texts like the Bible no longer require a traditional reading inclusive of a doctrine of the soul as a substantial thing.[47]

Biblical Reasons for the Existence of the Soul

More specifically, do we have biblical reasons to believe in the soul? Such a question may seem rather strange to some. For those who take the soul to be an apparent biblical truth, raising such a question is kind of like asking the questions: "Do birds fly?"; "Do fish have gills?" or "Does the Bible teach that humans are generally sinful?"

After all, isn't that what it means to be human? It's just basic to human nature and the human story. Of course humans have souls. It may be surprising to some that the popularity of souls is on the decline.

Souls in Decline

The popularity of the soul has declined for a variety of reasons. As science gains more credibility in suggesting that physical processes explain much of how the world works, Christian scholars are reexamining the biblical/theological data in fresh new ways and arguing that the soul really isn't all that necessary for making sense of biblical and theological data.

Motivated by what she sees as responsible scientific reasons, Nancey Murphy says this about the soul:

> So the strongest point I can make here is to claim, as I did in the preceding section, that physicalism—along with an eschatological hope for resurrection of the body—leads more naturally to a concern for the physical world and its transformation than does dualism.[48]

The term 'physicalism' (or 'materialism') is just a sophisticated way of saying that humans are purely physical objects: their bodies. In contrast, dualism is most commonly the view that humans are souls with bodies. Murphy concludes by saying that the overwhelming evidence (e.g., biblical, theological and scientific) suggests that we do not need souls.

Are Science and the Bible at Odds about What Humans Are?

Biblical scholar and Christian materialist Joel B. Green reaches a similar conclusion in his book *Body, Soul, and Human Life*. In it, Green rightly assumes that the question of the soul, a question often posed in the biblical study of anthropology, is a second-order or derivative inquiry into biblical texts. This is so because the biblical material is arguably not directly concerned with specifying the constitution of humans. In this way, motivated by recent neuroscientific concerns, Green reexamines the biblical data.

He argues that instead of presuming that science and the Bible are odds, science can help or "underscore" the biblical data on humans.[49] For Green, recent scientific study suggests that human functions were previously attributed to the human soul, but are now detailed and attributed to physical processes in the brain.[50]

I seek a *via media* that responsibly handles the Bible along with science, philosophy, and tradition.

Green offers several biblical reasons why Christians should reassess the so-called dualism of the past and consider materialism as a live biblical option. While not favoring a purely biblical approach that seems to exclude, at least initially, other theological sources of knowledge to the question of human constitution (e.g., tradition, philosophy, science, and experience), I am convinced that Green's approach, driven in many ways by contemporary science, is also flawed. Instead, I seek a *via media* that responsibly handles the Bible along with science, philosophy, and tradition. I would like to offer some brief reflections on Green's arguments and offer some reasons why Christians do in fact have biblical grounds for belief in the soul.

Dualism Versus Holism? Reflections on Joel Green's Arguments Against Dualism

Green argues that the widespread belief in dualism among Christians is "undoubtedly" due to the importance theological tradition has placed on dualism (13). He argues, however, that we must pay careful attention to the Old and New Testament witness to human embodiment (14). Furthermore, he argues that the creation account found in Genesis 1 and 2 offer us no reason to believe in the soul, a view that has gained notable support amongst Old Testament scholarship.[51] Instead, the creation story and its view carried along in the Old Testament is a view of humanity as physically embodied, holistic and relational, not soulish or immaterial. Why think then that there is *any* place for a soul in the Old Testament? Green's argument in his book and his more recent work seems to amount to the following.

1. The Old Testament/Hebrew conception of humans is holism.
2. Dualism excludes holism.
3. Therefore, dualism is not the OT/Hebrew conception of human nature.

Yet, nothing in the above argument necessarily rules out dualism! Furthermore, why think this is the end of the story? The defender of dualism should respond by claiming that holism does not exclude dualism.[52] Simply because the Old Testament nowhere teaches, entails, or necessarily yields dualism does not mean it *precludes* dualism. If dualism is not excluded as an option faithful to the Old Testament witness, we may have additional reasons from the New Testament, guided

47

by theological tradition and good philosophy, for belief in the soul. This is precisely what I wish to argue in a moment. But, before I do so, I want to ensure that I am being fair to Green's argument. It may be that he is arguing something along the following lines.

Reformulating Green's Argument Against Dualism

More charitably, Green's argument, reflecting a tradition of modern and contemporary reflection on the biblical narrative, is something like the following:

1. The biblical narrative gives us no reason to think that dualism is the appropriate ontology of humans.
2. Scientific data suggests that humans are monistic in nature (monism is the view that humans are not two kinds of things but one).
3. The biblical data highlights humanity as holistic, relational, and embodied.
4. Thus, it is probable that dualism is not the biblical teaching. And, monism or materialism remains the most viable option.

Does Science Suggest that Human Beings Are "Monistic"?

Whilst I am not a scientist by training, premise 2 seems to be open to further discussion. It is not at all clear that the scientific data suggests that humans are monistic or materialistic in nature. In fact, we have no reason whatsoever to believe that desires, ideas, intentions and the like are attributable to the brain or a physical process, despite what some might suggest today. Philosopher Daniel N. Robinson has pointed this out in more than one context. In one place, he states,

The brain has no motives and seeks no solace. That actual

persons—possessed of brains and other anatomical structures—are, indeed, motivated and do, indeed, strive to find deeper meaning in an otherwise indifferent cosmos is beyond dispute. That such motives and longings are somehow enabled by the brain should be readily granted but not as a fact that would give the motives and longings to the brain or locate them in the brain. Such inferences might well trigger activity in the anterior cingulate cortex in any creature expecting propositions to be meaningful.[53]

What Robinson makes clear in this pithy quote is what is held so persistently by persons. Persons, as minds or souls, are the kinds of things that have phenomenal experiences and from this emotional place they long for higher transcendent realities, make choices accordingly, and act in ways that cannot be explained by the neural cortex. Such a frame provides a conducive and fertile context for considering religious data on the nature of persons.

Back to the Biblical Data on Human Persons
But my primary concern here is with the biblical data. It may be true that humans are portrayed holistically, relationally, and bodily in the biblical story, but, once again, this doesn't rule out dualism.

Do we then have any biblical reasons for the soul and dualism? One might argue that dualism effectively makes sense of the biblical data while materialism simply lacks the resources to do so. Such an argument is a tall order and too ambitious to make good on in this context, so I simply wish to offer a couple of reasons for thinking that belief in the soul is biblically viable.

Two Ways the Bible Supports Belief in the Soul

1. Belief in the soul is motivated by theological tradition.

Belief in the soul is motivated by theological tradition, and thus we would be wise not to dismiss the belief too quickly. As noted earlier by Green, the popular belief in the soul is motivated by the fact that theological tradition teaches it. However, I want to suggest it is not arbitrarily motivated by tradition. One can make an even stronger claim about the church's consistent belief is in the soul throughout history. Arguably, the tradition has had a longstanding inclination toward belief in the soul that is rooted in biblical reflections. And it has been helpfully guided by good philosophy, in order to accommodate the biblical teachings on human transcendence over the physical world—especially in light of humanity's creation in the image and likeness of God and the human purpose to see and experience God in the afterlife.

There is one particular passage that clearly teaches this view of human transcendence, which constitutes the second reason for embracing belief in the soul.

2. The Intermediate State: Human transcendence of the physical world in 2 Corinthians 5:1-10.

The traditional readings of 2 Corinthians 5:1-10 correspond to and support the notion of human transcendence and thereby provide a basis for belief in the soul. This passage has traditionally been interpreted as supportive of what is often called the 'intermediate state' of human existence. By positing an intermediate state, theologians suggest that humans will continue to exist after physical death and before physical resurrection. Hence, there is an interim period between the life that we presently live and the new life of physical re-embodiment. 2 Corinthians 5:1-10 states,

1 For we know that if the earthly tent we live in is destroyed, we have a building from God, an eternal house in heaven, not built by human hands. 2 Meanwhile we groan, longing to be clothed instead with our heavenly dwelling, 3 because when we are clothed, we will not be found naked. 4 For while we are in this tent, we groan and are burdened, because we do not wish to be unclothed but to be clothed instead with our heavenly dwelling, so that what is mortal may be swallowed up by life. 5 Now the one who has fashioned us for this very purpose is God, who has given us the Spirit as a deposit, guaranteeing what is to come.
6 Therefore we are always confident and know that as long as we are at home in the body we are away from the Lord. 7 For we live by faith, not by sight. 8 We are confident, I say, and would prefer to be away from the body and at home with the Lord. 9 So we make it our goal to please him, whether we are at home in the body or away from it. 10 For we must all appear before the judgment seat of Christ, so that each of us may receive what is due us for the things done while in the body, whether good or bad.

Earthly Tent, Heavenly Home

While space is limited, a few brief comments on this passage are in order. The language of an earthly tent has often been interpreted to refer to the present human state, which will be replaced by our heavenly homes with God. But, as we see in verse 2, there is this unique state of waiting for the clothing (i.e., the body). And while it seems clear that this is referring to an interim state of human existence, the passage has often been taken to refer to something higher than our state on the earth, as we see in verses 6-8, thus pointing us to that transcendent aspect of humans.

I maintain that we have no positive reason to reject the tradition's belief in the doctrine of the soul and we may have at least a couple of reasons lending credence to the belief in the soul doctrine.

Traditionally this passage is cited as support for the 'beatific vision' (i.e., the eschatological, heavenly vision of God for the saints), which is assumed to be experienced during the interim state between bodily death and bodily resurrection.

Thomas Aquinas, representing what would come to be a common traditional reading, explicitly affirms this and sums up 2 Corinthians 5:1-10 by saying:

> Therefore, the answer is that the saints see the essence of God immediately after death and dwell in a heavenly mansion. Thus, therefore, it is plain that the reward which saints await is inestimable.[54]

Assuming this is the best way to read 2 Corinthians 5:1-10, we have one clear biblical teaching that yields support for belief in the soul because it requires not only that some thing exists beyond the body, but also that this entity experiences the vision of God in the intermediate state in a way that transcends bodily life. So, here the NT gives us a reason to affirm the belief in the doctrine of the soul as undergirding human transcendence in the afterlife.

In contrast to Green's suggestion that the biblical narrative provides no such reason or motivation for belief in the soul, I maintain that we have no positive reason to reject the tradition's belief in the doctrine of the soul and we may have at least a couple of reasons lending credence to the belief in the soul doctrine. Unfortunately, it is true that most contemporary biblical scholars reject the tradition's doctrine of the human soul (as seen in Green's analysis), yet the arguments for such a conclusion remain unconvincing. In the next chapter, I consider some additional reasons in the context of science and theological discussions that favor a soul as the core of persons.

Chapter 3

Bodies and Souls: Why we matter

(Portions modified and adapted from "The Soul and Science: Challenging the Consensus," *The City*, special edition: "Christianity, Mind, and Mental Health," Winter/Spring 2019)

For centuries, the question of the soul was assumed as a part of the dogmatic core of the major monotheistic religions and something cherished by humans as the vehicle for the survival of human life beyond the grave. While this notion of the soul is challenged today, it holds important place in the debates beneath our debates. For all the major contemporary debates about politics, society, race relations, and medicine presume something about a deeper question of what it means to be human.

Are we souls, bodies, or some combination of the two? Even raising the question anymore is met with similar responses of raising questions about current longstanding government programs. Once you have them, it is hard to consider alternatives. And, even when they are practically overturned, their shadow is often still with us. Something like this has been occurring for a long time in scientific communities. For one to raise the question about souls is to suggest that spooky entities (e.g., ghosts and angels) exist, which is to challenge the prevailing, or the 'supposed' prevailing, consensus in some circles that all of reality under investigation is material in nature, i.e., a little more than flesh and blood machines.

For one to say that the soul has been under attack, would be an understatement. Since the rise of logical positivism, the attitude to the soul is likened to the attitude toward God. Logical positivism is the philosophical thesis that we can only know that which is empirically verifiable, which excludes the statement: "God exists," because it is not verifiable empirically, at least not directly. Logical positivism may not hold prime authority in philosophy and science anymore, but the shadow of logical positivism remains in some academic circles. Closely related to it is the belief in materialism of some sort, namely, the philosophical stance that the reality under investigation is wholly material in nature, mechanistic, and is governed solely by regular lawful events. And, it is often supposed that belief in the soul, if not in contradiction with it, is not supported by science.

One famous critic of the soul, Nancey Murphy captures this 'leftover' attitude quite well:

> While body-soul dualism is a hot topic now in conservative Christian circles in the United States, the debate over dualism versus physicalism is thought to be settled by scholars in a variety of fields... [B]iblical scholars called body-soul dualism into question beginning a century ago (but given the current popularity of books for and against the soul, they apparently neglected to inform their congregations!). The concept of the self has long served as a replacement for the soul in a number of disciplines, such as psychology, and in ordinary language as well. No significant neuroscientist has been a dualist since the death of Sir John Eccles.[55]

Making several appeals to authority, Murphy gives the reader the impression that dualism is simply not taken seriously anymore by anyone credentialed in respected scientific fields. But this just isn't the case. As Murphy mentions, the esteemed Sir John Eccles took it that humans are soul-body composites. What Murphy doesn't tell us is how important Sir John Eccles is to neuroscience. Instead, she gives the impression that he is one "significant" neuroscientist among many, but, sadly, this would be mistaken. In fact, he is one of the most significant neuroscientists of the last century as a Nobel prize winner in 1969. Unfortunately, in many ways, he was and still is ridiculed for his belief in the soul.[56]

So, are there *any* other significant neuroscientists who advocate for a soul? What about Mario Beauregard? Beauregard (PhD, University of Montreal; https://drmariobeauregard.com/bio/) has been involved in several projects that call the scientific "consensus" into question by re-envisioning science in a post-materialist way (i.e., science is not beholden to a worldview that is governed mechanistically, and is non-intentional and non-experiencing all the way down).[57] And, Beauregard is famous for showing that our emotions, which are presumably not physical in nature, can actually change our brain states (meaning that there is not only a something that is distinct or over and above the physical states or neurons firing in the brain, but a thing that has some causal power that itself is not conceivably the brain or the parts of the brain)—even more they can affect our epigenetic patterns. But, Beauregard certainly isn't the only scientifically-minded intellectual who believes the soul exists and has some important role to play in our investigation of the world. So also does Jeffrey Schwartz (MD, research psychiatrist at the University of California at Los Angeles; https://jeffreymschwartz.com/about/).

Schwartz is a famous psychologist who has argued for the soul as an important datum that informs our way of thinking about humans and the world. In several places, Schwartz has argued that you are not your brain, but, in fact, you are something more or above and beyond your brain. You are something other than your brain illustrated by the fact that your brain can be shaped by you—it's almost as if you are an outside force that can shape and form your own neural patterns. Scientists have referred to the neural phenomena as neuroplasticity (i.e., the view that our neural patterns are malleable), which Schwartz has deployed as a way of showing that we are the kinds of agents that can change our brain states.

This begs the question: If we grant that Murphy is right about the neuroscientific consensus, what does *that* prove? Arguably, neuroscience has very little to say that is direct about our mental and internal lives. It might tell us about various neurons in our brains and what those neurons do, but neuroscience tells us little about the nature of consciousness, thought, virtue, experience—you know, all that interesting human stuff. Comparatively little that is of bearing regarding the soul or mind is the object of neuroscientific study. In fact, it is more likely that neuroscientists are often not directly concerned with the soul question at all. Even if they have a settled opinion that the soul doesn't exist, their own discipline tells us very little about the nature of the soul; at least not directly, so their belief may be misguided. Why then should we take Murphy's authority claim seriously? Simply put, we shouldn't. For, Murphy's claim that no neuroscientist believes in the existence of souls is little more than an appeal to authority for something else going on in the discussion. Take another look at the quote above.

Murphy suggests that biblical scholars have begun to change their language from the use of soul to self in part because of the scientific consensus and also in part because there is no need for a soul anymore. Her passing statement: "but given the current popularity of books for and against the soul, they apparently neglected to inform their congregations!" amounts to a kind of paternalistic condescension of lay people sitting in their pews who don't know any better. One might be inclined to say thank you for those "intellectuals," like Murphy, to show us how we've been so wrong. By disabusing us of our infantile beliefs, we can move on to more mature beliefs about human nature informed by rigorous standards of "science"! However, Murphy gives us a place to start for thinking about the soul. She states that the common man (or woman) in the pew believes in the existence of souls. Why is that? Well some psychologists have confirmed that this belief is supported by our own cognitively inclined dispositions.

Renowned and respected psychologist Paul Bloom (PhD, Professor at Yale University; https://psychology.yale.edu/people/paul-bloom) has argued in more than one place that children naturally develop a belief in God and soul. Bloom goes so far as to suggest that these beliefs are often a package deal. As we develop as young infants, we naturally form dualist beliefs about who we are. When a child begins to recognize her hand, she instinctively makes a distinction between her *hand* and *her* hand.[58] In one article, Bloom calls this initial and naturally developed belief in dualism "common-sense dualism" because the belief comes about as a natural operating orientation, which comes from our cognitive apparatus. He proceeds to point out that the first thing we learn in introductory psychology is that substance dualism isn't true and that nearly all scientists reject it.[59] Bloom offers no additional reason why we should concur with the consensus of the scientific community. Beyond our common-sense belief that we are distinct from our bodies, there are other sophisticated reasons for thinking that I am a soul and not simply a body.

Why should we believe in the soul?

While Paul Bloom has given us an initial reason for believing in the existence of the soul, we can gain additional reasons by taking a deeper look at our natures. Upon further reflection, it appears that the material realm just doesn't provide us with the reasons for explaining those features that are most central to our internal lives. In other words, the material just doesn't cut it as an explanation for the life of the mind. Picking up on a thought above, we can consider the various parts of our body and, like the child developing her cognitive abilities, we naturally develop the belief that we are distinct from our bodies or the parts that comprise our bodies. On further examination, it appears that we try to find a candidate that adequately describes who we are as persons, minds, and conscious beings, but we come up short of an answer when looking at our bodies. We can consider our hands, but not only do we develop the belief that we are not our hands, we could also conceive of those hands being somehow lopped off and we would remain the self-same persons.

There is a deeper fact that explains why it is impossible for us to conceive of the fact that we are not identical to the body or the parts that comprise our bodies. The fact is that we are simple (i.e., indivisible) beings unlike our material bodies. The nature of our internal lives is such that it is not characteristically complex and, in principle, divisible in the way that material things are divisible. Conceivably, the body could be divided into smaller pieces, and, for that matter, all material things are divisible into smaller parts. However, one's own consciousness does not work that way. For what would it mean for a soul's thinking to be broken down into parts? Again these qualities of persons are not quantities to be measured by external instruments, and the same goes for the soul that is having these qualitative experiences. There is something about it that it is unlike the physical brain of which it interacts. The brain can be split, and there are certainly all sorts of interesting facts that follow from a split brain worth considering concerning the impact it has on consciousness, but consciousness itself is an individual singular—and it cannot be split like the brain. As Descartes himself famously stated, "we can't conceive of half a soul."[60]

Another argument supports the fact of our indivisibility. Thomas Nagel has recently argued that the prevailing paradigm in science, namely materialism, doesn't have the resources to account for consciousness. He states: "The existence of consciousness seems to imply that the physical description of the universe, in spite of its richness and explanatory power, is only part of the truth, and that the natural order is far less austere than it be if physics and chemistry account for everything." Part of the reason the material or natural order lacks the resources to explain consciousness has to do with what Nagel calls "subjective appearances."[61] There is something of what it is like to me in my own conscious experience of the world that simply cannot be captured by the material world or by science as it is often described. There is another reason. My conscious experience brings with it a qualitative feel that is not captured by the material realm. The deeper question is what is it that explains these "subjective appearances" and the qualitative feel of our conscious experiences of the world? I suggest to you that this answer to this question is found in a deeper fact about souls. Each individual soul appears to contribute something novel to the world that is otherwise non-capturable in the material order. Such a fact presses us to think about the world beyond the bounds of the material order of mechanistic causes and effects. This gives us a second reason for believing in the existence of the soul.[62]

There is a third reason. If you are a Christian or a theist generally, then you likely believe in the afterlife. Following Paul Bloom's argument, the belief in an existing soul comes as a package deal along with the belief in God's existence and a belief that we will exist after death. He states in the context of talking about religious belief and soul-body dualism that, "These biases make it natural to believe in Gods and spirits, in an afterlife, and in the divine creation of the universe."[63] John Cooper actually argues that souls are presumed in Scripture because of its teaching that we survive our death. In his famous book, *Soul, Body, and Life Everlasting*, he develops the most sustained defense to date for dualism and the existence of persons after death from a biblical perspective.[64]

Some in the scientific community, like Murphy, may have you thinking that the soul is *passé* and no longer scientifically reputable. Three challenges present themselves to Murphy's claim. First, science, especially neuroscience, tells us very little about the features often associated with the soul, which concern features like consciousness, thought, experience, and values. Second, there are a number of scientists, psychologists, and neuroscientists who believe we have lots of reasons to think that there is a soul or, at a minimum, something above and beyond our present embodiment. Third, for these and many other reasons, not only have the scientists offered little that refutes the existence of the soul, but we seem to have good positive grounds for thinking that, in fact, souls do exist.[65]

Chapter 4

Why neo-Cartesian Selves?

If you are of the mind (no pun intended!) that souls are passé like the unwelcome guest described earlier, then all the worse for Cartesianism with its strong distinction between the mind and body. The benefits of Cartesianism in addition to its being the common-sense view is that it provides a metaphysically elegant view that bears the mark of simplicity (not to be conflated with metaphysical simplicity)—a value cherished by scientists. For these reasons, those inclined toward a belief in the soul should consider it as a viable option. This is my preferred option of which I will give several reasons favoring it in what follows in contrast with complex and what I will later call 'obscure' dualisms. Yet, my preferred view is not beholden to all the commitments found in Descartes (e.g., his commitment to the fact that animals lack souls, or his crude understanding of the body as mechanistic), but it is committed to his core assumption that personal identity is rooted in the soul which is distinct from the body. That Cartesian premise is actually hard to deny once we take seriously the nature of consciousness in relation to personal identity, and it is one that scientists, materialists, and naturalists must contend.

A Philosophical Defense of Cartesian Souls
Consider, once again, the well-known thought experiment originally proposed by Frank Jackson. Mary is a brilliant scientist living in a black and white room who has studied color, the physics of light, its relation to color, and neurophysiology. Yet she has never experienced the color red. When she steps out of her black and white room, she experiences the color red. At this point, she exclaims: "I see red." At the point that she

sees red it is argued that she gains a new concept/mental item of knowledge that is distinct from her knowledge of red prior to seeing red. Accordingly, we know that there is a duality in Mary's knowledge: one that derives from a posteriori as it concerns a new item of knowledge and one that is a priori as it concerns a presupposed item(s) of knowledge.[66]

Considering the items within her purview suggest something beyond the original motivation for the argument. They suggest not only property dualism (i.e., that she has properties of a mental sort and a bodily sort, revealed to her in her new item of knowledge about color), but they suggest that there is a unity to the field of the new knowledge.[67] Chisholm has argued along these lines for the mode or presentation of mental properties. He says that there are two properties distinct with every piece of knowledge or concept. Those properties include the thing directly in the purview of one's perceptual states and the self as presented with the perceptual state. The property of presentation or consciousness he calls "self-presenting properties."[68] Self-presenting properties go some way in forming the I-concept, i.e., what it is that makes me me. This is the concept that we have of ourselves directly, and immediately attending all other concepts and properties in light of the property of the object presenting itself to the self. When Mary sees red, she can know by reflecting on the concept that *she* is having an experience of red and she gains a new item of knowledge—phenomenal-red, but also that she sees red or at least upon reflection she can know that she sees red. Knowledge and subject-hood seem to be foundational to the knowledge of red and everything else. Thus, knowledge and self-consciousness is co-terminus. Following from this, Mary's experience seems not only to support the inextricable connection between mental items and minds, but also the duality of the body/brain with persons who think and have characteristics of persons. I argue that on this basis the 'I' or self is a metaphysical simple distinguishable from a complex self.

Arguably, she can introspect about the fact that she endures through the phases of time and can reflect back on the same concept of her self.[69] The fruit of her reflections reveal something stable and enduring about the self.[70] Her mental items of seeing red are just that, her mental items of seeing red. One could apply similar thought experiments to other items of knowledge and realize that there persists this 'I' that provides the unity to the phenomenal field of awareness and endures through time. While the purported counter objection from Buddhism may be raised that I could exist sans thought (i.e., 'sunyata'), this highlights rather a distinct concern from the one raised here. The point is that from thought to thought, some*thing* persists that accounts for the continuity of thoughts—quite apart from the possibility of the Buddhist thought-experiment given. Even supposing something like stage theory of metaphysical persistence (where there must be a subject of these thoughts), it might be advanced that there does not need to be the self-same subject of thoughts. In response, what guarantees that this is the self-same subject just is the designator that we will discuss in more detail in a moment. If I have an 'informative' designator or what I advance as a 'sufficient' designator at different moments of time, then it is I as the self-same subject that is aware of this fact across the phases or stages of time.

Both material things and bundles consisting of purely property-things do not have the persistence conditions to account for my having the property of coexisting with all my concepts/mental items. Pace Hume, there has been this notion that there is no subject present (i.e., the bundle theory), but this defies common sense, introspection and the fact that sensations are bound and unified by something.[71]

We have several reasons for denying the bundle theory. First, if one considers the unity-of-consciousness argument, namely, the notion that a person's conscious field of awareness is unified and singular then we have reason to think that a bundle view cannot account for this—but instead requires a subject of experience. Bundles do not have the tight unity reflective of our conscious mental states. Bundles of properties lack the internal depth characteristic of a conscious field.[72]

Second, mental items are unified in a phenomenal field rather than loosely related or related as an information rich system tied by an attention schema. In other words, these are not qualitive particles bumbling around in the brain or in immaterial space. Third, there exists a subject of consciousness that has access to the items of knowledge, hence there exists a distinct power descriptive of a distinct kind of substance from a bundle thing or a material thing—this might be called the privileged access argument, offered by Richard Swinburne.[73] Using his coined term informative designator (i.e., the view that a term is informed to describe a proper noun), Swinburne rightly argues that the physical property of a sensation is not logically equivalent to that of the mental property of experiencing the sensation. On one, we have access through brain scans, and the other it is a subject or person of experience that has access alone. Swinburne argues that mental events, like in the cases above when Mary sees red, are mental properties that are accessible only by substances.[74] The knowledge argument reveals property dualism, but something deeper is presupposed that we can know through reflection on our interior states of phenomenal awareness and recalled through memory, which is that the self as a substance has access to that which is not physical.

Fourth, a bundle of material and/or immaterial properties does not adequately account for the close relation between concepts and conceivers, as discussed briefly above. Bundles do not have ownership of things the way a mental thing has ownership of a concept. Rather, it appears that it is a pure substance unlike the material.

Connected to the above, the experience of knowledge/mental items as simple, irreducible to the physical and intrinsically nonphysical in conjunction with self-presenting properties seems to yield a metaphysical simple. If concepts are simple, intrinsically nonphysical and dependent on the person/mind, then it seems natural to infer as one did above that persons are simple because of a singular binding thing that unifies the phenomenal states of consciousness rather than a property-bundle.

Considering the difference between propositions and concepts, it is not as if I am adding a proposition from the abstract realm to my mind. Concepts do not come from anywhere else but my mind, *sui generis*.[75] *Sui generis* things are deeply foundational, new (i.e., not derived or coming from something else), and simple in nature. The phenomenology of my mental items is deeply dependent on me not anything else, and if there is a pure mental property to be had it seems it is had by a pure immaterial thing because the pure property is had by a thing and the characteristics of that thing resemble a simple immaterial thing not a material thing—thus we have a pure or simple mental subject.[76]

The property I have access to is the property that is instantiated by a pure mental subject. In order to bring out this intuition more clearly we could draw from Descartes' useful thought experiment.

> I saw that while I could conceive that I had no body... I could not conceive that I was not. On the other hand, if I had only ceased from thinking... I should have no reason for thinking that I had existed. From this, I knew that I was a substance the whole nature or essence of which is to think and that for its existence there is no need of any place, nor does it depend on any material thing.[77]

If I can conceive of a situation like the one on offer by Descartes, then it buttresses the belief already had about the informative designator—that which makes me *me* and that which only I have access. Having said this, the property that I have access to directly is a feature of the subject that has access to his/her mental states immediately and what is characteristic of this subject is that its fundamental nature is not a quantity measurable but a subject of qualitative experience.

The above notion that my concepts/mental items are simple ties to the unity of consciousness argument for substance dualism that when I experience red I do so in one unified field of awareness.[78] Furthermore, we can say more about the subject of these phenomenal experiences based on what we have access to through introspection. This substance of consciousness is a metaphysical simple that binds the plurality of items in my field of consciousness.[79] The self as soul furnishes the metaphysical glue for the experience of concepts and the unity of conscious mental states.[80] What I have shown about the nature of the soul is effectively a version of Cartesianism. Next, let us consider the possible relationships between the soul and the body through a Cartesian lens.

Cartesian/PBSD Variants

If you are familiar with films like *Planet of the Apes, Guardians of the Galaxy,* even *Transformers* then you are familiar with this pull toward the imaginative possibility that animals have or could have consciousness like you and me. This is certainly motivated by the view that humans are closely related to the rest of the physical world and came from it. From the rise of evolutionary theory, the continuity of species and the similarities between humans and animals there has been a paradigm shift in our philosophical and theological constructions of human persons. Hume's "Enquiry Concerning Human Understanding" has a lot to do with this shift in our understanding of humans in relation to animals.[81] In fact, Hume thought that humans just were bundles of properties that are highly complicated. As stated above, this trend has and continues to make its way into philosophy, theology, and the social sciences to such an extent that there has been a complete revision of our understanding of humans from what the ancients once thought. Arguably, this distracting trend highlights something about our natures as partly bodily, but overextends itself in the near elimination of what it truly means to be human. In what follows, we will consider different ways of understanding the soul in relation to its animal-part (i.e., the body) and why we should, once again, contend that humans are souls at their core.

Pure, Compound, or Composite Substance Dualism: Disambiguating Terminology

I wish to distinguish two broad views on substance dualism. The first is strict or 'pure' dualism (PSD) and the second is compound or composite dualism.[82] Pure dualism says that I am strictly identified with my soul/mind yet contingently attached to the body.[83] There may be some ambiguity in communicating that the soul has existence apart from the body because it tends to convey the soul as a part of the person, but on PSD the soul just is an individual person.[84] This has been called Person-body dualism (PBSD) in the Plato-Augustine-Descartes tradition, yet, I will suggest that there are variations within PBSD that fall under pure varieties of substance dualism (which might be construed as compound structures or substances in terms of human nature) in contrast to composite variations.[85]

The second is compound or composite dualism. Whilst these two terms often refer to one position in the philosophy of mind literature, I suggest that there are some sufficient distinctions between the two. On a compound view, as I describe it, human beings have two parts but the essential part of the person is a pure mental ego that has a part in terms of a property-nature (I call this CSD). Composite dualism is the notion that I am composed of both body and soul, and both are essential or necessary in some sense (hereafter, COSD). In discussing the nature of these substances, I am interested in the question of what kind of thing is in Latin called an ens per se (i.e., existence that is not dependent as a property) rather than ens per accidens (i.e., accidental existence).[86] This will move us some direction to furnishing a ground for making sense of the self as a pure substantial soul distinct from the body.[87] On a broadly Cartesian view, the soul substance has an ens per se kind of existence in a strong sense, i.e., it is independent and does not exist as a property of another thing. Proponents of most varieties of composite dualism maintain that the soul substance is not a proper substance, but exists in some important way on the matter of which it is related. Rather, it is incomplete in its nature when apart from the bodily organism. The composite dualist contends that the soul substance is properly unified with the body as a human person and the soul substance may have an ens per se kind of existence in a weak sense, yet more naturally is an ens per accidens as it is united substantially with the material organism.[88]

This distinction is important for clarifying the nature of Cartesianism from other variants of substance dualism. While some have suggested that there are just two types of substance dualism, namely radical versions in contrast to holistic versions, I will expand some of the options in what follows.[89]

Compound/Composite Dualists and Confusion

There is significant confusion about how to parse the relationship between soul and body.[90] Richard Swinburne provides us with insight into the soul-body relationship that is both illuminating in one sense and, potentially, confusing in another.[91] Swinburne states,

> That truths about persons are other than truths about their bodies and parts thereof—is, I suggest, forced upon anyone

who reflects seriously on the fact of the unity of consciousness over time and at a time. A framework of thought, which makes sense of this fact, is provided if we think of a person as body plus soul, such that the continuing of the soul alone guarantees the continuing of a person.[92]

It is not clear from this statement and others like it whether Swinburne takes the person to be strictly identified with his soul or the soul and body.

If we are to be charitable to Swinburne, then we could say something along the lines that the soul simpliciter can expand to include the body (accidentally) for certain phases of time.[93] Swinburne's statement above and in other places is consistent with this, but what he says does not necessitate this interpretation, hence the concern for clarity. But this does provide an opportunity to clarify some of the options.

Swinburne and Modified Compound/Composite Substance Dualism

Swinburne provides additional clarity in his: "From Mental/ Physical Identity to Substance Dualism".[94] He develops a view of persons as metaphysical simples and pure substances that have a robust functional relationship to their bodies and brains.[95] He explicitly states this: "My final claim is that human beings, you and I, are pure mental substances (which do not supervene on physical substances)."[96] Yet later on, somewhat confusingly, Swinburne refers to the human person as a pure mental substance that is a "composite of substances of two genera."[97] What is Swinburne saying about the nature of the soul-body relationship?[98] Interestingly, in various places, Swinburne also affirms that the body is a contingent part of me, which might suggest that I am identical to the body + soul, but this would be absurd if we take seriously Swinburne's modal intuition that the person can survive via the disembodied soul.[99]

Taking Swinburne charitably, it may be best to interpret him as affirming something in between a pure radical dualism and a composite or complex dualism where the soul can expand to include the body, albeit contingently and not essentially.

Swinburne retains intuitions that are often compatible with both Aristotle and Plato, i.e., that I am either a compound or complex entity (with Aristotle) or a simple (with Plato).[100] Swinburne does this because he assumes a more finely-grained role for mind on brain dependence.[101] There is a difficulty with affirming this. While it is natural to affirm the functional dependence of mind on brain (and it comports well with neuroscientific findings), it is also clear that there is no theory that is able to explain or correlate mind and neural connections and it is likely that there never will be.[102] This, naturally, raises the question as to whether or not there is an unnecessary empirical constraint placed on his understanding of the soul and its powers.

In another place, Swinburne discusses the relation in a distinct way when describing the stories of souls and bodies compared to telling the story of human beings.[103] The two stories are distinct because a soul can have a history that is distinct from the body. However, this is not quite right if we take it that the body is an accidental, or contingent, part of the human being, then the narrative of the body would be the narrative of the human being that begins with a self as soul.[104] Using the terms 'compound' or 'composite' is not entirely clear, but it is a common way of capturing that we are both bodies and souls.[105]

This raises an additional worry that often perplexes philosophers, namely, what properties are properties of me in contrast to my soul and/or body. Take for example the property of weight. My body may weigh 160 pounds, but some may contend this is not true of persons literally. On a composite version, one could argue that I am 160 pounds because the body is a part of me.[106] On some versions of a pure soul as person distinct from the body, it would be accurate to say I am 160 pounds via (or derivatively) from my body, but I am not, strictly speaking, 160 pounds. However, on the story we told above where souls expand, as it were, we could say that I, a self as soul, am 160 pounds, but this is only a contingent part of me subject to change (and we all know that this can fluctuate quite significantly). This raises another important question about why we should expect to retain a connection to our body, if the body is nonessential to personal identity.

On PSD (and other pure varieties of dualism), as I have described them, the soul is naturally and normally attached to a body without a necessary relationship between the soul and body of which there are four reasons to believe this to be true. First, from an empirical and experiential standpoint we have every reason to think that we are naturally and normally attached to bodies. From the beginning of our existence we are embodied, at least, so far as we are aware. Embodiment, minimally, furnishes the soul with powers and virtues that are conducive to the soul's existence and functioning.

Second, we have a theological reason to think that we are in fact naturally and normally embodied according to religious texts like Genesis, if you take seriously these texts as Divine revelations.[107]

If one were to affirm that the soul comes into existence with a body (i.e., the essentiality of origins), then we may have reason to affirm a kind soul (namely, that souls are created kinds that fall under certain categories in virtue of a property(s)) that has some unity with a body. The soul does come into the world with an essential origin relation to a body.[108] A relational soul might be construed as a generic soul in its own right that can change, adapt, and mold to a particular body. In this way, souls do not have an intrinsic relation to bodies, but are able to become embodied. In this way, relational souls, you might say, are not essentially human. Instead, they bear a relation to a human body when embodied. Kind-souls are distinct in that souls have a kind relation to bodies. Bodies and souls are fitted for the other, so that there are particular kinds of souls that are fitted to particular kinds of physical entities, e.g., a human kind-soul and a human body. A hybrid view would say that human souls can exist on their own as a substance like relational souls, but have intrinsic aptness for a human body. One could think of this as a first-order property or dispositional property that is only actualized (i.e., second-order properties) when embodied.

For those who are interested in a more detailed analytic argument for my version of Cartesianism, see the following, but for those who do not wish to wade these thick waters, they can skip to the next chapter.

In what follows, I build on the tradition of F. Brentano, J.P. Moreland, Roderick Chisholm and others who argue from the transparency of the mental compared to the material as a context that furthers the rationale for thinking that I am not my body, the parts of my body, or the body parts interacting at some high-level of specified complexity.

Defining Terms

TT=Transparency thesis: phenomenal consciousness reveals the nature of the mind.

ETT=Extended Transparency thesis: qualia implies a more fundamental feature that characterizes the subject of conscious experience.

FPP=First-person perspective: some knowledge about the physical world from second properties are given to the mind. I can think about them.

S=Subject of conscious experience:

- private (that which is accessible by the subject of conscious experience)
- inner (that which is internal not external or spatially located)
- self-presenting (a property that is directly available, accessible, or aware to me)
- intentional
- Some subjective states of consciousness have this s-set.
- No physical things have this s-set.
- S-set properties are not identical to the material.

SD=Substance Dualism: every person/subject who has experiences is an immaterial substance. An Immaterial substance is: (1) essentially the person, (2) foundational to the mental or conscious life, (3) does not have many of the properties characterizing physical/material things.[109]

OD='Obscure dualisms': those views that give primacy to the mental, yet either deny the transparency thesis or advance a position that implies a non-transparency thesis. Under this title, I include the following: pan-experientialism; micro-psychism; pan-psychism; hylomorphism; absolute monism.

HN=human nature or the essence of what it means to be human is an abstract object. In the case of humans as soul-body compounds, we address what it means to be a soul-body compound in relation to the nature of human beings.

HO=human origins. HO supplies a story for how it is that an individual HN comes into existence through a process.

An Argument for Primitive Immaterial Subjects

1. The transparency thesis of phenomenal experience is

directly available and accessible to the FPP.

2. Only a primitive 'S' particular (i.e., subject of conscious experience) accounts for the transparency thesis because of the fundamental first-person powers that are non-multiply exemplifiable.

3. 'Obscure' dualisms do not have this fundamental power that is non-multiply exemplifiable.

4. Therefore, 'Obscure' dualisms cannot account for the reality of the transparency thesis.

The Primacy of the Mental

Working within the psychological tradition of personal identity in contrast to the animalist tradition, substance dualists often take it that thinking, consciousness, and other mental items are indicative or pointers to that with which we as humans are identified. And this for the simple reason that there is not any garden-variety physical object that we can point to and say that's me! Instead, there is some essential core that makes us who we are at a time and across time—the immaterial center of conscious experience.

An initial definition of a basic subject is given by John Foster. He states,

> We already know what conditions something has to satisfy to qualify as a basic subject: to qualify as a mental subject, it has to be something to which mental states or activities can be truly ascribed; and to qualify as a basic mental subject it has to be something which features as a mental subject in the philosophically fundamental account—something which is both ontologically basic and whose role as a subject of mental states and activities is not reducible to factors of a different kind.[110]

A subject is a mental subject or a subject of conscious experience.

A fundamental account of the subject or self is what I am after in the following discussion, which begins in 'introspective' dualism or common-sense dualism. Introspective dualism takes its starting point in what is most apparent and clear as indicative of what is true in reality, namely the FPP. Common-sense dualism is similar in that it takes its starting point from that which is the most obvious, apparent deliverances of our reasoning about the world—namely that there exist differences between mental and physical things, and that the contents of my mind are more apparent than the physical objects. It is a given of our phenomenal experience, hence the reason for beginning with consciousness when trying to ascertain the meaning of who we are. The TT is the thesis that the contents of my mental life are more obvious than the contents of the physical world because of all my experience (and that of the scientist investigating the physical world). Hence it is consciousness that is the starting point for considering the identity and meaning of subjects. For what it is like to experience the physical world, say the flower and all its properties, is basic. As Philip Goff describes TT as our direct phenomenal transparency.[111]

There is one key part of John Foster's definition that is important and one for which I am concerned when adequately assessing the TT. John Foster states: "it has to be something to which mental states or activities can be truly ascribed." It is the qualifier of 'truly' that is important here. What is it for qualities or properties truly to be ascribed? The aspect of subjects that makes each individual subject *this* subject and not *that* subject begins with introspection, according to the 'introspective' tradition of substance dualism. To this we turn as the vehicle for accurately understanding the nature of consciousness—hence, personal identity.

Building on the successes of 'introspective dualism' (i.e., the argument that there are items of knowledge through direct acquaintance of the world and its objects that prefer a dualism of subject and the body), the TT is the thesis that the unique nature of conscious knowledge is directly available to the conscious agent. Yet, the TT that we will consider in more detail below is often limited in its scope to phenomenal transparency and needs extending. When we extend the transparency thesis, it becomes clear that substance dualism (or idealism) accounts for the TT in a way that 'obscure' dualisms do not. TT, then, provides evidence for the primacy of the mental when determining the meaning and identity of subjects.

Primacy is used as a term to describe grounding relations in metaphysics. The relation of dependence between the grounded entity and that entity's grounding is concerned with primacy. The primacy relation says that z is grounded in y, y is primary over z and y metaphysically explains z. In the case of the primacy relation within consciousness, the mental is primary over the physical concerning consciousness and metaphysically explains consciousness.[112] Considering the mental life of human beings, the TT is the most obvious fact about our experience of the world and supplies us with immediate FPP evidence for the primacy of the mental over the physical.

Common-sense dualism is important for defending the primacy of the mental over the physical concerning consciousness. Following Roderick Chisholm, John Foster and others, when I enter into my conscious states of awareness, I am aware of the objects of the world before me in my perceptual states. I can actually pick out the various items in my field of awareness. I can introspect about those items and consider all the features or properties that each object has. When I enter into my states of awareness and consider all the items presented to me, I realize upon reflection that I am neither those objects nor the objects of my body that I, too, can reflect on as objects within the presentation of my consciousness (i.e., what is commonly called self-presenting properties in the introspective dualism literature), which indicates the primacy of the mental existence over the physical and the properties of the mental. I experience them as distinct from myself. The 'natural' conclusion is that I am a distinct consciousness that is different from these objects.[113]

Considering the nature of color fits well here. The fact that I seem to have direct acquaintance with the color green in the grass that I perceive provides *prima facie* evidence that I, in fact, have the color of the green grass directly within the purview of my conscious field of awareness. I am aware of the green colored grass and I have the power to access those properties directly in my conscious field. These properties, again, are called self-presenting properties describing the phenomena that I am directly acquainted within my conscious experience, and these are ones for which I can further inspect through introspection. And these sets of properties are descriptive of a set of properties for S. While they may not be the intrinsic properties of the grass itself, the point is that I have access to these properties via conscious experience. Clarifying the nature of the color green in grass is not confused with these self-presenting properties (where the grass appears greenly to me). Whatever one makes of the actual color green in the grass (i.e., primary qualities) as intrinsic to the grass and objectively the case in the world, this is distinct from the phenomenal qualia (although they may be causally related) of green in one's perspective of it.

In order to move from *prima facie* to *secunda facie* justification of my conscious perception, I can investigate the properties further. By moving closer to the green grass, I can inspect it more closely to see if the properties of my conscious powers of perception are functioning properly. Further, I can speak with others to see if my experience of the green grass is the same as their experience of the green grass.[114]

This raises a distinct issue in the literature that needs addressing. The phenomenality argument is the argument that phenomenal qualia are basic, fundamental and accessible to the mental life of individuals.[115] This is commonly the view of contemporary philosophers. But it appears to me from my FPP that phenomenal qualia, while it offers an avenue into the mind's nature, fails to capture what is most fundamental in terms of the mind's essence. There is an alternative feature or characteristic that seems to encompass more than the qualitative feel of color, taste, smell or the hand-felt nature of grass when I touch it with my hands; it is subjectivity.

Subjectivity seems to be an apt descriptor of that which covers phenomenal qualia, but encompasses additional features that get us closer to the essence of minds. This is true of other features of physical objects in the natural world that resist reduction like ideas, aboutness, and teleology within the physical world (all features or properties that require an explanation beyond mere machinery). Subjectivity captures qualia, but it also captures the place that I occupy (not to be confused with Descartes' objective physical location), the perspective I have, the interpretive angle I take, the contribution that I make simply in virtue of the fact that I am me and not anyone else. If there is such a thing as subjectivity as I have described it, then there is something that is more fundamental to mental nature than phenomenal qualia. The subject is prior to the general characteristic of mind. For there are no generalized minds or properties of minds that are universalizable, but there are S's (again primitive immaterial subjects of conscious experience).

Both qualia and the FPP presume something more fundamental about the properties of conscious experience. Implicit in the FPP is a substance or what philosophers have called bare particulars (i.e., those substances that have no properties in the abstract). For it is these properties that depend on and are predicated of something in particular. That something I argue is a metaphysically simple substance. Following Quine's dictum: "there is no object without identity," which I will take as a basic fact, becomes mysterious when we apply it to persons.[116] For persons, there are no physical parts with which we are identical. But the case is even more mysterious when there are no generalizable features or properties that describe me or make me *me*. Instead, there is a primitive fact that I am me—something like Chalmers's primitive indexical fact.[117] E.J. Lowe offers a helpful definition, when he says: "A non-composite or simple substance—one that has no component parts—must, it appears, have no criterion of diachronic identity."[118] While a substance might depend for its functionality on a complexity of parts, it does not entail that one's identity depends on that same complexity of parts, and, in fact, the argument from replacement suggests just that fact about persons that we could lose the various parts of our body (and possibly all of the body) and remain the self-same existing entity, which means that the parts lost are nonessential to the identity of the self/subject.[119]

Yet, the issue already alluded to is related to the argument for a simple substance from mereological replacement. What underlies the parts and properties is an actual substance that grounds them (the ETT). This particular that we are directly aware of and can access precedes even the properties in our minds. In other words, what makes sense of the properties of qualia is the S as a metaphysically simple substance, a primitive particular. Moving in this direction alleviates another concern prompted by SD.

According to Geoffrey Madell, the simple view of personal identity presumes the criterial gap issue.[120] Accordingly, 'A is F' and 'I am F'; 'persons are souls' and 'I am soul.' In other words, the generalizable terms always presume the gap between the objective and the subjective. Implied by this proposition is the 'contingent truth issue,' which says that the truths that we ascribe to the objective order of things involving persons always miss the more important primitive fact about those persons. Finally, all of this means that there is a problem with self-ascription. The uniqueness of the S's consciousness is that there is never a way adequately or sufficiently to describe the person because of the primitive nature of selves. While the FPP and other generalizable facts may come close, they will always fail adequately to ascribe the sufficient feature(s) of the S due to the primitive fact about them.[121]

Apparent problems exist on Madell's thesis. One apparent problem is that it is unclear if there is a substance present. Another problem is that there is no way to determine that there is a substance of consciousness present. Madell clearly believes that something exists, as a subject of experience is the most obvious thing in the world. However, a subject, as substance, is a rationally necessary entity that explains the qualitative experiences of individual S's.

Further, there is some evidence in addition to what seems a rationally compelling reason to assume that there is a substance of a particular sort that grounds these properties of consciousness. In addition to the fact that there is some ground for qualia, there exists some phenomena in the world that are non-universalizable, i.e., they have no explanation apart from a primitive particular. Consider for example the fact about taste. In some cases, there is no further explanation grounded in one's biology or in properties that accounts for one's individual liking of certain tastes. There is no further analyzable fact that explains the fact that I might taste something different than another as the account for my not liking x or the fact that I taste x in the same way as another person but I just do not like x. The only fact that seems to ground this experience is the primitive fact about me, an S. To clarify, the principle of sufficient reason demands a rational explanation of substances and all properties in the world, including phenomenal qualities.

In keeping with the subjectivity argument, the above rationale prompts the question about the essence of S's. There are two views open for consideration. One view, following Madell, is that there is no-essenced (or so this is how I am interpreting him) bare particular, which is consistent with the primitive indexical fact without a sufficient designator. The alternative view, and the one I am inclined to, is an individual essenced bare particular (or a haecceity). I have already advanced some reasons that we actually believe that minds have this more fundamental fact. If so, then we have a primitive fact of the self, namely S's.

The most obvious fact about the world is that my mind is transparent to me. This fact undergirds all other facts in the world. The ubiquitous nature of minds is present all around and accounts for what is clear and direct to my experience. Additionally, the fact that colors and smells have a particular felt quality to them grounded in a subject captures something of the ubiquitous nature of the mental as central to explaining the nature of the world. The fundamental or primitive nature of minds is that they are subjects.

If this is the case, then modifying Madell's numerated challenges concerning the simple view of personal identity is important to making sense of the world of conscious experience. I have to this point advanced a case for a version of SD with specific attention given to S's as primitive immaterial subjects of conscious experience, a Cartesian view. While Madell advances a Cartesian thesis that presumes the metaphysical simplicity of selves, he does so without giving a sufficient explanation for those selves. For a modification of Madell's challenges assuming S's (with FPP's) have a haecceity that makes each S *that* S, see the following.

1. Criterial Gap Issue: 'A is F' when the *user* ascribes to himself this property.[122]
2. Uniqueness issue: No account of conscious perspective is from a purely objective frame apart from the user.
3. All truths about the world are contingent upon the user using them rightly as it pertains to him/herself.
4. There is no problem of self-ascription when the user uses

the terms to refer to him/herself, if s/he has adequate grasp of herself. Otherwise, the gap is simply one between DeDicto and DeRe.

In other words, the gap between the objective order of things and the subjective order of things is closed within a proper understanding of the Cartesian thesis. If the Cartesian thesis about mental essences is correct, then it rules out any of the 'obscure dualisms' because they by nature deny the ETT or they entail the denial of TT. Consider that both hylomorphism and neutral monism assume that which underlies mental essences is something that is not directly accessible, but rather something that disposes or gives rise to minds.

Hylomorphism presumes that all matter has an organizational structure (i.e., form) or a component part that provides the organizational structure (i.e., form) that will eventually give rise to minds at some level of neural complexity and structural organization. Neutral monism presumes that there is some underlying ontological structure that grounds both the physical and the mental. There are properties that are dispositional in nature, but the underlying ontology is unknowable and this is what supplies an explanation for minds.

The same applies to pan-experientialism or panpsychism. On pan-experientialism, higher-order minds are composite products of lower-level mind-lets (i.e., dispositional properties that give rise to minds). On one understanding of panpsychism (which I am casting under the net of pan-experientialism), all of reality is experiential, but what is known about the experiential is dispositional properties. Similar to materialism of the mind, panpsychism is confronted with the combination problem like all bottom-up approaches that have no underlying primitive minds. On all bottom-up approaches where minds are the products of a high-level composition of lower-level physical parts, mysterious properties underlying both the physical and mental, or the combination of other lower-level minds, the how of a simple or unified mind from a complexity of parts is parasitic on all these approaches to the mind. In the final analysis, at a minimum, the evidence for the basic Cartesian thesis is the fact that all the other accounts are lacking as explanations for the mind.

Part II

Where do selves come from?

Chapter 5

Origins of the Self, A Religious and Contemporary Problem

(Drawn from, adapted, modified selections, and substantially rewritten portions of the following for purposes here: Joshua R. Farris, "Considering Souls of the Past for Today: Soul Origins, Anthropology, and Contemporary Theology," in *Neue Zeitschrift fur Systematische Theologie und Religionsphilosophie*, vol. 57, issue 3, 2015)

For the contemporary ear, discussion of the soul's origin is likely met with quizzical eyebrow raising. For many, it is undoubtedly as strange as trying to resurrect Plato's recollection theory of the soul. However, this dated discussion demands revisiting in light of recent science-engaged theological discussions. This old discussion points us in the direction of a part of reality that is currently being submerged by naturalism or the dominate physicalist paradigm found in scientific communities—now creeping into philosophy, theology, and, worse, the social consciousness of the common man. It is this discussion that helps us see afresh the mental reality that is central to what we care about most.[123] Research into the philosophy of mind, especially into emergentism, prompts a reconsideration of older options in light of newer ones.[124]

The simple contemporary question: "where does consciousness come from?," actually finds original footing in this older discussion. As seen earlier, we have good reasons for taking it that consciousness is not a property, state, an event, nor is it reduced to neurons or brains. In fact, we have a more refined question to answer of which this old discussion aids: where do conscious selves come from? Do they emerge from neural events? Do they come from other souls? Or, as I address in the remaining parts of *The Creation of Self,* do they come directly from a personal being, like God (or alien powers that are non-natural), who simply causes them to exist?

Defining terms

Before we dive into discussions about the soul-body connection in relation to the soul's origin, we need to define some terms. Creationism is the view that God creates the individual soul directly and immediately. God is directly the cause in the sense that he utilizes no other cause to bring about the soul. Thus, God is the terminus of the causal chain. By immediate, I mean that Divine action is without mediation through other causes or events. For the creationist, the creation of the soul is directly rooted in a Divine choice-event, not a process that exists prior to the choice-event.[125] Traducianism is the view that God creates one or two souls immediately and each successive soul, secondarily or mediately, through the generative process from one generation to another. One's metaphysical assumptions about the relationship between body and souls will lend itself to interesting implications concerning the theology of the soul's origin.[126] Let us turn now to consider these assumptions in more detail.[127]

The Mind-Body Problem, Substance Dualism, and Implications for Origins

The mind-body problem has a long history of variegated discussion on the nature of the mind and its relation to the body.[128] In other words, what follows is not a piece of historical philosophy, but an exercise in the metaphysics of the mind in relation to the theology of the soul's origin.

In previous chapters, I have gone some way to show that there are two concrete particulars, a soul or mind (of which the self is carried) and the body.[129] The variants of materialism will not be discussed here as a result, but I will come back to these in the next chapter when I give an exposition of emergentism and panpsychism.

The problem for a substance dualist is similar in that both must supply a bridge for the properties of the soul in relation to the properties of the body, yet different in that materialists have the additional challenge of explaining mental properties via the physical base on which they stand. Substance dualists do not encounter this problem, at least not obviously, because they assume that there are distinct kinds of property-bearers.

Mental property-bearers are distinct from physical, or material, property-bearers. And, this impinges on the origins question in that the meaningful relation between the two parts presumes something about where they originate. Mental property-bearers are characterized by subjective qualia, privacy, internal access, and first-person awareness. Material property-bearers are radically different. Property-bearers of a material kind are characterized by public access or public knowledge, third-person knowledge, and characteristics predicated from the physical sciences. Material things or properties are accessible by anyone and everyone. They are thus distinguishable from property-bearers of a mental sort.[130] The problem faced by the substance dualist is that both property-bearers are radically different. The two are not different in the same sense that two colors are different or in the sense that flowers are distinguishable by differing characteristics, but property-bearers of a mental kind and property-bearers of a material kind are fundamentally different. The two do not overlap. For the mental and the physical there is not merely a lack of physical and spatial overlap, but a seeming lack of fundamental ontological overlap.

Now, establishing the dissimilarity between the two sorts of property-bearers is only one part of the problem. The other part of the problem is one of influence. That is the two seem to interact causally. For instance, when I bump my knee on the chair I not only have observable sensations and effects on my physical body, but my mind thinks new thoughts of 'ouch' or at least this is an internal sensation that is distinct from the observable aspects in terms of my body. What is more, when I have thoughts or intentional states of mind it seems to affect or causally influence my body. So, when I have the intentional state of desiring to have a cup of coffee and intend to make a cup, then my body moves when I bring it about as a choice-event. The fundamental cause seems to be my mental state of intending to enjoy a cup of coffee not the physical sensation that then causes the mental state following with other physical causes.[131] When I intend to make a cup of coffee and do so, my body acts. Other physical sensations follow from this act. Thus, the two seemingly distinct kinds of things interact in a deep and intimate manner. David Robb and John Heil state the problem in terms of causation quite well, when they say:

> The philosophical significance of mental causation goes beyond general concerns about the nature of mind. Some philosophers (e.g., Davidson 1963; Mele 1992) insist that the very notion of psychological explanation turns on the intelligibility of mental causation. If your mind and its states, such as your beliefs and desires, were causally isolated from your bodily behavior, then what goes on in your mind could not explain what you do. (For contrary views, see Ginet 1990; Sehon 2005.)[132]

The dilemma for the dualist is clear. Dualists have an intuitive challenge of supplying an explanation for the interaction between two distinct parts and showing the plausibility for a two-way causation. This is what many philosophers have called the interaction problem because some sort of bridge is needed to explain the interaction. According to Hasker: "This argument may hold the all-time record for overrated objections to major philosophical positions. What is true about it is that we lack any intuitive understanding of the causal relationship between Cartesian souls and bodies."[133] The motivation behind this common objection arguably comes from a Humean (i.e., the famous modern philosopher David Hume) view of causation, roughly, that there is a continuous regularity of succession between objects. The problem for the Humean is that it lacks an explanation as to why there exists a regularity of succession. The problem is similar for the materialist who affirms the reality and distinction of a mind, in some sense, from its brain. Hasker rightly shows that this is not an utterly unique problem for the dualist.[134]

All dualists agree that minds and bodies interact.[135] Some form of causal interaction is real, but lacking a theory of how this precisely works is not a good reason to deny the truth that there exists a mind that is related to a body.[136] Consideration of the mind-body solutions in relation to the origins debates opens up afresh the space for considering newer options in light of older options.

Pure substance dualism is a radical form of substance dualism in terms of the distinctions between bodies and souls.[137] Olson defines this view according to which persons are souls and are intimately connected to bodies, although bodies are not parts of persons.[138] The two parts do not mingle in their respective essences, but, as many would argue, all that is needed is a singular relation between the two for there to be an interactive relation.[139] Others will argue that the relation is merely a brute (what philosophers use to refer to something that has no further explanation or more basic relation or ground).[140] One can argue that in order for the objector to isolate the problem specifically aimed at dualists would require a greater clarity and facility of the nature of the mind and the body without which it is difficult to motivate this common objection. An additional explanation that can be offered is that the relation is simply rooted in Divine intentionality that the two interact causally.

Composite substance dualism supplies a distinct option.[141] On such a view, minds and bodies are more intimately related.[142] A common way to make sense of the two is to posit that there is some matter-form relation between the soul and the hunk of matter it informs, following Aristotle and Thomas Aquinas.[143]

Emergent dualism is another solution and one which has gestured in the direction of the discussion concerning the origination of souls.[144] This is the most recent and radical of all three varieties of substance dualism in the sense that it posits a view that is similar to non-reductive materialism, yet remains a live option in substance dualism. On this view, souls are synonymous with minds or selves. The apparent benefits of emergent dualism advanced by defenders include that it grounds a more natural relation between mind and body and is more economical in explaining the soul in relation to the brain because it is the soul that emerges from a brain, thereby avoiding the interaction problem altogether—arguably.[145] The view has similarities to non-reductive physicalism in explaining the origination of minds, but, as a unique option, it maintains a robust substantial distinction.[146] The soul is conceptually and modally distinct from the body/brain.[147] Importantly, it is distinguished from other dualist options in that the soul comes from and depends upon the brain as a result of emerging from it.[148]

Each option in conjunction with variations of soulish origins has interesting implications. Let's consider some of the options and their implications.[149]

The Origin of the Soul and Options

Traditional-Traducianism[150]

It is not uncommon to identify traditional dualism with

creationism, but this does not capture the panoply of options reflecting traditional views of souls.[151] There are versions of traducianism that might be considered traditional in nature. One important theologian in Ecclesiastical history that affirmed traducianism is Tertullian who said that human souls were passed down from parents.[152] He also stated that this occurred originally from one created Soul—Adam.[153] Many others affirmed the basic traducian positions that souls are generated from one created soul.[154] Here are some traditional possibilities that, arguably, have Ecclesiastical and Scriptural support.[155]

A traditional-traducian view says that God created one human soul directly and immediately that somehow contains all other un-individualized human souls.[156] Souls are thus propagated primarily through a generative process becoming individualized souls.

Traditional-Traducianism: the notion that a parent or at most two parents generate a soul that ultimately derives from God is creating one soul directly and immediately. All successive souls obtain as individual souls from the first soul that was created. The process of generation is not all at once (i.e. synchronic), but it is across time (i.e. diachronic).

As stated above, pure and composite varieties of substance dualism could coherently work with traducianism. In what is to follow, I discuss two variations of traditional-traducianism: fissile variations and parturient variations.

The first variation is the notion that the soul is fissile in nature. To say that the soul is fissile is to say that souls or persons fissile or split-off and are fused with other material to form a person and/or soul. One version of a fissile traducianism can be grasped in the mental picture of a lump of clay. The lump of clay represents one soul that can become more than one soul as when clay is divided. With the lump of clay, one can take a piece of clay from it, and, then, take a piece of clay from that piece of clay and one can repeat the process. Souls work in a similar fashion according to the fissile traducian view. God creates one soul that generates other souls similar to a lump of clay. Souls on this view split-off and become new souls from the previous soul.[157] The new soul has the potential, again, to split-off.

A second variation of Traducianism is parturient in nature. The idea here is that somehow souls give off parts, and generate new souls not that souls split-off. The soul and persons are generated from a previous generation in a line leading back to one created soul. The gamete-like view holds that the parents generate soulish parts that are carried on through human seed. The notion here is that the parents in virtue of the gametes through the seed carry on souls and DNA. Additionally, souls and persons are compound and complex in nature not simple in nature.[158]

Within parturient traducianism, the process by which persons come into being could be something along the following lines. The unifying process of the soul and/or person takes place in the process of gestation in the mother's womb when the proper parts come together in syngamy.

One example of an emergent and parturient form of traducianism is a version of hylomorphism (arguably a version of composite substance dualism as I define it above).[159] Hylomorphism that is also a kind of substance dualism does not entail traducianism, but it could work as a version of traducianism. Hylomorphism is a form of constituent ontology where the parts have liabilities and potentialities that are actualized in relation to other parts (e.g., the necessary constituents include the biological organism that has latent active capacities and passive liabilities, and the soul).[160] There are two constituent parts, body and soul, that constitute the composite person.[161]

The picture of origins on hylomorphism may be something like the following. One could view the soul and body as spatially present with the other, but two different things. If hylomorphism is construed according to natures as powers, then natures are complex things made up of parts. When various parts come together those parts become a new nature. A rational soul with a body composes human nature. When these parts unite, a new nature comes to exist. Both the soul and body are able to self-breed or reproduce under certain conditions in a similar fashion. Alternatively, it could be that the gametes carry soul-stuff that come to inform the new body.

The picture of a modified Cartesian might also be a form of traducianism and parturient emergentism.[162] While Cartesianism often entails creationism and most Cartesians happen to be creationists, Cartesianism (broadly construed) does not entail creationism. Cartesians could affirm that souls are carriers of soul-stuff.[163] On this modification, a Cartesian soul is a complex not a simple and could undermine what has been argued thus far concerning the fact that persons are simples that are not composed of more fundamental parts.

Simple Creationist Soul (Special Creation)[164]

The traditional-creationist view might also be termed the 'Special Creation' view (SC). This view finds much support in Ecclesiastical history and, arguably, Scriptural support.[165] Cartesian dualism is normally thought to be a form of traditional-creationism, and most Cartesians are creationists.[166] It seems that a simple or pure form of Cartesianism entails some sort of creationism, but it may be that some variations of composite substance dualism cohere with a simple-creationism or traditional-creationism. There are other views similar to Cartesianism that are also variations of creationism. I discuss this as a live possibility reflecting a traditional-creationist view of the soul's origin.[167] For my purposes here, I intend to give a picture of how these souls originate. Let me first offer a tentative definition of traditional-creationism (hereafter, SC).

> SC: As a matter of logical priority not temporal priority, God creates the soul as the primary cause of the concrete part/soul. He, then, attaches the soul to the concrete part-body that is generated by a parent(s) at the moment the body begins to exist.[168] Alternatively, it could be that God creates the soul, and at the moment, God creates the soul it is causally interactive with the body. The soul is not generated or emergent from a subvenient base of physical matter and/or non-physical stuff.[169]

Peter Lombard, it seems, articulates something along these lines, "The Catholic Church teaches that souls are created at their infusion into the body."[170] A contemporary example of this kind of creationism that might fit with much of Ecclesiastical tradition is John Foster. John Foster in pressing in on the metaphysical relationship of the body and soul argues that there exists a brute relation grounded in a Divine personal explanation. Thus, there is a direct and vertical link/relation between the Divine and human on this view of origins. Foster explains it this way,

> An apparent difficulty for the Cartesian view is that there seems to be no remotely plausible way of accounting, in natural terms, for the existence and functional role of the postulated nonphysical subjects. Biological life begins at conception, when an ovum and a sperm fuse to produce a new unitary organism. However, it is hard to see how this process, or the subsequent development of the organism, could create an additional nonphysical substance and functionally attach it to the organism in the relevant way. The answer, it seems to me, is that we should explain these things by appeal to the creative role of God... it is God who creates the nonphysical

96

subjects and arranges for their functional attachment to the appropriate organisms; and, at least in the case of human beings, theology can offer some account of God's purpose for doing this, and of why that purpose is rationally appropriate to his nature... Theism enables the Cartesian to explain the existence and role of the nonphysical subjects; and, because this is the only satisfactory explanation, the argument for the Cartesian view becomes itself a powerful argument for the existence of God.[171]

It is important to note that in Foster's novel argument, he begins with the relationship between the body and soul, and then moves to the actual existence of the soul as explanatorily grounded in Divine intentionality not in matter or something sub-set of fundamental parts. On this view, the challenge as we have seen is that there is not an obviously natural connection between the two such that the further removed problem of the soul requires an explanation outside of the physical domain and its processes. This explanation is rooted directly in a Divine choice-event one might argue, which furnishes a connection between simple/ pure substance dualisms in the mind-body literature with that of origins, and it becomes a unique option—a direction in which I lean in what follows.

The picture that applies to traditional-creationism is the idea that God creates each individual soul directly and immediately, and attaches/infuses that soul to a body. God is not the secondary cause with the primary cause being a physical evolutionary mechanism. This soul is a concrete particular or a substance made up of essential properties that are internally united as a substance of an immaterial kind.[172,173] Hence, it is distinct from traducianism where souls are generated from one created soul.[174] Therefore, this view of the origin of souls provides a distinct picture not only of souls, but also of God's relationship to those souls.[175]

The bare substrata or particular view, as philosophers call it, says that there are concrete particulars that have causal powers and are property-bearers, but these particulars are not composed of the said properties. Instead, the substrata or bare particular underlies all properties predicated of it. Michael Loux defines substrata this way:

> Substrata are not bare in the sense of having no attributes; they are bare in the sense that in themselves they have no attributes; and what this means, he will claim, is that none of the attributes that a substratum has figures in its identity; it has a 'being' independent of all of them.[176]

Whilst I am referring to the bare particular view, I am not referring to any old bare concrete particular, but, specifically, to a mental/soulish bare concrete particular.[177] A substrate to some extent has an existence all on its own distinct from its attributes.[178] If mental substrates or bare particulars are coherent and plausible then it seems that there is a need for a creation of these kinds of things.[179] These are not the kinds of things that emerge and these are not complex entities made up of lower-level substances and properties. They are basic brute realities that require some sort of explanation. God as creator seems a plausible explanation of such entities.[180]

Another option is a form of essentialism with respect to the soul. This view is a middle path between bare particulars and bundle theories. Essentialism holds that there is a subject who has a set of essential properties that comprise the subject and are internally united in the subject. This is distinct from a bare particular that is not comprised of essential properties. On this view, the picture would look something like God bringing all the necessary and essential properties together to form a soul, and at the moment, the body reaches some sort of complexity, then God either creates the substance/soul in the body or creates the substance/soul and attaches it to the body.[181]

Cartesianism naturally works along the lines in terms of the above-mentioned kinds of substance. Cartesianism would look something like God creating the bare substrata or fashioning the soul with essential qualities, and then attaching it to the body. Moreland defines it this way:

> According to Cartesian creationism, egg and sperm are merely physical-chemical entities and the PR[182] conditions are sufficient for the generation of a human's body, which, you will recall, is merely a physical object. On the Cartesian creationist view, at some point between conception and birth, God creates a soul and connects it to a body that results entirely from PR conditions.[183]

This naturally fits with variations of Cartesian-like views of souls that are traditional and creationist in nature. A proponent of simple or traditional creationists-souls holds to such radically different natures between souls and bodies and connected to these radically different origins for bodies in contrast to souls that there is no obvious, necessary or sufficient condition tying the two together. It may be established by Divine fiat, but beyond that, there is no additional explanation.[184]

William Hasker and Emergent Dualism (EDMO): Materialist Generation of Souls

Hasker is not the only person contending for emergent substance dualism (hereafter EDMO) but he is the recognized authority on this position.[185] To begin let me offer a tentative definition of EDMO and materialist origins.

> ED and Materialist Generation of Souls: the notion that souls are generated primarily by at least one and at most two parents, and only secondarily created by God via an

emergent mechanism whereby God so structures and creates the physical matter with conscious stuff that a soul emerges at some suitably complex neural state. A mechanism directly causes the emergence of a new sui generis unified subject that sustains or has mental properties and powers.[186]

The creation story of persons within emergentism is along the lines of God designing physical matter with the plurality and diversity of different life, such that at some complex level of biological evolution human persons would evolve. Emergent dualism is a new view in the discussion on the origin of souls. As a unique version of substance dualism with some virtues in its favor, it deserves consideration in the debate over origins in theological anthropology.

While it is similar to traducianism, it is not accurate to categorize it as such. It is traducian-like in that a soul is generated in a physical-like process. First, on all variants of traducianism throughout church history, discussed above, it seems that the soul-progenitors have some direct involvement or contribution to the successively generated soul. Second, on the variants of traducianism, it appears that God contributes at least one new soul (if not two souls; namely Adam and Eve) that brings about a new chain of events generated from the first progenitors.

Emergent dualism is also similar in some respects to non-reductive physicalism in that the mind/person comes about from lower-level physical processes. Emergent dualism with material origins is distinct from non-reductive physicalist views in that it actually affirms a new substance, what philosophers call *sui generis* (fundamentally new) substance obtaining from a material substance at some level of neural complexity.[187] Similar to non-reductive physicalism, emergent dualism supplies an arguably natural relation between mind and body.[188] However, from where do conscious-stuff or qualities of an immaterial thing come? This is essential to understanding EDMO.[189]

William Hasker in a somewhat recent essay touches upon the relationship of the soul to the body and its implications in terms of human souls and their origins. After working through materialism and traditional substance dualism, he offers a possible solution to both the mind-body problem and the problem of the soul's origin. Hasker states this:

> Here is an initial proposal: a viable solution needs to consider the mental lives of human beings and animals together, rather than separately. The reason for this can be seen in some of the views we've already considered. To those who begin by thinking just about the minds/souls of humans, especially when the topic [is] viewed in a religious context, the very idea of 'soul' tends to have some rather lofty, 'spiritual' connotations... On the other hand, thinkers more inclined to naturalistic or materialistic views tend to start with animals and reduce the psychic life of human beings to what can be explained in the same terms they apply to animals.[190]

Hasker affirms that souls are intrinsic to the evolutionary process. This is the overarching benefit to his view over traditional alternatives of the self. In some way, material has a propensity to give rise to souls in the process of biological development. A sufficiently complex brain will serve as a proximate cause of the soul.[191] The benefits of Hasker's view include the fact that it provides a natural bridge for the soul and brain and it connects human souls naturally to lower level animal souls. These are important desirables in our present context, and they open up afresh space for reconsidering the origins of selves as souls. The concern with Hasker's view, and others like it, is that it fails to provide an informative designator, and more importantly, a sufficient explanation for the particularity of persons, which we will consider in the forthcoming chapters.

Part III

Emergent-Selves

Chapter 6

A Survey of Materialism, Emergentism, and Panpsychism

Mary Midgley talks about something like the notion of "empty and idle fancies" from Francis Bacon, as mentioned earlier. She describes the tendency within scientific communities as an impulse toward a synthesizing of all data with a universalizable test (i.e., a "universal acid test"). It is the notion of natural selection from Darwin that is applied universally to all things, even beyond the intentions of Darwin. Unfortunately, like the impulse found in atomism to explain all things by their underlying parts, this common impulse ends up explaining away several realities that we historically assumed in a fuller and more vibrant picture of reality—something we need to retain and maintain. By applying Darwin's ideas in the ways that he would have perceived as inconceivable we end up blinded to a portion of reality.[192] Even sadder still, these ideas and this impulse have moved beyond the sciences in such a way as to be normative in much philosophical and theological discourse.

In contemporary science-engaged theological conversations, there is a new attempt to provide what some will call 'bridge' programs between science and religion. The perceived distinction between the language and reality of science and religion can be overcome, purportedly, by building bridges. Bridges need building, some think, between a world that functions according to deterministic laws of nature, or by indeterministic laws of nature that are consistent, regular, and predictable along with other realities from consciousness, morality, spirits, angelic beings and gods or God.

The bridge that many helpfully conceive oscillates around the nature and origins of conscious individuals. For consciousness, as an arguably late development in biological evolution, is what represents or gives rise to a host of complex and abstract notions already mentioned, like spirits, morality, and religion.

It is consciousness and its attending properties, powers, and capacities that introduce into biological evolution the fact of religion (and whatever that entails). It is also consciousness that is foundational to entering into deep and meaningful relationships with other persons, including God. Consciousness is foundational and necessary to morality, free will, conscience, and accessing other transcendent realities (from platonic universals, angels, and divine beings).

So, it is no surprise when we find bridge programs that attempt to bridge the natural world of cause and effect with that of consciousness. This is a *natural* (not to be confused with natural as with the natural world) starting point. Further, for many who are committed to a non-interventionist account of God's relationship to the natural world, it is commonly consciousness that opens up space for God to act without messing about in the universe. This is one version of what some have called the causal-joint account of God's interaction with the universe (with the assumption being that God can act as the cause of events in the natural world as well natural processes, regulated by laws, can be the causes of natural events). As the name suggests, causal-joint is a term representing those spaces where it is conjectured that God meets the physical world.[193] Causal-joint theories are of two kinds. One kind takes it that God must suspend the laws of physical reality in order to act in the natural world, i.e., an interventionist account.[194] Another kind takes it that God does not intervene in the world, i.e., non-interventionist account. There are of course a variety of causal-joint accounts that take into account quantum mechanics that open up space for immaterial agents acting in the natural world, yet this too takes into account the importance of consciousness as the bridge between the two dichotomous realms.[195]

Physicalists try to find a bridge, but often this is just a disguised nod to the reality of consciousness without having to actually deal with it and its implications. As we have already discussed, there are a variety of different types of physicalists. The most prominent examples of contemporary physicalists concerning the problem of consciousness (specifically, the hard problem of consciousness) have a number of responses. One is to affirm a form of identity physicalism that conscious mental states are identical to brain states interacting or to provide some reductive explanation for consciousness. Both accounts amount to an elimination of consciousness because phenomenality is basic to the nature of consciousness itself. The hard problem of consciousness is the problem of explaining qualitative experience through quantitative measurements in the physical world. But, there is and, never will be, a way to explain qualitative experience with triggers and pulleys, quantities, mass, and charge. These are not identical to the properties consciousness. Some reductivists will have you believe that there is such a thing as consciousness, but that is not to be conflated with 'phenomenal' consciousness, and assert that it is a "fiction written by our brains."[196] The problem is that when we understand consciousness we know that it just is qualitative and phenomenal in nature. Otherwise, there is nothing descriptive about the nature of consciousness and it is simply a fiction.

Before pressing on, let me complicate the reductionistic picture just a bit so as not to pass over it too quickly. There are different types of reductionisms recognized and at play in the physical sciences that are often either 'consciously' or 'implicitly' behind the scenes in scientific study. Nancey Murphy offers a helpful schematic listing of the different types on offer as a context for exploring variants of emergentism.[197] The first is methodological reductionism, which takes it that research into a subject scientifically (which applies to other domains as well) would be conducted by breaking everything down to the smallest parts to analyze. The obvious problem with this is that most scientists recognize the importance of environmental conditions that inform holistic properties, states, and functions of organisms that must be studied to gain an adequate understanding of them. The second is epistemological reductionism. This is the view that all higher-level laws are deducible from lower-level laws, and, for many, what this means is that physics is the ultimate explanation of everything. The philosophical view of positivism adopts something like epistemological reductionism, which is closely related to linguistic reductionism (i.e., the view that all states can be articulated using the language of the lower-level physical sciences as adequate and comprehensively descriptive of all higher-order systems). The third is causal reductionism, which takes it that the parts of a system or organism are determinative of higher-level states and deducible from them in a cause-effect logic. The fourth is ontological reductionism. According to ontological reductionism, there are no novel properties, states, things, but all higher-order are deducible from lower-level parts that comprise the whole—i.e., as if stacking a deck (i.e., H_2O is just the sum of the parts). A more radical version says that there are no higher-order structural units, instead all that exists are the lower-level parts.[198]

Unfortunately, all of these reductionisms eschew the reality of consciousness. Consciousness, as phenomenal experience of what it is like, cannot be captured in the language of physics because it is ontologically basic and distinct from the physical parts. Further, it opens up other powers that are not deducible to the lower-level parts like the ability to realize what it is like to experience water, and the further ability to adjudicate between the features of one's conscious experience about the drinking of water (i.e., whether it is tap or filtered), what cup it is found in, and what all is going on in the environment around it.

Others have moved in what is oft called a non-reductive

physicalist direction or an emergentist direction because they realize that the powers following from consciousness, particularly first-person consciousness, are not reducible to lower-level parts, but rather are the product of those lower-level parts interacting in a way that something novel and unexpected arises (e.g., consciousness, freedom). They believe this is the starting point for providing a bridge between science and religion. The final solution that moves beyond these options is another option that historically developed as a final naturalistic solution, namely panpsychism.

What is non-reductive physicalism? Non-reductionism parallels reductionism in that as a research program, practitioners recognize the different types of non-reduction. For example, one could still be an ontological reductionist of a sort, but recognize that there are unexpected, non-predictable, novel patterns, powers that come about from lower-level physical parts interacting but are themselves causally new and can have an influence on the lower-level parts—e.g., if we consider the analogy of an elevator system that once the elevator reaches the top, then it can causally affect the bottom on its way back down. We might also consider the patterns of RNA from DNA. Such an example philosophers have called downward causation because the higher-order property can actually change the lower-level interactions of the parts in a way that is not derivable from the bottom nor is it causally determined by the bottom. The obvious concern amongst philosophers is that on non-reductionism of this sort the higher-order property appears to always have a causal link to the lower-level parts interacting, which would suggest causal determinism. There is a further concern of overdetermination with higher-order patterns that are caused by the parts in the whole.

But, this is where things are interesting in non-reductionism. Terrence Deacon describes the "configurational regularities affecting constituent interactions," as an important feature of some systems in nature that explains something that atomists or physics cannot explain.[199] He describes emergence as seen in natural systems with teleology, information, and semiosis. All of these explanations are discernable in nature and are attributable to an evolutionary system where organizational systems are built, in some sense, from the ground up through natural selection, adaptation, and other evolutionary mechanisms like genetic drift.

The obvious concern as a comprehensive explanation of some of the most important phenomena here is that some of these phenomena are indistinguishable from other ways of explaining the phenomena, e.g., when we consider information theory as a designed reality or as a created reality.[200] The mechanisms in these cases are invisible in nature, but emergent mechanisms for nature's novelties are not discernable, which is why some hold out hope for a reductive explanation or describe such phenomena as magic.

This is what Mary Midgley has described as a "universal acid." When Darwin's dangerous idea of natural selection is used as the universal lens in which all else is explained and seen. When this occurs it functions as a kind of acid that eats away at other legitimate explanations.

Emergentist Timothy O'Connor describes this higher level of emergence, or strong emergence, as states, patterns, properties in a way that they have something like their own grammar, rule, and laws at this level that are no longer explained at the lower levels of interaction. O'Connor is clear to point out that we do not know what these mechanisms are that give rise to these higher-order emergent phenomena, especially when it comes to consciousness, but it is clear that they exist. Even though we do not know how consciousness emergence works, we recognize them as products of emergence within nature that parallels other novel emergent features in nature. This rationale furnishes justification for believing in them, according to O'Connor.

O'Connor is also clear about the unified nature of consciousness posing the most unique feature within nature that we have no parallels for. Everything that we know about physics and biology has some explanation in the parts, parts interacting, and holistic states. However, the unity of consciousness is a novelty that is not only *sui generis*, but it requires not only the complexity of parts interacting at some unified structural state but something else.[201] This is where something like a thisness that describes, unifies the conscious experience is not only not predictable in nature, but it demands a new thing altogether.

There are some historical cases that precede our contemporary discussions that overlap with religious and scientific considerations. Some theories are so extravagant that they extend all the way up to God himself. And, here we find not only a bridge for how it is that God acts in the world without messing about in a system of laws, but an ontological explanation for the existence of God. The famous naturalist emergentist Samuel Alexander develops just such a view. He describes in the following,

> For any level of existence, deity is the next higher empirical quality. It is therefore a variable quality, and as the world grows in time, deity changes with it. On each level a new quality looms ahead, awfully, which plays to it the part of deity. For us who live upon the level of mind deity is, we can but say, deity. To creatures upon the level of life, deity is still the quality in front, but to us who come later this quality has been revealed as mind.[202]

Everything according to Alexander is explained by Darwinian evolutionary mechanisms, including God. This is the most exaggerated view that takes seriously the universalizing effect that Darwin's dangerous idea explains everything. It begins in mind, but it encompasses God's mind of which God becomes a part of Nature.

Such a view need not be the view of all emergentists. Most are satisfied with simply explaining creaturely or human consciousness by way of evolutionary mechanisms. This is exotic enough.

The most notable science-engaged theologian committed to neo-Darwinianism, God's acting in the world at the level of consciousness, and human consciousness emerging as a higher-order product of biological processes, is Philip Clayton. That said, Clayton recognizes what Thomas Nagel has pointed out so clearly that a pure naturalism, with its attending physicalism commitments, is insufficient to explain consciousness.[203] In other words, and this is an improvement on some physicalists, Clayton invokes theism as the explanation for the emergence of consciousness. The leftover from a neo-Darwinian picture of the world remains, however. Clayton is committed to the idea that most of the world is explained by lawful processes within biological evolution, and human consciousness is the outcome within nature. He calls his view a version of emergentism or non-reductive physicalism because as he articulates it, consciousness emerges as a highly complex configurational state from the brain. The mind, for Clayton, is a product and property of the brain.[204] So, while he firmly rejects metaphysical naturalism as inadequate to explain consciousness, he remains, nonetheless, committed to some of its key assumptions about the processes in which things come to be in the natural world.[205]

The concerning implication is that there is no, in-principle, reason to reject the fact that conscious selves could be produced by ensuring that the same biological conditions are met (assuming we could set up all the biological conditions). Ironically, the picture of a scientist in the lab establishing a neural network that was sufficiently complex as a human brain would, in theory, give rise to an individually conscious self at some point in its biological history. Furthermore, unless some reason is given for why it must be organic material, then this logical system would support the possibility of setting up AI neural networks that could eventually be self-conscious. Now, some emergentists may ultimately opt for a non-natural, even theistic explanation, by punting to design, but there would remain no principled reason why this could not occur. Some see this as an obvious weakness of the emergentist paradigm.

But, as Joanna Leidenhag rightly claims, these bridge projects between science and religion are not really bridge explanations, but rather bridge "paradigms." Why? Because they really don't explain consciousness or how consciousness comes to be in a natural frame so unlike it.[206] This is precisely where panpsychism has come on the scene. It is a development that arises out of the frustrations with the non-reductive physicalism paradigm.

Panpsychism comes in a variety of articulations and postulations, but it is ultimately the view that posits something like physicalism in that it is committed to the fundamentality of physical particles as well as the fundamentality of the mental. Ironically, it begins with consciousness known and imposes that consciousness on the lower bits of reality. The structure of the physical, it is supposed, has these properties of consciousness, even though we have no reason to believe that they are there and have no access to them. In this way, it resonates with physicalism as well as dualism. How it understands the mental is still being discussed. The mental may be the product of an underlying substance that is neither physical nor mental (i.e., Russellian Monism, attributed to the famous Atheist analytic philosopher Bertrand Russell), the fact that particles are conscious, or the fact that particles have a dispositional property toward consciousness that at some higher-level of neural complexity will give rise to consciousness (i.e., constitutive panpsychism, which retains emergentist elements). This is why it is not surprising that some emergentists have turned to panpsychism of some variety for help after confronting the inadequacy of their physicalism.[207]

However, panpsychism, at least most varieties (excepting Absolute Monism or Cosmopsychism, more on these later), runs into a similar problem parasitic on physicalism. It too runs into what is commonly called the combination problem or the too-many thinkers problem. In other words, the too-many thinkers problem is that problem that there are too many thinkers that come to comprise one new, higher-order, emergent thinker that is composed of lower-level thinkers. Similarly, it runs into the problem of explaining the problem of how it is that a combination of thinkers could come together in a way that a new singular, unified thinker exists. As we know from our own conscious perspectives, we are neither a sum of a complexity of physical parts, as in physicalism, or a complexity of multiple thinkers—but we are one, singular, unified thinker that has a novel thisness that binds together all the conscious phenomena within a first-person perspective. However, we will look at the combination problem a bit more below, and expand on it when we consider what philosophers call thisness (i.e., an essence or nature of an individual thing). There is a unique thisness that not only ties together the complex bits in a unified phenomenal perspective, but is undergirded by a different kind of thisness that explains what we all care about most deeply, that which makes me *me*.

Chapter 7

Emergent-Selves: Created or Magical, A Survey of Religious Concerns with Emergentism

(Drawn and adapted from, "Creational Problems for Soul-Emergence from Matter: Philosophical and Theological Concerns," *Neue Zeitschrift fur Systematische Theologie und Religionsphilosophie*, volume 60 (2018), 406-427)

While these novel emergentist options appear to be clothed in sophisticated updated science, what I will show in what follows is that they, quite provocatively, yield a form of creationism. The implied question then to the reader is what version of creationism has fewer liabilities and which one is less likely to be true. The present chapter explores some of these rather knotty issues that focus our question for the self on the problem of what concluded the last chapter, namely what philosophers call 'thisness'—the nature of individual things. Here we get closer to an understanding of personhood or the particularity of persons.

Presently, two significant theories of an emergent mind have helped to re-motivate what was once a thriving topic in philosophical and theological discussions, namely mental origins. They include, first, Timothy O'Connor's emergent-materialism (or as he calls it, emergent-individualism), which is the view that humans are material objects wholly comprised of material simples that bear novel emergent properties at some complex neural arrangement. Second, William Hasker develops a variation of emergent dualism (i.e., a version of substance dualism, and what one might call a deviant form of Cartesianism), which is the view that human minds are novel substances as the logical outcome of lawful processes or are causally produced by a complex neural arrangement—the product of which is not comprised of material simples.[208]

Both O'Connor and Hasker are seeking to distance themselves from traditional options in the philosophy of mind, namely, reductive materialism and classical or stronger versions of substance dualism. While new and exciting, several philosophers remain dubious about their success, but they do open the door to potential alternatives. In the present article, through an exposition of the most sophisticated versions of emergentism, I raise some noteworthy challenges to Hasker's view and within that context I will later advance a robust version of creationism. By creationism, I refer to minds that are created *directly* by God. Such a view is likely found in the Cartesian (as a term of art) camp—roughly the view that humans are identical to their souls or minds that have some relationship (albeit external and causal) to their bodies.[209]

William Hasker raises some noteworthy concerns for Cartesian substance dualism from mind on brain dependence and evolution. Furthermore, Hasker has argued that Cartesianism fails to offer an account for any "intrinsic" or "essential" relation between the soul and body.[210] Through a critical engagement with these two emergentists, I intend to show some of the deficiencies in their views, and that Cartesianism, coupled with a particular view of emergentism, can provide a more satisfying alternative with an "essential" kind property that makes natural the union of soul and body. In these ways, I suggest that constructive theologians should consider taking up and engaging more seriously with a model of Divinely created souls that takes into account the benefits of emergentism in our scientific age because the desiderata satisfied includes the desirables of emergentism along with the fact of particularity informing personhood via the soul.

Emergence and Soul Origins

In a recent discussion on emergence and human origins, Hasker raises the question, "Is Materialism Equivalent to Dualism?"[211] This is an important question, no doubt, but one that might surprise the reader. It is not uncommon to read the delineations of materialism and dualism as radically distinct. Materialism, in anthropology, is the view that human beings are wholly material or physical beings.[212] Distinct versions of what have been called reductive materialism are on the table for discussion including, but not limited to, identity type or token materialism, functionalism, and behaviorism.[213] I will not concern myself with these directly here, given my aims. By way of contrast, substance dualism is the view that humans are comprised, somehow, of two distinct property-bearers—body and mind.[214] It is important to define substance, property, physical, and the mental. A substance as I understand it is a property-bearer that has causal powers and liabilities. A property is a universal that can be instantiated in multiple and distinct substances. All substances bear properties. The physical is a distinct type of substance that is non-mental, public (i.e., its properties are accessible by persons). Minds are distinct types of substances from the physical, and bear one unique feature (or non-universal property distinct to particular minds), namely, the feature of my having and experiencing my own particular experiences, of which no other substance could have or experience. In other words, my mind or soul as substance is distinguished from other minds or souls as substances in virtue of its being private, and having an insider's perspective or restricted access in virtue of my experiencing my experiences.[215] Debatably, there are other versions of dualism that are not easily categorized as either materialism or substance dualism, but may fit into some alternative monist category, materialism broadly construed (for example Timothy O'Connor's view it has been argued fits in an alternative monist category but others have argued that it remains within materialism), or substantive dualism (i.e., not quite as strong as substance dualism because the two concrete parts are not actually distinct, even if they are conceptually and/ or modally distinct).

Substance dualists agree that the two property-bearers are evident in our basic phenomenological experiences. The case for the mind's distinction from the body has been made on the basis of a variety of arguments for the *uniqueness* and *centrality* of consciousness.[216] As indicated above, substance dualism is normally construed as Creationist because it seems to require a causal explanation outside natural forces wherein some agent-cause is the direct cause. Interestingly, on this point, both Hasker and O'Connor seem to ride a razor's edge in their attempt to bring together what was previously thought to be incompatible. In his recent article, Hasker seeks to establish the similarity and distinction by considering what he construes as the "best" (i.e., animal human continuity, mind-brain union, and an accounting for a full mental life) options within dualism and materialism.[217] I will briefly describe both "emergent-materialism" and "emergent substance dualism" for the purposes of carving out a distinct option that remains Creationist. I suggest below that emergent-materialism ought to be called emergent-monism as it does not fall neatly into what is often construed as materialism because new properties instantiated in an *immaterial* thing emerge and these properties are not contained within a closed system.[218]

Based on an understanding of Hasker's emergent substance dualism, I argue that O'Connor's articulation of the emergent individual seems to require some variant of substance dualism to account for consciousness and the individual essence of persons. According to Hasker's categorization, the human mind is emergent 1_b and emergent 2, which means that the mind is a novel substance that is quite radically different from the material substance that produces it. Hasker distinguishes this from what might be construed as a lower-level emergence, emergent 1_b, where novel properties come to exist from the interaction of the lower-level parts but are comprised of material simples (e.g., emergent-materialism).[219]

Emergent-Materialism or Individualism

In an attempt to carve out what they see as the most sophisticated option in the philosophy of mind, Timothy O'Connor and Jonathan Jacobs advance an emergentist version of what they call materialism.[220] On this view, humans are biological objects; yet calling their view materialist is a little misleading for it is in tension with other central features of what is commonly referred to as materialism (e.g., reductivism, non-reductivism, and the constitution theory of persons).[221] It is doubtful whether the substance with these emergent powers is, strictly speaking, still material in nature.[222] Human consciousness is not reducible to the brain states. It appears, instead, that the material simples do not constitute human consciousness because the product is new. Rather, human consciousness is emergent from the material, yet distinct, evident by the fact of novel powers which require a novel substance.[223] O'Connor's and Jacob's defense of mereological particularity, then, seems, I suggest, insufficient. Along these lines, it appears that a better description would be emergent-monism, as stated above, but it is difficult to ascertain what this vague referent is given the limits of our knowledge.

In one important quote O'Connor and Jacobs offer the reader a careful description of their view. I will cite it in whole, then briefly discuss the salient points.

I am indeed a biological organism, but some of my mental states are instantiations of simple, or non-structural, properties. A property is 'non-structural' if and only if its instantiation does not even partly consist in the instantiation of a plurality of more basic properties by the entity or its parts... Emergent features are as basic as electric charge now appears to be, just more restricted in the circumstances of their manifestation. Further, having such emergent states is, in general, a causal consequence of having the requisite type of intrinsic and functional complexity. The emergent state is a "causal consequence" of the object's having this complexity in the following way: in addition to having local influence in a manner familiar from physical theories, fundamental particles and systems also naturally tend (in any context) towards the generation of the emergent state. Their doing so, however, is not detectable in contexts lacking the requisite macro-complexity, because each such tending is, on its own, incomplete. It takes the right threshold of complexity for tendings, present in each micro-particle, to achieve their characteristic effect jointly, the generation of a special type of holistic state.[224]

Mental states are instantiations of non-structured properties or parts that emerge from them, and are basic, thus non-reducible to the material. These properties are *sui generis*, which means that they are of their own kind, wholly different from the properties otherwise instantiated in the material simples comprising the body. And, the mental state is an emergent state causally brought about by the material object in its complex configuration. Important, though controversial, the authors assume that the material parts have "tendencies" toward emergent states.

If we were to summarize, then the following features would seem to comprise the essentials that factor into how O'Connor and Jacobs understand "emergence" in this context.

a) Persons are biological objects.
b) Conscious/mental states are non-reducible and non-constituted by material parts.

c) Conscious/mental states emerge from the material as unique holistic states.
d) Conscious/mental states are basic.
e) Human Persons are fundamental like material simples but not aggregates.
f) Implication: Conscious persons have the capacity of downward causation.
g) Material particles have intrinsic tendency toward emergent states.

The above comprise the main features of emergent-monism or so it seems to me.

Hasker raises an important challenge for this version of emergentism. If we take the unity of consciousness seriously, then a question emerges (no pun intended) concerning the previously articulated emergentism. How is it, then, that O'Connor and Jacob's emergentist view accounts for the unity of consciousness? What or who is it that is aware? On their view the emergent mental states are not reducible to or constituted by the simpler material parts that comprise the person. So when I experience the various objects around me while sitting in the barber shop, where I am at present, *I* experience all the various objects in one unified field of awareness and it is not the parts that are individually experiencing the various objects around me, just *me*.

A variant of the unity of consciousness argument follows. (1) I, as a subject, am experientially aware of the field of green as a unity. (2) Functionally, I, as an embodied being, experience the field as a whole being rather than the parts that comprise my being/system experiencing the field. (3) Thus, the subject is a whole not a system of parts. If my brain is comprised of synapses firing, then that would be insufficient as a ground for being experientially aware of the field of green as a unity. The brain is comprised of various parts and synapses firing, so it would follow that I am *something* distinct from the brain and, additionally, I am different from other material parts of my body. One might object that the belief that I am distinct from my brain is solely what follows, but if we have a first-person perspective that just does have a unified consciousness of the field, then more than mere belief follows. The kind of unity I have consciously/perceptually is different than the material it is interacting, so it follows that I am not my brain or any other material part.

Given the unity of consciousness, a *thisness* is required, yet not in the parts or the structural composition comprised of the parts—something Hasker rightly points out.[225] Hasker shows that a mind is or requires a unified subject, a subjective or phenomenal unity. It requires a substantial unity that has powers, and the subject of these new powers can influence the parts.[226] In other words, this would seem to yield substance dualism of the Haskerian variety, or some similar view, where we have a distinct substance of a different kind. Thus, rather than the assumption of emergent-materialism, or monism, we have an emergent substance—despite O'Connor and Jacob's belief to the contrary.[227]

Related to this, several other questions seem unavoidable, and deserve additional attention, if the emergent-materialist or monist is to reject emergent substance dualism. Where is the conscious substance if not a substance of a new kind? The answer seems to be that it resides in and beyond the space of the physical particles comprising the brain and the nervous system, which, once again, sounds a lot like a new or distinct substance altogether. If 'thisness' is attributable to the mental states, then one has a unified consciousness not simply a structural/holistic emergent property. Given all that we *seem* to know from science about physical stuff functioning holistically in what is described, emergent-monism is in tension with modern scientific knowledge of physical objects.

Hasker summarizes this sentiment when he says, "the problem for emergentist materialism is that the holistic behavior is attributed to something we already know a great deal about, almost all of which lends itself to being understood in atomistic fashion."[228] Hasker is clear that the mental substance is wholly distinct from objects exhibiting holistic behavior. I will return to a similar argument when I raise a significant worry for Hasker's emergent substance dualism, and I show that his view seems to amount to a variant of Creationism.

Hasker's Emergent Dualism (i.e., Substantial Dualism)

Like Cartesianism, Hasker affirms that there are two different kinds of things, one mental and one physical. Like O'Connor and Jacobs, Hasker affirms that the immaterial substance is not created directly by God, nor does it emerge as a unique holistic property from the material, but it emerges from a sufficiently complex neural state as a *sui generis* substance. Motivated by Karl Popper's emergent dualism, Hasker understands the mind to be a new substance not simply a new set of powers or properties, although *it* has those.

Hasker understands it that the soul is the highest and most exotic form of emergence in the physical world. As such, he is aware of its challenges, which I address below.[229] He claims,

I will sketch out a theory of the mind, which makes the mind both emergent$_{1b}$, since it is endowed with novel causal powers, and also emergent$_{2}$, since it possesses libertarian free will.[230]

In other words, Hasker is stating that his theory not only allows for novel causal powers (thus it is distinct from non-reductive physicalism which says that there are higher-order physical properties). It is also more exotic than both emergent-monism and dual-aspectism in that there is a novel power of libertarian freedom, which is only predicable of substances (emergent mental substances, i.e., persons).

Hasker distinguishes his view from Creationist and Cartesian dualisms. He defines a Cartesian view in the following manner, "Cartesian dualism simply accepts the chasm, postulating the soul as an entity of a completely different nature than the physical, an entity with no essential or internal relationship to the body, which must be added to the body *ad extra* by a special divine act of creation."[231] It may be accurate to define Cartesian dualism as having no "essential" or "internal" relationship to the body, but I will lay out an alternative Cartesian-Creationist view that souls have a natural relationship to their bodies. While souls may not have an essential relationship to bodies, I intend to convey that souls have some distinct kind-property reflected in the fact that souls necessarily depend on bodies for the actualizing of specified properties and powers. In this way, a Cartesian theory is, potentially, on equal footing with Hasker's emergent dualism. Before turning to Cartesianism, a summary and critique is in order.

Summary:

a) Persons are novel substances (i.e., basic mental substances).[232]
b) Persons have novel powers and properties distinct from their bodies.
c) Material has endowed potency.
d) Material, in certain arrangements, has designed ends.
e) Persons are non-reducible to and non-constituted by their brains or bodies and the interaction of the material parts.
f) Persons originate from their bodies and are sustained by them.

With this summary fixed in one's understanding, there are reasons why one might not be fully satisfied with Hasker's variation of emergent dualism. The first worry concerns the nature of emergence and God's role in the process, which, granted, is a concern for theists alone. The second worry concerns the nature of a particular or subjective *thisness* not simply an *immaterial* thisness that is universally instantiated. Given these concerns, Hasker's view is in deep tension with modern science as I argue briefly below, and Hasker's view is in tension with our basic experience of self in the world. It seems that Hasker's dualism encounters some significant challenges—similar to the O'Connor and Jacobs alternative.

One theological concern for Hasker's emergent dualism, and others like it, is the problem of material creation ex-nihilo. Hasker's emergent relation seems to yield the notion that an individualized material has the power to produce a soul (i.e., a novel substance with distinct causal powers). O'Connor claims, "The present sort of emergence... would involve the generation of a fundamentally new substance in the world—amounting to creation ex nihilo."[233] Such a state of affairs would be problematic, most importantly, because it would deny that power to God alone—which those within the Christian, Jewish, and Islam tradition maintain. Ironically, however, it is not only strange, but the defender appears to commit a category error. Arguably, if immaterial things are contrary in nature to material stuffs or things, coupled with the assumption that one is not a subset of the other, then it is difficult nigh impossible to conceive of one thing having the power (attributable to God) to cause the existence of something it is not—again, unless we ascribe the power of creation *ex nihilo*. Hasker has a ready response.[234] He advances an interesting, albeit questionable, response that the objection is minimized when we conceive of God as the one who *endows* the material with special powers, and we conceive of the material outcome—the mind—as God's designed intention.[235]

Philosophers sympathetic to Hasker's proposal might have a ready analogy to help Hasker avoid the consequent. Consider a music box that has the power to make musical sounds once it is wound up. Once wound up, the music box brings about the sound. Like the creation of material that has an intrinsic design that will give rise to a novel substance, the music box has the machinery that under certain conditions will give rise to sound. However, it is not clear that the sound is a sufficient parallel to a novel substance. Rather the music box seems to have dispositional properties such that under certain conditions it makes sound, according to its design. The sound is explicable in terms of the machinery that gives rise to it in one sense, but the qualia and significance of the sounds is dependent on persons experiencing them. The sound is not in itself a new substance that contains its own intrinsic power. Hasker's emergent soul is far more exotic in that the complex material gives rise to a novel substance with new properties and powers non-attributable to the material, which gave rise to it.

As illustrated with the music box, Hasker's response to the charge of material creation ex-nihilo is less than fully satisfying. First, his response begins to resemble something like a creationist view of the soul, assuming the material does not instantiate the power of creation ex-nihilo because something else is creating or contributing to it as a sufficient causal condition. If God has placed these alien powers in or around the material, in question, and God creates the matter with "propensities" toward the emergent-soul, then the power seems attributable to God rather than the material we intuitively take to be distinct from the soul. The significance of bringing emergence into the solution is to exclude 'spooky' entities from the equation, which seems odd in light of Hasker's suggestion that God imparts the propensities to matter. By making the move of attributing the material power to God's unique action, however, Hasker's view is starting to look a bit different than what is normally taken to be an emergentist account in that it is not simply properties that emerge but a substance. In this way, Hasker is able to have his cake of maintaining a coherent natural process for human development, which allows for a substance that is similar to a Cartesian substance without its baggage. It appears that Hasker must bite the bullet, however, and accept the consequent that the material has the power of creation ex-nihilo. Hasker may contend that this is not a grave concern because God designs the material to give rise to a diversity of things under necessary and specified conditions. Furthermore, while this is not the traditionally assumed position by Christian theologians throughout the ages, one might argue that in our scientific age where all sorts of novel things emerge it is not all too serious to suggest that a mind emerges from the material.[236] With this in mind, an important question presents itself. If one is willing to bring God back into the process in some *robust* way, then why not just affirm Creationism? The obvious response is to say that there is space in creation for a diversity of things. This much is true, but it is one thing to say that material substances give rise to distinct and more complex material substances and quite another to say that it gives rise to a fundamental something it is not.[237]

At some level, theists believe that all things are created by God even when God creates something that generates a chain of events or substances, but making the claim that created things can cause entirely new things out of nothing is, arguably, problematic.[238] This will depend on one's ordering of theological authorities, but it raises another question. What kind of power within the material would it be that is also consistent with what we seem to already know about material things? It is unlikely that we would ever have an answer to this question due to the mysterious nature of substantial emergence. Hence we have a unique challenge for a materially produced soul in contrast to the classical view.

The presence of conscious human subjects might be surprising if, in fact, minds are more closely related to God's nature—central to and foundational to the world, which is a common philosophical assumption throughout the history of Christian theology. This is especially true if we take it that God is a mind as human beings are minds, and what is central to being persons is the immaterial mental substance in question. To suggest that something higher comes from something lower seems especially exotic.

If we take it as theologically problematic that a soul could come from matter, then a coherent and plausible explanation can be found in soul-creationism. Unless we contend that matter has mental properties or proto-mental properties, we have theological reasons for rejecting the materially produced soul and considering an alternative option, e.g., soul-creationism. Assuming the reader is unmoved by the concerns above, there is another significant concern for Hasker's version of emergentism, which seems to *require* some kind of creationism.

Earlier Hasker raised the topic of mental *thisness* as a problem for O'Connor's emergentism, but it appears that he runs into a similar problem from what I will call *subjective* or *personal thisness*—haecceity. This kind of haecceity is a primitive intrinsic property or feature of an individual thing that describes the thing in question, and is available only from an insider's perspective. In a famous article, Robert Adams describes what a 'thisness' or a haecceity is for an individual,

A thisness is the property of being identical with a certain particular individual—not the property that we all share, of being identical with some individual or other, but my property of being identical with me, your property of being identical with you, etc. these properties have recently been called 'essences', but that is historically unfortunate; for essences have normally been understood to be constituted by qualitative properties, and we are entertaining the possibility of nonqualitative thisnesses.[239]

128

In other words, a haecceity or thisness in this sense is not simply a quality or attribute of an individual, but it is a distinct property of the individual in question. It does not take away from one's kind-essence. It is an individual essence that is not shared by other individuals. While one might have an individual essence composed of underlying qualities or relations or properties of the individual's history, what is needed is more than this for an individual human mind. In two helpful statements, Lynne Rudder Baker helps articulate an understanding of thisness. She says, "haecceity, roughly, is 'thisness', a nonqualitative property responsible for individuation. I want [...] to take an haecceity to be the state of affairs of someone exemplifying a property." And she continues to describe the haecceity as non-descriptive of a thing's whatness, "a haecceity does not add to the 'whatness' of a thing but distinguishes it from other things of the same kind."[240] If she means by this that the haecceity is non-substantial, then dualists would disagree.[241] It seems acceptable to say that the haecceity could factor into the personal and/or subjective nature of the individual all the while contributing to (i.e., substantially) what the *thing* is in question. As humans are individual minds with bodies (however one wishes to describe the mind-body relation does not seem directly relevant here), there is some fundamental fact (i.e., property or feature) about persons as minds that supplies the metaphysical contents of this one mind, where other minds have their own distinct thisness (for they have their own feature). And, this feature of minds is not universally predicable of other minds and sufficiently informs the concept of a particular mind (e.g., President Obama's mind is fundamentally distinct from President Trump's mind). Additionally, it is this feature that distinguishes minds from other objects in the world.

I say property or feature for a reason. Properties are normally thought of as universals, and the kind of thisness necessary to an individual mind is not a universal. In fact, given the simplicity of a human soul or mind, this kind of thisness is not a universal at all. In this way, it seems more appropriate to call it a feature, even a brute feature of minds. It is a feature that is unique to the individual mind itself.[242]

Taking a page from Swinburne's development of rigid designators in terms of informative designators, it seems that we can say a bit more about mental haecceity. A term that refers to a particular object and is true in every possible world is a rigid designator. So, a name for a particular person would amount to a rigid designator (like Richard Swinburne) where a title is a non-rigid, and accidental property, term (like Professor of Philosophy of Christian Religion). An informative designator is a term for an object that is true in every possible world and sufficiently describes the object in question.[243] When considering mental substances, arguably, they contribute something fundamental to the world that is distinct from other kinds of objects in the world. Each individual mind contributes some fundamental fact to the world that is sufficiently knowable or accessible to minds alone. In this way, there is some essential and fundamental fact in the world that provides some content to the world. So, it is not entirely accurate to describe such a view as non-informative. In fact, it is informative yet it is informative to minds. The question that concerns us is whether or not minds have them, and if they do Hasker's emergent dualism encounters one significant problem.

It seems in fact that humans do have a personal or subjective thisness. As a substantial subjective mind, I have an insider's perspective to my own mind as a pure mental substance. I am the kind of thing that thinks, that unifies the variety of thoughts I have simultaneously, and I can exist causally at different points in my body and different times in history. I am, it would seem, a simple. All the while, it is *I* that is present at each one of my thoughts and at each moment of my existence. If this is the case, then *I* am a substance that instantiates a unique feature—a haecceity—that distinguishes me from any other mind that does exist or might exist.

Furthermore, it is a primitive feature of a metaphysically simple substance (i.e., a soul) that I seem to be aware of (i.e., I have an inside perspective), which grounds *my* existence. If it were the case that I, as a mind, emerged as a new substance directly from a body, then my body would either carry the property itself or it would have the power to produce a radically new kind of thing—hence creation ex-nihilo. Yet, material parts do not seem to have haecceities, at least not in the sense described here.

The practice of the natural sciences seems to support this idea that material substances do not carry along the kind of thisness listed above (i.e., as a primitive personal or subjective thisness). Material substances are complexes comprised of various divisible parts unlike mental substances, so far as we know from science. As it were, a material substance is not a satisfying alternative to the notion that a mental substance has some fundamental aspect that is non-complex, non-qualitative, non-divisible and distinct from a set of properties. Rather, material parts are publicly observable in principle, or at least this is a common assumption in science and philosophy. One practical assumption when experimenting within the natural sciences is that the powers and properties of what is under investigation is that the properties/features of material things are discoverable through testing. This is not so of minds. Minds are known primarily from an insider's perspective—and this provides a fundamental and essential fact about individual persons. Another related yet distinct challenge would follow for Hasker's dualism if minds had properties that were, in principle, public and discoverable.

If material parts could produce individual minds, then it seems plausible that such a state of affairs could be re-duplicated in principle.[244] If it can be re-duplicated in principle then what we have is not a non-qualitative, non-divisible, subjective thisness (i.e., a haecceity) that captures the nature of the individual mind, but we have something that is qualitative. We have universals that are discoverable by science. This isn't a mind, however, in the way defined above. Keeping all that has been said in perspective, I am merely raising the concern that on Hasker's version of substance dualism rather than have a novel mental substance with a subjective thisness, we have something else. In this way, Hasker would seem to have a choice between the endorsement of a subjective thisness in which case creationism (e.g., Divine creationism or material creationism) would seem to follow or he could deny that minds have this distinguishing feature and affirm that we are natural products.

On Hasker's view, it is not clear at all that a subjective/personal thisness would come from a material object. Instead, it seems that thisness of this sort would need to exist already in the material, but material particles themselves do not seem to bear haecceity. Rather than instantiating *subjective* thisness, material individuals bear properties (i.e., universals that are multiply-exemplifiable), and based on common assumptions in science about the lawful repeatability of material products, it would seem that particles lack any sort of primitive thisness and are distinguishable based on external relational properties alone.

The objector might respond and argue that it is precisely these complex arrangements that give rise to an individual thisness, but if this is the case, once again, then with a sufficient amount of knowledge we could reproduce the same results. By reproducing the same conditions, in principle, we could bring about the existence of the same individual. But, my having insider's perspective to my mind would exclude the possibility that another individual would be the self-same individual as I am, hence a contradiction.

Let us assume that haecceity can be produced as a new

complex haecceity. Something like a hylomorphic view of matter would be the assumption here, but this would not be Hasker's version of emergentism. This raises a distinct problem. If we assume a hylomorphic view of matter, then we would never know the distinct essence of physical particles. Such a feature would be invisible (the invisibility problem). Humans lack that ability to access the inside of things (apart from one's own mind, but even that is metaphysically questionable on the view proposed).

Furthermore, the success of the sciences seems to be predicable on the fact that physical matter is publicly accessible, as stated earlier.[245] Given the nature of subjective *personal thisness*, if souls as pure mental substances exist, then we have one good philosophical reason for affirming creationism.[246] There is at least one emergentist-creationist-dualist view worth exploring, which can account for a *subjective personal thisness*. The challenge for a creationist view is commonly noted in the literature is its ability to maintain the organic integrity of mind-brain relations.[247]

Conclusion

In what precedes, I explored the relationship of two emergentisms and their relationship to persons and mental states. I noted the strengths and weaknesses of each view. While I did not attempt to disprove the first two views, I did raise significant concerns, which should cause the theologian or philosopher to consider another option for serious consideration, namely, creationism, and particularly the view that the soul or mind is created by God. However, if we take our consciousness seriously in a way that does not eliminate the 'appearances' of our consciousness and the items therein, then we have good reason for rejecting something like emergent materialism, emergent monism or emergent individualism with its basis in a materialist framework. Along these lines, then, we can take more seriously the prospects of emergent dualism—similar to what William Hasker lays out above as a live option that not only accounts for consciousness (and the entailments to personal identity), but we actually do have something like it when we give some analysis or description to our phenomenal consciousness. Alternatively, and what I will argue in a moment, is that we should move beyond phenomenal unity to an actual object or substance that provides the unifying role to our consciousness, yielding a view that begins to look like a traditional soul, and assumes the Divine creation of souls.

Chapter 8

Why Selves are Probably Not Generated: An Initial Objection to Emergent-Selves (or Mere Emergent Dualism)

(Drawn and adapted from Joshua R. Farris, "Souls, Emergent and Created," *Philosophia Christi*, 2018)

Theology has something to tell us about the origin of souls (i.e., minds),[248] and yet much of contemporary literature on the soul's origination would suggest otherwise, having us believe that minds are the products of high-level physical processes. While a minority report affirms a creationist-soul alternative, it is often advanced by adherents of stronger and/or traditional versions of substance dualism (i.e., Thomism or Cartesian dualism).[249] In an attempt to avert both emergent versions of materialism[250] and stronger versions of substance dualism, some have attempted to include the benefits of both in what is often called emergent dualism. This is the view that the soul is indeed produced by a sufficiently complex brain, but is nevertheless not reducible to the interactions of the neural parts. However, common articulations of emergent dualism, with its quasi-naturalistic explanation, face a significant problem that requires a creationist explanation.[251] In the present chapter, I articulate one version of emergent dualism that is also a version of creationism by specifically focusing on the nature of the emergence relation.[252]

In this paper, I make two claims: First, I argue that while emergent substance dualism is gaining a following, it is insufficient to procure an explanation for the particularity of the soul. In this way, Divine creationism is a necessary condition for that particularity. Second, I articulate a version of emergent substance dualism that is also a version of creationism. On this view, both neural and Divine action are necessary for the emergent mind, thus bringing about a sufficiency relation in the conjunction of the brain-event with the Divine-event.

Now, a note about emergent dualism (ED) is in order. Once again ED is neither materialism nor a traditional version of substance dualism, but it is a *via media* between the two. ED is similar to emergent materialism in the following ways: (1) the mind is non-reducible to the interaction of neural parts (i.e., what Searle calls emergent 1b for novel powers; emergent 2 for a novel substance),[253] and (2) the mind is a product of the brain. Emergent substance dualism is also similar to traditional substance dualism in that it posits the reality of two substances (i.e., property-bearers) each of which is irreducible to the other. I will call this view *mere* emergent substance dualism or mere emergent dualism for short (hereafter MED) in order to distinguish it from a distinct variation of emergent substance dualism, which I will advance below.[254]

The advantages of MED have been clearly communicated in a variety of contexts. Several have argued that it carries with it an in-built explanation for the natural and intimate union of mind on brain, which is situated in biological evolution.[255] This later point is relevant to the biological data that appears to securely establish a continuity of humans with higher level animal species. Thus, on MED, there are two assumptions worth grounding in an emergent explanation: (A1) Animal-human continuity in biological evolution; (A2) A natural and intimate mind-on-brain dependence. Furthermore, I will argue for a third assumption that MED excludes, but without it, one is unable, on MED, to explain at least one important fact about souls. In this way, there is a need for a third assumption (A3), as I argue below, where soul emergence requires creationism.

MED and the Problem from Particularity

To motivate MED, defenders have raised several objections from the non-natural relation between soul and body from traditional construals. Hasker states in the context of discussing Cartesian substance dualism, "In rejecting such dualisms, we implicitly affirm that *the human mind is produced by the human brain and is not a separate element 'added to' the brain from the outside.*"[256] In Hasker's assumption given here his intent seems to be one of safeguarding the organic integrity of body and soul. I will offer an account that appears to safeguard the organic integrity of the soul and brain, with a different picture in mind, and, more importantly, avoids a more significant problem for MED.

Not only does the relationship between the body and soul on MED seem implausible, but there is also a fact about the world for which MED simply cannot account. The fact of the soul's property or feature of particularity (i.e., souls have primitive thisnesses: intrinsic and available only from an insider's perspective or from God's perspective) provides a forceful reason to move away from MED to an alternative ED with *divine creationism*. Each individual soul, as a metaphysical simple, just is different and what makes each different is this feature/property that only the said soul has, and through which the soul has an *inside perspective*. Call this a subjective or personal thisness, which I and, presumably, each of us has. This feature supplies the metaphysical content that makes me-*me*. If this is true, it is impossible, or near impossible, that the brain could produce personal souls because there is no material thing that has a primitive thisness of this sort.[257] Nevertheless, if we are already willing to accept Hasker's exotic view (or some similar view)—that minds actually emerge from matter—then why not also accept that souls emerge with thisness, however implausible that might sound?[258] The reason is simply that there is an incompatibility between the primitive thisness described here and the lawful relationship between mind and brain required by MED.[259]

Consider the possibility that Joshua exists on the earth and twin-Joshua exists on world Z. Consider further that all of the qualitative and public properties of each individual are the same, even their thoughts (at least as they are verbalized for others). Let's also suppose that their spatial location is arbitrary because each Joshua could just as easily occupy one space over another (i.e., the same relative position in each world), which would also mark the arbitrary nature of each individual's modal properties. What is it that would individuate these two individuals? It seems to me that there must remain one primitive fact that is also intrinsic to each individual that makes *this* Joshua on earth distinct from the *other* Joshua on world Z.[260]

Notice how this is different from material objects that are, in principle, publicly available. Assume we have particles with the same qualitative properties, perceptually distinguished by their relational occupation in the universe. Commonsensically, there is no qualitative distinction between this particle and another particle, apart from its spatial location. Each could have easily and arbitrarily been assigned to another spatial location, and each could have the same relative spatial location in parallel universes. We could take a number of different physical objects as illustrations of their identical nature (separated only by their relational occupation). Consider a coffee maker of a certain type, the Nespresso VertuoLine coffee maker. Presumably, the Nespresso VertuoLine coffee maker is one coffee maker with multiple instantiations of the same exact object with the same exact function. Now, the creators of Nespresso make the assumption that by using qualitatively identical parts in the appropriate configuration they can create a machine thousands of times over that will perform the exact same function. Not so for the individual mind. Each individual mind is distinct in terms of its particularity, which becomes apparent to the individual that has an inside perspective to her thoughts. Thus,

I have or instantiate a particularizing property/feature that is non-multiply exemplifiable. This raises a further question. Is it a possibility that I might have emerged from a set of complex physical conditions (PC)?

Given the uniqueness of *this* particular mind compared to another particular mind, it seems that PC could not produce a particular mind without the intervention or injection of the primitive particularity. Barring a hylomorphic view, where matter-form relation provides an intrinsic distinction between different arrangements of matter, PCs, it would seem, are insufficient for the production of a mind.[261] It is worth noting that the hylomorphic theory would cause some problems for the state of science, given the un-detectability of material essences, but let us set aside these problems in this context. There is one way in which PCs might be sufficient for the production of a mind, namely by proposing laws in the world explaining the production of each particular. However, a consideration of what this lawful relationship must be like introduces the worry that it would require some additional agency (e.g., a supernatural agent).

Assuming the same outcomes of lawful events are repeatable, presumably, these laws could be applied numerous times over with the same result, as with my Nespresso VertuoLine. The key idea is that if persons are the result of general laws, then the process of the same resulting individuals could emerge more than once, but this conflicts with our sense of credulity. Assuming I am my soul that has a particularity that sufficiently supplies the metaphysical content of what I am, if I was produced from the underlying material it would seem to follow that I could be reproduced with the same conditions in place, which is problematic if I am a non-universal that was produced by physical laws.

However one understands the laws of nature, a problem occurs for the defender of MED. On a determinist understanding all events are causally necessitated by their preceding events, and, past, present, and future events are contained within one causally closed system. This would fit on what is oft called the classical picture of the world in classical mechanics where the world is a machine. On the classical picture all particles are fixed as to their positions and the outcomes. On an indeterminist understanding of the laws of nature, what we arguably have on a quantum picture of the world, physical events occur in a lawful way, but while lawful events are not fixed they are predictable—based on probabilities.

First, let us look at the deterministic option. On the present view of souls, in a determined physical universe, this would entail that there would be over 7 billion separate fundamental laws because there are over 7 billion individual persons (and more to come!). It is not clear, though, that these laws would sufficiently explain who *I* am because that would be hidden from public view. Assuming these laws were in place, it does seem to follow, in fact, if I have a distinct particularity that sufficiently informs who *I* am that this lawful emergence would only occur once. In theory, a contradiction would ensue if, presumably, the same law could produce Joshua on earth and that same law could produce twin-Joshua (with all the same perceptible properties) on another world. More problematically, in a deterministic universe, there would need to be distinct laws for every individual, making the discovery of the laws highly unlikely, even if the lawful events occurred only once in the history of the world. One problem for this single occurrence that would arise is that we would never know for sure that this law created this person, aside from actually checking with the person herself. Furthermore, it is not clear that these are laws in any sense of the term, given the generalizable nature of laws. Hence, there is a problem for MED in a deterministic frame without some additional explanation.

Second, an indeterminist option would require that physical

parts lack the sort of particularity ascribed to the soul, so that it allows the repeatability of products. It would seem most scientists presuppose in practice that physical particles along with complex objects lack the sort of particularity ascribed to souls, and philosophers of physics assume that physical particles lack this sort of particularity.[262] The problem is that the present option disallows the kind of causality that is non-repeatable, and that the products are discoverable, at least in principle. In other words, if an indeterminist process produces you once, it is logically impossible that it could do so twice, even if it were within the bounds of statistical possibility. My particularity, the fact that I have immediate insight to this one pure property (i.e., subjective thisness), is determinate and could not be produced by a physical process in an indeterminist world.[263] Thus, an indeterminist world of physical causes and effects fails to explain this fact about souls.

Thankfully there is an explanatory option that provides the resources for souls. Both the deterministic and indeterministic options are accommodated in theism. On the deterministic option, God would at creation of the world establish the laws that give rise to you. On the indeterministic process, with the PC conditions in place, God simply acts by way of making determinate your particular soul.

With these points in mind, it is clear that creationism is a necessary condition for an emergent soul, and the sufficient condition for a soul's particularity, if the conditional is true. There is one viable response for the defender of MED who denies the primitive thisness view described above. She could understand the soul's thisness in a similar fashion to other physical products. On this understanding, souls are individuated by spatial location, and distinct complex arrangements of particles. A soul, in this case, could inherit its unique structure from biology, but there is a cost here if one takes it that this is the way in which one individuates one soul from another. It seems to me that my consciousness yields a distinction between *my* mental substance, which is a non-universal and a product of a non-generalizable event, contrasted with material substances that exist as products from lawful events, which, themselves, are generalizable in nature. The defender of MED, then, would need to deny what seems most apparent to her own mind. It would also seem to follow that two perceptibly identical persons could be just that—identical, distinguished only by their spatial occupations and the modal properties that follow.

Swinburnian Superiority to MED

We are left then with some version of creationist-souls. The challenge, as some have made quite clear, is that creationist versions of substance dualism lack the explanatory resources to make sense of animal-human continuity and a fine-grained dependence relation of mind-on-brain. But, one might question whether we should take these scientific assumptions as constraints on our philosophical theorizing.

It seems to me that we do have reason to take (perhaps tentatively) the scientific consensus on mind-brain relations as a constraint on our theorizing and so Hasker and Swinburne are right to do so. First, one might take it that the sciences have served a corrective role on our theorizing in history.[264] The overwhelming successes of the sciences in providing some profitable explanations have helped us to better describe the world as it seems to be. On the important issue of the mind-brain relationship, there is a growing consensus amongst scientists and many philosophers that matter has a tremendous amount of diversity and potential that was otherwise undetected in previous generations. It is this *growing potential* that has given philosophers additional resources from which to develop coherent explanations of the relationship between mind and brain. Second, the fine-grained dependence relation corroborates the scientific data with our common-sense experiences of mind and brain relations, where minds are functionally dependent on brains.[265] Take for example my running into a door frame and hitting my head. If I run into it hard enough, I will surely find myself unconscious lying on the floor. The scientific data tells me that something occurs in the neurons, while common sense tells me that what happens to my head intimately affects my mind.[266]

There is one creationist option that stands out as an option that appears to satisfy A1 and A2 given above. Richard Swinburne advances a more satisfying version of creationist-dualism that takes more seriously the findings of neuroscience and the data from biological evolution.[267] In this way, Swinburne has crafted a creationist alternative that begins to resemble MED, but it is not clear that his is a version of ED in any robust sense, even if it allows for a finely-grained dependence relation (A2). The problem is that Swinburne's theory appears to be 'inconsistent' in places.[268] Inconsistent or not, there are some clear oddities that one would hope could be resolved.

In several places, Swinburne seems to suggest that souls can pop in and out of existence.[269] Several related thought experiments are given from bodies sleeping and the severing of the corpus callosum, which he raises as conceivable possibilities for soul-cessation. On the latter thought experiment, it is suggested that the severing of the corpus callosum could bring about the emergence of a new soul.[270] For some this clearly seems unappealing, or worse, at odds with his creationism.[271] Swinburne's theory is arguably unappealing because it apparently presumes a messy origination process, where unique laws are required for each soul-body arrangement (see above). Despite such challenges, it seems to me there is a way to harmonize MED and creationism: combining them would make MED no longer MED, but another form of ED.

Emergent Creationism or Creationist Emergentism

One could conceive of an alternative ED along the following lines. As the creator of souls, *via* the materially configured neural structure, God creates human bodies to have a law-like or lawful relation to particular souls that he divinely intends to come about at a specified time. Divinely intending the actuality of the soul's particularity, then, is necessary to bringing about the existence of individual humans. God's bringing about *this* particular soul fulfills A3, but the *manner* in which the soul exists resembles MED. These two events are individually necessary and jointly sufficient for the origination of the human soul and so we have a theory that provides a natural explanatory ground for A1 and A2.[272] More can be said in order to add some additional analytic flesh on the theological bones of the soul. For a viable emergent relation between a body and a soul, we need to consider laws.

An emergent law would look something like the following. Biological conditions or physical conditions, what I will call (BPC) (i.e., the determinable), are required for the general features of the *originating* mind (OM). At some specified time t, the BPC are met, and a law establishes the union of *this* M to this brain. The emergent story does not end here because as shown above the BPC are insufficient for the originating M. Another necessary condition is required for the individual OM.

The divine act (determinate) of providing the particularity is an additional necessary condition, and the sufficiency condition for the soul's particularity, for the OM. OM must have originators (or originating causes), namely, BPC and Divine act. The sufficient conditions are met when BPC meets the Divine act in the specified way.

What emerges is not simply a novel set of properties and powers (emergent 1b, where novel properties/powers emerge from the interaction of low-level properties of material things), but a novel substance that did not previously exist.[273] The present view, call it emergent creationism or creationist emergentism, is not simply emergent 1b with a novel law, but is a higher form of emergence, which requires the presence of Divine action.[274] In the end, the mind emerges in one of two ways: First, it emerges by the confluence of BPC with the uniquely established law for each individual (where this unique law is established by God or some other agent). Potentially, defenders of MED could endorse something like this option, but it seems that they would need to give more credence to Divine action as a causal explanation in a soul's origination. There is another more obvious cost, however. The first option is, no doubt, unattractive because these sorts of laws go against well-attested theories of physical laws, so let us consider the second option. Second, it emerges by the confluence of BPC with the Divine injecting or imparting the particularity within the biological process. On this way of thinking, BPC is necessary for the emergence of souls (particularly human souls), but the Divine act is sufficient for a soul's particularity.

There remains a particularity problem for defenders of MED, which requires Divine creationism or some other supernatural agency. I have offered a couple of ways forward for MED, but it is not clear that MED would retain the 'mere' descriptor because some additional agency is present to or with lawful physical events. Furthermore, I have given reasons why these solutions are unsatisfactory. Yet, some version of emergent substance dualism with creationism seems preferable. The view I have advanced should not be confused with alternative origin stories. According to this view, physical events are not manifestations of the Divine acting in a specified way, thus the view advanced here is not a version of Divine occasionalism. Neither is it the case that mentality exists in physical particles, excluding micropsychism. Additionally, the assumption is not that the BPC has within it the powers to produce the mind, which also excludes MED. Thus, we have a distinct origin story of the mental. What needs further distinguishing is the fact-maker serving as an individuator of souls and the causal framework that plausibly grounds the origination of that fact-maker. More on that in the chapters to follow, but before moving on there was an exchange between William Hasker and myself about his views in response to my understanding of thisness. For those so inclined, they can look at this in more detail or skip to the next chapter.

Hasker responds to Farris

Hasker recently responded to the argument given above by effectively side-stepping the more fundamental issue of particularity that stands under the nature of our consciousness. You can see Hasker's response, here: *Philosophia Christi* (20:1, 2018). I provide a summary and response to Hasker's original response article in what follows, which provides additional clarity to my notion of how we should understand the particularity of persons.

(Additional response to Hasker's response published on the EPS web project, The Philosophy of Theological Anthropology)

In one place, I argued that Hasker's understanding of the emergent mind would be more hospitable in the context of a traditional view of the mind, which requires that it be created by God or some other agent rather than natural causes.[275] Working with the view that souls possess a primitive particularity (i.e., a fundamental and absolute thisness), I argued specifically that the lawful nature of natural events is incompatible with Hasker's view that the soul emerges from the body/brain. In other words, souls do not emerge as regularities. Instead, they appear to be singularities (i.e., irregularities) caused by chance or some non-natural agent. Hasker responded by denying my version of thisness as a primitive particularity of the soul. However, there are two main problems with Hasker's response. First, he does not give good reasons to reject a primitive particularity view of the soul. Second, he fails to offer any account of the soul's particularity. And, it is this second point with which I am most interested. Even if Hasker finally rejects the "Farris view of particularity," how he accounts for the soul's particularity remains a profound mystery. My immediate hope in this paper is to elicit what, I think, is a much needed response from Hasker on how he accounts for the soul's particularity—the fact that Hasker's soul is *Hasker's* soul and not any ol' soul. But, specifically how does Hasker respond? While I cannot deal with all the issues in that paper for the sake of space, I will give attention to the notion of a primitive thisness, which is at the heart of Hasker's particularity problem.

There have been several paths to emergent dualism.[276] William Hasker—who is known in the philosophical community for his commitment to substance dualism, evolutionary continuity of animals and humans, as well as the doctrine of mental emergence—has taken several different paths in his understanding of the nature of consciousness and matter.[277] Much of these have to do with the developing discussions on the origin of minds. Recently, the discussion has taken a turn to the problems with the material creation of minds (i.e., the claimed ability of matter to create minds or to act as the sole primary cause of minds).[278] In a previous article, I argued that Hasker's understanding of the emergent mind would be more hospitable in the context of a traditional view of the mind, which requires that it be created by God or some other agent rather than natural causes.[279] Working with the view that souls possess a primitive particularity (i.e., a fundamental and absolute thisness), I argued specifically that the lawful nature of natural events is incompatible with Hasker's view that the soul emerges from the body/brain. In other words, souls do not emerge as regularities. Instead, they appear to be singularities (i.e., irregularities) caused by chance or some non-natural agent. Hasker responded by denying my version of thisness as a primitive particularity of the soul. However, there are two main problems with Hasker's response. First, he does not give good reasons to reject a primitive particularity view of the soul. Second, he fails to offer any account of the soul's particularity. And, it is this second point with which I am most interested. Even if Hasker finally rejects the "Farris view of particularity," how he accounts for the soul's particularity remains a profound mystery. My immediate hope in this paper is to elicit what, I think, is a much-needed response from Hasker on how he accounts for the soul's particularity—the fact that Hasker's soul is *Hasker's* soul and not any ol' soul. But, specifically how does Hasker respond?

There are two claims in his response to take note of moving forward. First, he raises some concerns with what I have elsewhere called emergent creationism, noting a couple of substantive concerns with creationism in general along the way. Second, and directly related to the central argument of my "Souls, Emergent and Created," he raises several concerns to my understanding of the mind and the nature of emergence. He rejects my central objection because he finds it unpersuasive, so he denies primitive thisness to minds. In my objection to emergent substance dualism, I argued what seems quite apparent regarding the incompatibility of emergent minds with natural/physical laws.[280] If one affirms that minds carry a primitive thisness (a haecceity), then minds would emerge as a result of chance or, more likely, by direct agential action that supplies the primitive particularity to the mental subject.[281] Rather than engage with the objection, Hasker dismisses it. While the response is unhelpfully dismissive of an otherwise potent problem for emergentist views at large, I am pleased that he has explicitly and publicly stated that he rejects that minds are the carriers of primitive particularity. Here we have another development in the evolution of

Hasker's own thinking on his emergent substance dualism. Unfortunately, there remain two problems with his response. First, he gives no good reasons for his denial of what seems so apparent to one upon reflection, which yields some practical consequences that need addressing. Second, Hasker fails to provide any accounting for the mind's particularity, which my original article was attempting to elicit. In what follows, I will develop each of these points using the order Hasker gives in his response by considering the concern of creation ex-nihilo, primitive thisness, and divine occasionalism.

Creation Ex-Nihilo

Hasker is right to draw attention to my sympathies for emergent substance dualism. I am sympathetic to his line of thinking that the emergent relation between mind and brain provides a natural bridge between the two and an explanation for the intimate fine-grained relationship between mind and brain. It is this point that gives us some reason to find the empirical data for an intimate dependence relation between the two quite plausible ("Hasker's Response to Farris," 93). This, as I made clear, in the original article, is corroborated by further evidence from our common-sense experiences that presume a dependence relation, which I am keenly aware of when, say, I hit my head on the door frame upon entering a room. C. Stephen Evans points this out,

> What, exactly, is it about these findings that are supposed to create problems for dualism? ... Is it a problem that the causal effects should be the product of specific regions of the brain? Why should the fact that the source of the effects are localized regions of the brain, rather than the brain as a whole, be a problem for the dualist? It is hard for me to see why dualism should be thought to entail that the causal dependence of the mind on the brain should only stem

from holistic states of the brain rather than more localized happenings.[282]

It is not clear why local dependence of mind on brain would be a problem for any ole dualism including non-emergent forms of substance dualism. Hasker does grant that the story I have offered grants plausibility to the fine-grained mind on brain dependence relation.

Hasker credits the fact that something like emergent creationism can accommodate the empirical data of our intimate dependence of mind on brain (94). Briefly mentioning a couple of ways this could occur, Hasker gives credence to the notion that created minds could be designed, that are somehow suited, for brains or even pre-adapted for brains. We might flesh this out even more by describing minds as natural kinds that actualize some properties in virtue of their relation to brains, and the causal relationship may in some cases be in the other direction. Certainly the properties of the mind move beyond sensual experience of the physical world to a functional dependence for some of the properties instantiated by the mind. At a minimum, this sort of view yields property dualism of a sort that specified properties are lawful outcomes of the functional interaction between mind and brain. This leads to another problem, he suggests, for my view.

Hasker is keen to take one windy path away from a Divine creationist mind view because of animal-human continuity. And, he is not convinced that the view I have advanced has the resources to provide an accounting of "animal-human continuity" (94). He is right that the benefits of continuity within evolution are more difficult to make sense of in light of my view, but only slightly. It is, no doubt, trickier to account for strict continuity of animals and humans if we deny that animals have souls, but it is not clear from what Hasker stated that there could not exist a continuous relation between animal bodies and human bodies that have a similar biological structure. There are also important discontinuities between animals and humans from robust first-person consciousness, moral awareness, and robust rationality.[283] These distinctions exhibit a quite radical discontinuity in the kinds of minds. That said, there are challenges to the belief that animals have souls, which I attempted to give some exposure in *The Soul of Theological Anthropology*, thereby leaving open the possibility either way. There is first the challenge from access, namely, access to other minds. If we do not have access to other human minds, other than our own, what makes us think we have access to animal minds? Second, and more challenging when it comes to animal minds, animals are unable to communicate verbally to inform other minds that they have some inside perspective (i.e., thoughts about their own thoughts). This is one important evidential difference between animals and humans. Third, the physicalist thesis regarding animals is, arguably, defensible in the sense that there are several theses (e.g., behaviorism, functionalism, non-reductive physicalism) that can account for the data without requiring that the animal have an internal life, an inside perspective, or continuity of consciousness. Taken together, there is a greater challenge with attempts to demonstrably prove the existence of animal souls/minds. Then, but even more now, I am quite happy to grant that animals, especially higher-order ones, like dogs and primates, have souls because some animal responses (e.g., the responses I see from my dog when I accidentally step on his paw) seem to reveal consciousness, even if it is a *weak* first-person consciousness.

One path I find promising is to ground the similarity between animals and humans in neurology. With that in mind, the physical continuity between animal biology and neurology could very well be strictly physically continuous on the view I have presented. And, given the fitting functional nature of minds (the brain provides the general features of minds) is dependent on brains, then these would be functionally similar to animal minds with continuity of neurology. It is unnecessary, in light of these reflections, however, to expect that one must establish a strict continuity between animal minds and human minds in biological evolution. Specifying that relationship much beyond what has been said is empirically underdetermined, and, arguably, inaccessible by the powers of introspection.

All of these discussions raise a more important issue about the origination of minds in general on Hasker's emergent substance dualism because of the radically distinct natures of minds and material things. The question is: where do these minds come from? If minds originate from something from which they are substantially distinct—namely, matter, then it seems we may have an instance of material creation ex-nihilo, which is the idea that there is no ground for the existence of mental substances such that the latter substance is created by matter from nothing. This seems impossible. Matter is an insufficient condition for the emergent-soul.[284] It seems to me quite clearly from the models of laws on offer that matter is an insufficient condition for the emergent-soul, which is what I argued in a previous article. Hence, we do not have material creation ex-nihilo of minds. Interestingly, Hasker has claimed in more than one place that his view does not amount to a material creation ex-nihilo view in which case it seems quite compatible with emergent-creationism or something near it, but, instead, Hasker has recently opted for an alternative route.[285] In a recent article, Hasker offers some interesting lines of reasoning as a way to respond to the theological objection from material creation ex-nihilo. Until just recently, Hasker has not offered an explanation as to how his view yields neither Divine creation of souls nor material creation ex-nihilo. Somewhat unsurprisingly, he now leans in the direction of panpsychism, which, ironically, faces the combinatorial problem parasitic on materialism in its ability to account for a single, unified consciousness.[286]

In light of his new path, Hasker makes two quite revealing claims in response to the theological objection to material creation ex-nihilo. He states: "First, emergent dualism does not specify in detail how the emergence takes place; the manner may not be at all similar to creation ex nihilo." In other words, Hasker is granting quite a lot of latitude for the how of emergence and the conditions necessary for it to occur. He goes on to ask if God *could* (i.e., has the power to do so) create matter with the potential for emergence. Said another way, he asks: why could God not do this? And, he makes the further point: "To some of us, the power to create matter of this sort would seem to be a rather remarkable power, one which (assuming it to be coherent) enhances the divine majesty rather than detracts from it."[287] In other words, he is suggesting that this would be far more majestic of God than some other means.

There are three points worth making in light of Hasker's new path. First, the fact that Hasker gives some latitude for the possibilities and conditions involved in the process of a mental emergence from matter seems to open the door to the possibility that God might be involved in the process in some unique way—a way that is similar to creationism or, at least, indistinguishable from it. Second, while he is right to argue that the objector could not rule out some variation of panpsychism (a view that it seems he must endorse if he wants to get out of the problem of material creation ex-nihilo), it is not clear why this solution would be at all superior to Divine creationism with respect to the mechanism(s) involved in emergentism, especially given the fact that it is much easier and simpler to imagine one single, unified mind (i.e., a divine mind) creating another single, unified mind (i.e., human minds) rather than a plurality of mind-lets bringing about a single, unified mind. More importantly, the questions he raises as to God's power to create matter with the potential for mental emergence seems rather odd. The objection from material creation ex-nihilo seems not to be a question of whether God has the power or lacks the power to create matter with such potential. Instead, it seems to be a question of what we know about matter in contrast to minds, and how this would simply not amount to a form of Divine creationism of individual souls. How and what it is that marks out the emergent mind as non-Divine creationism and nonmaterial creationism ex-nihilo is unclear, as I argue elsewhere.[288] So, in opting for panpsychism, Hasker doesn't really offer any additional clarity on the mechanism, but, instead, seems to muddy the waters between the material and the immaterial. This is not very favorable to a position wanting to maintain *substance* dualism. Hasker would either need to posit a brute fact between panpsychism and particular minds or provide a more fine-grained account that illuminates the relationship. More importantly, the manner for mental emergence offered by Hasker is not only deeply mysterious in nature, it is *prima facie* indistinguishable from creationism regarding the empirical data that needs explaining. Third, his final point about God creating matter with the potential for mental emergence as signifying God's majesty seems, to me anyway, less majestic than God simply creating minds out of nothing. The latter action reflects far more power than God's using some created thing to bring about the existence of something new, but this is just one concern with Hasker's emergentism that seems to favor some version of Divine creationism. All that to say, in the way that panpsychism is a last resort for atheists to make some sense out of consciousness, so, it seems, it is a last resort for Hasker's account of mental origins (i.e., magic with a magician (a supernatural agent) is more plausible than magic without a magician).[289] His problems don't end here. Things are even worse for Hasker's emergent dualism; if minds are the carriers of primitive thisness, which I will show that they are, then Divine creationism follows.

The Challenge from Thisness

Emergentism and Primitive Thisness

I argued in the original article, beginning the discussion with Hasker, that a natural emergent mechanism cannot provide us with the results we desire.[290] I will not rehearse the objection here, but let me summarize it. Given the models of laws we have on offer, it seems quite apparent that those laws are inconsistent with or would never bring about the emergent-mind (with a haecceity, i.e., a primitive thisness). The fundamental problem is that haecceities are primitive particulars, but laws bring about generalizable events that, in theory, are duplicatable.

On a deterministic understanding of laws, an odd consequence ensues that primitive particulars require their own unique laws. This is problematic for at least two reasons. First, this requires that there are 7+ billion laws at present and more to come, hence a violation of Ockham's razor because these don't appear to be lawful regularities at all, but rather singularities— non-lawful. Second, this understanding of laws does not map onto any of the models of laws we have on offer. It is not clear that these laws would explain the primitive particular, as well. These events, rather than looking like regular events, which is needed for emergentism, look, instead, like irregularities (although common irregularities that are partially explained by regularities) in the world if minds are solely dependent upon physical and natural causes.

On an indeterminist understanding of laws, either primitive particular minds emerge by chance or by some additional agency. If the latter, then the mind would not depend solely on physical or biological conditions. If the former, then the mind could, in theory, be reproducible with all the same physical and/ or biological conditions in place. Problematic as this sounds, the situation is worse for the emergent dualist—where souls emerge solely from material events. Two results would ensue.

First, duplicate souls could emerge by chance, yet no ultimately distinguishing fundamental fact could distinguish one soul from the other soul. Second, identical souls would emerge, but this would seem to amount to a contradiction. However, without a primitive thisness there would remain no truth maker that ultimately distinguishes *this* soul from *that* soul.

Hasker responds to the above objection by denying that mental particulars are fundamentally and primitively distinct. By making this move, he avoids the consequent of the objection to his theory. But, his response is unsatisfying, once again, for the two reasons listed above. It is unsatisfying because it seems that we do have a primitive thisness, and he gives no good reasons for denying primitive particularities to minds. It is unsatisfying because Hasker gives no particularity account for minds, here or in his other writings.

Why we almost certainly have Primitive Thisness – If not Primitive Thisness, then what?
Apart from the claim that it is our properties that distinguish us, it seems there are two ways to account for individuation of minds. First, there is what one might call the brute particularity that I am simply different from another particular in view of the point of reference I occupy, and this depends neither on properties nor thisness (unless we assume a point of reference is the specifiable property that distinguishes one mind from another mind). Two consequences follow if Hasker endorses this view. What would follow is that there is no ground for my being *me* (i.e., no truth maker); and, while I could instantiate all the same properties as a distinct particularity in another world there would be no fact of the matter that sufficiently distinguishes *that* particular from me. Second, mental subjects do appear to be primitive particulars.

In order to motivate a case for primitive particulars, we should consider what is most apparent to our own minds. Considering all the features within one's own phenomenal awareness, there does seem to be one feature that ultimately distinguishes my mind. As a mind with my own first-person perspective and, as I have called it elsewhere an inside perspective, it does seem to follow that there is some feature or ground for my being me that is not dependent on properties. There would not be a contradiction in the idea of 2 distinct individuals even if they had all the same qualitatively identical thoughts, yet it appears that there would remain two sets of thoughts and not one set of thoughts because there are two subjects. Instead, my inside perspective is dependent upon a fact of the matter that is not dependent on properties or a material particular— the latter Hasker surely grants. This primitive particularity is not dependent on the capacity for an inside perspective, but rather the capacity is dependent on the former. Let me offer an argument for mental primitive particularity.

Assuming I do exist through time (which I do experience as basic to my being me and my apparent memories), it seems that something makes me *me*. We could run similar thought experiments as in the original article to show that *I* am not dependent on my properties. If I were dependent on my properties, then it is possible that I exist twice because it is conceivable that another mind could exist in a possible world instantiating all the same properties I instantiate in this world. Yet, this amounts to either a duplicate of me or one identical to me. That said, there would exist no fact of the matter to make determinate that I am me and not the duplicate in another possible world. But there is a fact of the matter, I am me and not the duplicate in another possible world. One can either assert the fact of the matter without a grounding or one can affirm a primitive fact—namely, that I am my own mind apart from any properties. I, as a primitive mind, exist and contribute something novel to the world quite apart from the properties I have, come to have, or cease to have.

Hasker raises another objection to the sort of thisness I advance, by claiming:

> An even more decisive objection, however, stems from principle (1). One's sense of oneself simply is not the right sort of thing to be a thisness as defined in (1); it is instead clearly qualitative—in Robert Adams' terminology, it is a suchness and not a thisness. For A to be aware of sense-of-self a and for B to be aware of sense-of-self b is just as much for them to be in different qualitative states as for A to be tasting hamburger and for B to be tasting asparagus. As a candidate for a primitive thisness, the sense of self is not even in the running. I conclude that, since there are no thisnesses in the sense required by Farris's argument, that argument poses no threat to emergent dualism.[291]

Hasker seems to muddy the waters here because the issue is not that there are two qualitatively identical senses of self, but two subjects. The sense would not make these two subjects identical for these properties would not provide the fact necessary to distinguish the two subjects. Hasker argues that my understanding of thisness is problematic and should be interpreted as a quality rather than a thisness based on the "inside perspective" or the sense of oneself. I take Hasker's point that there is something of what it is like to be me, and only I have an inside perspective on the fact, but this does not prove his point because there are two subjects quite apart from the identical senses they may have of themselves. Rather, this helps make the case that there exists primitive thisnesses independent from one's spatial location, the body one has, and the properties one comes to have. While it is true, I can come to bear properties that other minds have like the tasting of a hamburger or the tasting of asparagus. The fact that A is in the qualitative state of tasting a hamburger and B is in a distinctive qualitative state of tasting asparagus presumes a fact about A as distinct from B that remains unaccounted for when discussing different qualitative states. Let us consider one important fact about qualitative states that remains unanswered on Hasker's account.

Consider the fact of one's qualitative experience of tasting coriander. It is true there are certain physical facts about coriander that have something to do with how coriander tastes, but there remains an unaccounted fact when I taste coriander quite apart from Hasker tasting coriander. There is a fact of tasting coriander that is distinct from the fact of Hasker tasting coriander that physical facts, properties could not explain.[292] Even if you have two qualitatively identical experiences of coriander, they are numerically distinct because of the subject of experience and the fact that experiences have different subjects. As E.J. Lowe has helpfully stated,

> [I]t is strongly arguable that the only *adequate* criterion of identity for mental states and events will be one which makes reference to their subjects... [P]art of what makes an experience of *mine* numerically distinct from a qualitatively indistinguishable experience of *yours* is the very fact that it is *mine* as opposed to *yours*.[293]

The point is that qualitatively identical experiences are insufficient when accounting for identical subjects. Even if one has an identical suchness, this would in no way determine identical subjects having the same experience. Going back to the experience of coriander, there would remain one fact unaccounted for, namely, the fact that makes me-me as a subject experiencing coriander and the fact that conceivably makes my duplicate a distinct subject experiencing coriander. And, what is more, the further notion that there is a sense of self would not itself account for my being my*self* quite apart from my duplicate not being a subject identical to me.

What does this all show? It shows that there exists one primitive fact about minds independent from properties. It remains that for these two to be two subjects with the same suchness, or qualitative experiences, one would require a primitive thisness (haecceity) that ultimately makes one subject *this* subject and the other subject *that* subject. Unfortunately, without it, it appears that there would be no fact of the matter distinguishing two distinct subjects who have all the same qualitative experiences. For the reasons listed above, it appears that I do exist, but not according to Hasker's view. And, according to emergentism, I could not come to exist apart from God (or some other non-natural agent) granting that particularity. If I came to exist by chance, then there is no fact of the matter that would make me *me* and would ultimately distinguish my*self* from another. It seems obviously false that there would be no fact of the matter that makes me *me*.

Hasker's Further Response

Hasker advances a further response to me, which can be accessed here: (https://epsociety.org/userfiles/Hasker%20rejoinder%20 to%20Farris-2-3.pdf), and provides additional detail in an argument to Swinburne of how he conceives of a related view.

In a recent and related discussion following my pointed concerns to Hasker on his problems with personal identity, Hasker responds to Swinburne's notion of informative designators, which I have elsewhere expanded upon to argue for a sufficient designator (presuming the principle of sufficient reason, see below). Hasker has one interesting exchange with Swinburne over the notion of the hypothetical Tubby-person. Assuming that co-experiences are owned by one unified subject of consciousness, let's assume that Tubby-person could experience a fission process in a lab. Such a process would bring about a split-off from Tubby-person into two persons, Tubby1 and Tubby2. Let's set aside the fact that this is exotic and may not be conceivable at all and consider it on its own terms. Swinburne argues that this would entail something like the fact that Tubby1 and Tubby2 were originally parts of Tubby. Hasker responds, rightly on his view, that this would not be the entailment. Instead, in an emergence process the person, Tubby, would split-off and become Tubby1 and Tubby2, but there is no reason to think that those 2 individuals would have originally composed Tubby. Rather, they would be the products and Tubby would be preserved in the sense that he would exist as Tubby1 and Tubby2.

While this is technically consistent with Hasker's emergent dualism because it allows for the process of reduplication and Hasker denies the thesis of metaphysically simple souls, it is not without its problems. It presumes that there is not a stable ground for the existence of Tubby. Further, the subjects of experience, Tubby1 and Tubby2, lack a fact of the matter that is rooted in the soul, and, instead, are left to the generable determinations of whatever happens to the body.[294] Despite the fact that this view leaves personhood susceptible to scientific control, it lacks the metaphysical content necessary to make determinate what it is that makes me *me*, which has the further epistemic implication that I do not know that I am me because there is no fundamental fact that makes it so, leaving me susceptible to the illusion that I am me when I could be someone else. The problem is exacerbated when we consider the perfect-duplicate problem, which I address in the next chapter. This problem is parasitic on all naturalistic models of personhood and clarifies what is not only needed but necessary and lacking on Hasker's view of the self as a complex phenomenal unity.

In the end, Hasker does not sufficiently take into account the concern from particularity, which was the main issue I have placed at his feet. First, he does not give good reasons to reject a primitive particularity view of the soul. Second, he fails to offer any account of the soul's particularity. And, it is this second point with which I am most interested. In what follows, I expand on this concern for particularity that sharpens the problem in a way that demands that one accept an obscurantist dualism that fails to satisfy a sufficient condition for personhood or consider taking up Cartesianism with its clarity concerning the metaphysical fact that makes me *me*.

Chapter 9

Do Selves Exist? Perfect Duplicates, A Problem for Emergent-Selves and Panpsychism

(Drawn and adapted from "Emergentism, A Novelty Without Particularity: The Problem from 'Perfect Duplicates,'" *Philosophy, Theology and the Sciences*, issue 7, 2020, 70-89)

Emergentism regarding the mind comes in two primary varieties, as we discussed above. On the first variety, the mental is a set of higher-order, novel neurological properties and capacities that include first-person consciousness and top-down causation that are non-reductive to the underlying particles. On the second, and more radical, version, the mental is a substance (i.e., a property-bearer) with a thisness that characterizes mental nature as a unique singular conscious substance with first-person consciousness and libertarian freedom.[295] While the latter has the advantage of accounting for the unity of consciousness—a common benefit advanced in the literature, both have a similar problem. This is a problem I will call the 'perfect duplicate' problem. In brief, the problem has to do with the particularity of the mental substance, which requires a metaphysical individuator (not simply an epistemic individuator) that makes me *me* and does not depend on properties (i.e., what philosophers refer to as universals that are multiply exemplifiable). Emergentist accounts of minds do not give us a sufficient reason for thinking that this mind is sufficiently distinct from *that* mind because an emergentist account of individual thisness depends either on properties or on a brute particularity that lacks a sufficient explanation. This is where the emergent mechanism is crucial in precluding the right sort of particularity for the origins of personal identity (see Jacobs 2012).[296] Emergentism fails as an explanation for the origins of personal identity, but a traditional variant of a mental substance which is not dependent on a generalizable or universalizable process does not fail, at least not obviously, as an explanation (i.e., creationism seems an apt explanation for the mind) (Farris 2018a and 2018b).[297] Let's consider the basic logical structure of the argument to follow.

Take for example the person Joan. Motivated by Descartes' conceivability logic that whatever is conceivable is possible—it is conceivable that perfect physical duplicates exist, but it is not possible that persons (with first-person consciousness and primitive haecceity exist) as perfect duplicates exist. Regarding persons, it is conceivable that there exists a physical duplicate that is perfect in all respects to another. Regarding persons too, Joan* could exist, but not Joan. That the whole world is entirely physical or a product of the physical, then, does not follow. The argument above is buttressed by the fact that most physicists acknowledge that there are perfect physical duplicates, even particles that have no distinguishing identity as with a haecceity—hence rendering panpsychism false. The conceivability of persons as actual persons is rooted in the fact of the first-person conscious access to one's individual nature. On physicalism, emergentism, and panpsychism, perfect person duplicates are, ironically, conceivable. Perfect person duplicates would render a logical contradiction. Perfect person duplicates are impossible. The reason this is the case is that every person is sufficiently explained by a primitive haecceity and primitive haecceities of persons are not duplicatable in principle.

Here is how I intend to proceed. First, I will lay out my view of haecceity and why it is preferable to other views. Second, I will raise an objection to mere emergentism, of the materialist varieties and the dualist varieties. Third, I will explore the objection from material creation ex-nihilo concerning emergent dualism by showing that it requires panpsychism or an alternative explanation of the mind, but even panpsychism fails as an explanation of the subject/person primitive mental particular.

1. The Particularity or Individuality of Mental Substances

There are, at least, three ways to understand the particularity of the mind. Minds are individualized, i.e., they have a thisness that distinguishes one mind from another mind. My mind is not your mind and vice versa. A thisness is a countable substance. Normally, the literature is concerned with epistemic thisnesses, but I am concerned with metaphysical thisnesses that serve as the individuator of a thing. In this case, that thing is a mental thing or substance. A mental substance just is that thing that thinks and experiences.[298] But what is it that makes one individual mental substance distinct from another individual mental substance? There are, at least, three approaches when answering this question.

The first option takes it that an individual mental substance is individuated by special property. On some accounts, that special property just is a modal property. I am *this* mental thing and not *that* mental thing because I exist with a set of modal properties that *that* mental thing does not have. For example, it is conceivable that I exist with the same body, ideas, and character traits as another in an alternative possible world, yet what would distinguish us are the modal properties.

The second option takes it that minds have an individual essence that is not dependent on properties. Instead, individual mental substances are distinguishable not by any property, but in virtue of being a brute bare particular without a sufficient explanation for each individual substance. It just is that way, full stop, for that is what it means to be a bare particular.

The third option takes it that individual minds have a

primitive feature (i.e., a haecceity). This primitive feature by definition is the kind of thing that just is distinct not in virtue of properties, but in virtue of a feature that individuates it. This feature makes it such that one mind is distinct from another mind quite apart from any of the mental properties had by each mind. I just am my own mental substance.

a. Arguments for a Primitive Mental Particularity

Apart from the claim that it is our properties that distinguish us, it seems there are two ways to account for individuation of minds that do not depend on properties. First, there is what one might call the brute particularity that I am simply different from another particular in view of the point of reference I occupy, and this depends neither on properties nor thisness (i.e., as an epistemic property). What would follow is that there is no ground for my being *me* (i.e., no truth maker); and, while I could instantiate all the same properties as a distinct particularity in another world there would be no fact of the matter that sufficiently distinguishes *that* particular from me (a seeming problem parasitic on views 1 and 2 as listed above; namely, for the property view of individual mental substances and the brute particularity view). Second, mental subjects do appear to be primitive particulars that have a sufficient reason or explanation for their existence.

In order to motivate a case for primitive particulars according to view three, we should consider what is most apparent to our own minds. Considering all the features within one's own phenomenal awareness, there does seem to be one feature that ultimately distinguishes my mind. As a mind with my own first-person perspective, and as I have called it elsewhere an inside perspective, it does seem to follow that there is some feature or ground for my being me that is not dependent on properties. There would not be a contradiction in the idea of two distinct individuals even if they had all the same qualitatively identical thoughts, yet it appears that there would remain two sets of thoughts and not one set of thoughts because there are two subjects. Instead, my inside perspective is dependent upon a fact of the matter that is not dependent on properties or a material particular. This primitive particularity is not dependent on the capacity for an inside perspective, but rather the capacity is dependent on the former. Let me offer an argument for view three of mental primitive particularity.

Assuming I do exist through time (which I do experience as basic to my being me and my apparent memories), it seems that something makes me *me*. We could run thought experiments to show that *I* am not dependent on my properties. If I were dependent on my properties, then it is possible that I exist twice because it is conceivable that another mind could exist in a possible world instantiating all the same properties I instantiate in this world. Yet, this amounts to either a duplicate of me or one identical to me. That said, there would exist no fact of the matter to make determinate that I am me and not the duplicate in another possible world. But there is a fact of the matter, I am me and not the duplicate in another possible world. One can either assert the fact of the matter without a grounding or one can affirm a primitive fact—namely, that I am my own mind apart from any properties with an individuating feature. I, as a primitive mind, exist and contribute something novel to the world quite apart from the properties I have, come to have, or cease to have.

Thomas Nagel helps motivate the case that minds are primitive particulars by challenging a naturalist paradigm to consciousness. He states: "The existence of consciousness seems to imply that the physical description of the universe, in spite of its richness and explanatory power, is only part of the truth, and that the natural order is far less austere than if physics and chemistry account for everything." Part of the reason the material or natural order lacks the resources to explain consciousness has to do with what Nagel calls "subjective appearances" (Nagel 2012, 35).[299] Subjective appearances, however, arguably imply the fact of a subject. The fact of these subjective appearances depends on a deeper truth about consciousness, namely a subject of consciousness that is prior to the parts and makes consciousness not an indistinct consciousness but a distinct consciousness. To tease this out further, consider the fact that some appearances are likely not dependent on the properties — the qualities of the subject in question. Instead some are explained by the fundamental or primitive fact concerning the mental subject.

Consider the fact of one's qualitative experience of tasting coriander. It is true there are certain physical facts about coriander that have something to do with how coriander tastes, but there remains an unaccounted fact when I taste coriander quite apart from my father tasting coriander. There is a fact of tasting coriander that is distinct from the fact of my father tasting coriander that physical facts, properties could not explain (Callaway 2012).[300] Even if you have two qualitatively identical experiences of coriander, they are numerically distinct because of the subject of experience and the fact that experiences have different subjects. As E.J. Lowe has helpfully stated,

> [I]t is strongly arguable that the only *adequate* criterion of identity for mental states and events will be one which makes reference to their subjects... [P]art of what makes an experience of *mine* numerically distinct from a qualitatively indistinguishable experience of *yours* is the very fact that it is *mine* as opposed to *yours* (Lowe 2012, 149).[301]

The point here is that qualitatively identical experiences (i.e., the perfect duplicate experience) are insufficient when accounting for identical subjects. Even if one has an identical suchness, this would in no way determine identical subjects having the same experience. Going back to the experience of coriander, there would remain one fact unaccounted for, namely, the fact that makes me-me as a subject experiencing coriander and the fact that conceivably makes my duplicate a distinct subject experiencing coriander. And, what is more, the further notion that there is a sense of self would not itself account for my being my*self* quite apart from my duplicate not being a subject identical to me.

In fact, there is another related fact in the experience of coriander that is unaccounted for if my mental particularity is dependent on properties. It could be that my father does not like the taste of coriander, but I do. Accounting for the experience of his not liking it and my liking it could be explained, in part, by the genetic difference causing his experience of coriander to taste like chalk. However, in those cases where there is no genetic cause for one's dislike of coriander, then we are left with the explanation of subjects. The fact that my father does not like coriander, but I do like coriander is explained by the simple fact that he does not like it and I do or it might be that we are tasting coriander differently, but there is no way to make objectively determinate that we simply don't like coriander (assuming it tastes the same) or that we are tasting it differently. We, then, have, at least, one instance where the explanation for experiencing something differently may not be dependent on properties. In either explanation, there is no publicly verifiable property that makes determinate either that my father is tasting coriander in the same way or differently.

What these thought experiments show is that minds are not merely explained by generic or common essence, properties, or one's unique relations, but by a primitive particularity distinguished by a feature (a subjective feature that just is distinct as a substance). Without this subject primitive particularity, there would not be a sufficient reason/explanation for the existence of two distinct subjective appearances that have no recourse to their properties. Further, there is some additional fact that is actualized in virtue of the explanatory power of a mental substance, according to view three, that contributes something novel to the world. This discussion prompts a further discussion about the 'how' or origination of personal identity. As asserted earlier, emergentist views seem to entail the possibility of 'perfect duplicates' that are explicable by views 1 and 2 and are indistinguishable explanations which result in either no explanation for an absolute distinction of individual mental substances or yield a contradiction. Hence, the discussion of origins becomes rather important for providing a causal explanation that is consistent with all the metaphysical facts of our world.

b. Objecting to Emergence and Complex Mental Particularity

Before proceeding to the different ways of accounting for individuation on emergentisms, it is important to say something about why it is that the 'I' finds its locus in the mind. To this point, I have assumed that it is the mind. I just am my mind (or if you like to use the word soul to refer to an immaterial mental substance that works as well). The argument here leaves open the possibility that it could be some other substance than the mind, but what that would be remains somewhat mysterious. Furthermore, if as the above thought experiments show that the primitive particularity has not parts or complexity, then it would follow that the 'I' just is the mind with this primitive individuating feature.

On an emergent mechanism alone, emergentism cannot provide us with the explanatory resources to make sense of the mind coming into existence, but more to the point for our purposes here it fails to supply a sufficient reason for how *I* originate and what it is in the complex material that makes me *me* (because on some accounts it is the body that individuates the mind) or what it is about the emergent-mind that makes me *me*.[302]

There appear to be two issues that make this the case for material individuation. First, the underlying physical particles that make up the fundamental parts of the natural world and give rise to higher-order properties and substances through natural causes in a regularly patterned way (hence pseudo-naturalism) themselves are likely not carriers of primitive thisness. Second, given the models of laws we have on offer, the natural occurrence of mental emergence would yield one of three problematic consequences: one that there is a unique law for each mind (on a deterministic understanding of laws); two that a potential contradiction would ensue; three, that there would be no fundamental fact that makes distinct one mind from another mind.

At this point, the reader might wonder about the role of matter or physicality doing the work needed for particularity. Taking a page from Aristotle, the reader might think that human minds are matter-form compounds and the matter does the sufficient work to individuate the mind by providing the properties needed to supply a sufficient reason for *my* existence. The form supplies the species to the matter. The matter then would supply the sufficient distinction between two particular minds. However, this does raise a concern. Most contemporary emergentists reject an Aristotelian conception of matter as matter-form compounds such that matter simply does not do the work that Aristotle once attributed to it.[303] Furthermore, this raises the question about the intrinsic nature of material particles themselves. For material particles to give rise to higher-order properties, or substances, these material particles must either be intrinsically differentiated by a primitive thisness and have the power to give rise to a complex thisness that is differentiated by the distinct matter that a form has. Here it is worth pushing against hylomorphism because the material stuff fails to give us a sufficient account of the individual mind in question, and if the thought experiment above regarding the insufficiency of qualities to distinguish minds persuasively holds then hylomorphism would lack a sufficient explanation not of the generables of the mind but of primitive particular minds (given that hylomorphic forms of minds, i.e., 'rational souls,' are comprised of complex thisnesses). Since most contemporary emergentists reject an Aristotelian hylomorphism conception of matter, this defeater should not deter us here (French 2015).[304]

The emergentists could opt for a similar thesis that is metaphysically neutral on the nature of matter itself. Instead of adopting hylomorphism Aristotelianism, the emergentist could simply say that the matter individuates one individual mind from another mind. But, really what does that give us? At best it gives us a brute explanation of the mental particular in question, because as the coriander example shows our minds are metaphysically primitive, and maybe that is all that the emergentist desires. The bruteness of the explanation for *my* existence presumes that there is no fact of the matter beyond the mental properties that ensue from lawful regularities.

Given the models of laws we have on offer, it seems quite apparent that those laws are inconsistent with or would never bring about the emergent-mind (with a haecceity, i.e., a primitive thisness). The fundamental problem is that haecceities are primitive particulars, but laws bring about generalizable events that, in theory, are duplicatable. On many standard accounts, see the above, a haecceity is a property(s) had by particular substances. The specific concern in the present article is that the property view(s) give us no sufficient reason for the existence of a mental particular as contrasted with another mental particular, and the emergentist view seems to depend on such an account, but if it does not it fails to supply a story that gives us a sufficient reason for thinking that naturally lawful events could produce a mental particular.

Presumably we could have a theory of laws that allow for the possible emergence of particular minds, if we assume that individual thisness exists at the level of physical particles. Physical particles are assumed to be the building blocks of the natural world, and if it follows that minds are products of high level complex physical processes, then they could receive their haecceity from the lower-level physical parts that serve as the conditions for the emergent mind. The problem for such a view is twofold already signaled. To repeat, first, most quantum physicists and philosophers of science of which I am aware presume that physical particles are not carriers of primitive thisness. They are certainly not primitive thisnesses, unless one assumes an especially exotic version of panpsychism, in the sense that mental particulars are primitive thisnesses. But the deeper metaphysical question is whether particles are intrinsically carriers of thisness at all. In this case, minds could be complex thisnesses comprised of the lower-level primitive thisnesses, but this would give us an ad hoc and brute explanation of mental particularity without a definitive way of determining one mind from another mind. Second, the resulting product from natural processes would not give us a distinct primitive thisness, but rather a complex thisness comprised of lower-level thisnesses (i.e., a gravitation toward mereological mental nihilism) (French 2019).[305] But let us consider how mental primitive particulars could result from a lawful emergent process. There are two broad ways to parse out an emergent view lawfully.

On a deterministic understanding of laws, an odd consequence ensues that primitive particulars require their own unique laws. Consider a deterministic universal regularity view (say the view of Tooley, Armstrong, and others called the relations-between two first-order universals view; namely, that F's are G's and F-ness and G-ness are first-order universals that are non-logically related and contingent necessities), where every y is followed by event x, past, present, and future (Carroll 2019).[306]

The view is deterministic in nature, and has an in-built constraint that would not seem to allow for a particular emergent-mind in that laws necessitate the emergence of universalizable events. If minds were to emerge naturally, then the results would be nothing short of fantastic, to speak modestly of it.

For minds to emerge, according to deterministic natural laws, is problematic for at least two reasons. First, this requires that there are 7.5+ billion laws at present and more to come, hence a violation of Ockham's razor. These don't appear to be lawful regularities at all, but rather non-lawfully produced singularities. These singularities are not like the law of gravity that is instantiated billions of times over because the mind's origination is non-regular. Second, this understanding of laws with its regular process of bringing about singularities does not map onto any of the models of laws we have on offer. These events, rather than looking like regular events, which is needed for emergent dualism, look, instead, like singularities (although common irregularities that are partially explained by the regularities of the mind's corresponding bodies) in the natural world.[307]

On an indeterminist understanding of laws, either primitive particular minds emerge by chance or by some additional agency. If the latter, then the mind would not depend solely on physical or biological conditions. If the former, then the mind could, in theory, be reproducible with all the same physical and/or biological conditions in place. Assuming all the same conditions were met, in theory, it would be statistically possible to repeat the same event that gives rise to a duplicate product because objects are distinguishable by their properties or by a brute bare particular. So if we are willing to assume that mental thisnesses are, potentially, naturally emergent products, we are left with two concerns. The first concern is that there is no sufficient reason for the origin of one mind over another mind because chance explanations in an indeterminist frame fail to supply a reason (while there are lots of reasons to think a person exists like s/he is standing in front of you, it is not a sufficient reason for *that* person's particular existence). The second concern is that chance does not give a sufficient reason for the origination of *this* mind versus *that* mind. In other words, we lack a sufficient reason for determining a difference between duplicates and identicals. Let us consider why this is the case.

On the former understanding, if minds are distinct via properties, then it could be that another mind is produced in the same context, meeting the same conditions, and by chance the duplicate would have all the same properties. In this way, as it is possible to produce and reproduce the same material objects, in principle, one could do the same with minds. A common thought experiment on the identity conditions for the ship of Theseus across time illustrates this problem (diachronically). Richard Swinburne has recently argued that the problem of the ship of Theseus across time—that the ship of Theseus at time t1 with the old wooden planks is the same or not the same at time t2 when it has new wooden planks. According to Swinburne, the identity conditions for a material object are ambiguous and lack a fact of the matter that would informatively designate that the ship of Theseus is the same at time t1 as time t2 because "there is no more to any substance than its parts (e.g., fundamental particles) and the way those parts are arranged" (Swinburne 2013, 35).[308] Swinburne rightly notes that we can tell the story of the history of the ship of Theseus in one of two ways—namely that it is the same ship because of its continuity across time or that it is not the same ship because it has lost the original wooden planks that once composed it. He states: "We can tell the story either way without anything being omitted (Swinburne 2013, 31)."[309]

Lynne Rudder Baker raises an interesting response to Swinburne's argument that the story could be told without anything being omitted (Baker 2014, 5-15).[310] By her lights,

Swinburne could miss important information about the ship of Theseus. There are certain facts surrounding the history of the ship that are relevant to the story like: who owned the original wooden planks, who owned the new wooden planks etc. Baker sees these as additional relevant facts to the history of the world. While Baker's point is generally important, she has not rebutted what seems to be Swinburne's main point. She confuses Swinburne's metaphysical thesis with her own epistemic thesis. Swinburne is not interested in all the historical facts surrounding the ship, but the fact that makes the ship the ship that it is—i.e., using his own language, is there a property/ feature that serves as the "informative designator"? And, the answer is unclear. For, we could say that the ship of Theseus at time t2 is the same because it stands in historical relation with the ship at time t1 and may even occupy the same space having been in a shipyard all this time. Alternatively, we could say that the ship at time t2 is different from the ship at time t1 because it has different wooden planks. In other words, the facts surrounding the ship, e.g., the history, the planks, the spatial occupation, are all accidental and fail to give us a determinative fact that comprehensively describes or sufficiently describes the ship (i.e., in Swinburne's terms the "informative designator"). Minds are different.

We could take any ol' material object (synchronically) and the problem is relevantly similar. Consider the fact that the CHI company makes hair straighteners that are produced in the same way, with the same features of weight, with all the same parts, and with the same function. And, let us suppose that two of the CHI-made hair straighteners are the same color. Presumably at this point we have exhausted all the properties that comprehensively describe each CHI-made hair straightener. The only other difference one might advance as an individuator is spatial location, but there are problems with the property of spatial location making determinate this individual hair straightener and a duplicate hair straightener.

Ultimately, the concern is that it is not a metaphysically necessary truth that spatial location factors into the constitutive identity of a material object nor is spatial location a logically necessary truth in this world (Black 1952, 153-64).[311] First, it is not clear that the spatial location adds any additional relevant information on the individual nature of the hair straightener. Second, it is not clear that when we switch the two hair straighteners so that each occupies the space of the other that the identity of each changes based on the changing locations. Third, there is no metaphysically necessary reason that spatial occupation of the individual hair straightener (or any material object for that matter) is a constitutive factor sufficient for its identity. For some further fact to make determinate this hair straightener from that hair straightener, we would need something beyond the properties themselves that factor into the identity of the item in question. But, what would that be? There is no further fact in sight.

Now going back to persons. In other words, the principle of the identity of indiscernibles does not apply to substances with a primitive particularity or haecceity. It could be that chance gives rise to a brute particular that is non-distinguishable by her properties. In this case, it just is the fact that this person is distinguishable not by properties or by the material part in question but by a mind that has no intrinsic features or properties beyond those that are multiply-exemplifiable. That doesn't mitigate the fact that there is a new mind present. It just means that there is no causally constitutive feature or property that makes it that way. In this case, while we could imagine the possibility of a chance event occurring where this mind was an emergent product of this brain, there is a significant concern. There would exist no sufficient reason for its existence nor is there a distinguishable event that causes its existence. There are, at a minimum, two problems. First, there exists no fact that makes one mind distinct from another mind. Second, and the further causally productive role of a physical thing that acts as the proximate cause for minds would fail to have a sufficient reason for bringing about *this* mind rather than *that* mind.

Ironically, in this case, it would be logically possible, even if probabilistically unlikely, that we could produce the same person or her duplicate. If we were to conceive of a world where we had a fairly exhaustive knowledge of a person's genetic makeup, then in theory that same person could be reproduced in a lab. Problematic as this sounds, the situation is worse for the emergentist, where minds emerge solely from material events. There are two results that would ensue. First, duplicate minds could emerge by chance, yet no ultimately distinguishing fundamental fact could distinguish one mind from the other mind. Second, identical minds would emerge, which would yield not two minds but one where the two minds had access to their own mind—but this would be absurd. Intuitively, once again, it would seem that there are two distinct minds, and nonidentical minds even if they had all the same publicly verifiable properties. Assuming the brute particular view, minds are understood as those that are distinct, but there is no additional sufficient fact beyond the perspectival space that I occupy in contrast to my potential duplicate. And, there is no particularizing feature that makes my perspectival space *my* perspectival space—for that's what it means to be a brute particular.

Without a primitive thisness, we lack a truth maker that ultimately distinguishes *this* mind from *that* mind and there is no sufficient reason for conceiving of *my* coming into existence. If one were to opt for a lawful emergence of minds solely from natural events, then the indeterminist option seems more satisfying as an option than the determinist option given its widespread acceptance amongst philosophers and scientists today. The fact that natural events occur by chance that are predictable probabilities of empirical phenomena seem to fit the present state of the consensus of the scientific community. This opens the door to consider the possibility of how it is that *my* mind comes into existence by way of creationism or by way of chance. It is here that we can see with clarity the problem from perfect duplicates.

2. Creationism or Chance

Three options for the defender of emergentism are open to further reflection, and all of these assume mind-body dualism. There are two obvious options, and one less obvious option. The defender of emergent dualism can accept that chance brings about the lawful event that *this* mind would come to exist. Alternatively, the defender of emergent dualism can affirm some version of creationism. Creationism supplies emergent dualism with some obvious resources for making sense of mental particularity. If she affirms a divinely created soul, then she could just accept indeterminism at the physical level, but accept that there is an underlying ontology that explains the emergence of minds. On this story, God, or a supernatural being, simply creates the mind directly by making it occur that one mind emerges rather than some other random mind, but if she rejects a crude version of divine creationism, then the emergent dualist could affirm that the mind is produced by the physical components that serve as a proximate cause of the mind.

If she endorses indeterminism and accepts that chance could produce individual minds, then significant challenges follow. In addition to the challenges mentioned above regarding the lack of a sufficient reason for *my* existence, there are concerns with the mechanism for how *my* mind comes into existence. Perhaps the most notable change is that physical events would produce individual minds by chance. While the probabilities for my coming into existence are low, there is a more important worry. The fact that there is no sufficient reason that explains why I came into existence rather than some other mind is significant. Notice that the challenge isn't simply the fact that any old mind comes into existence, although that is a concern, but the fact of a particular mind's origin. Why should we think that this one mind would come to exist rather than another mind?

Considering an indeterminist explanation, through quantum mechanics, Alex Pruss lays out the standard interpretation of the general problem on indeterminism. He states: "The problem, then, is that it seems we cannot explain why the electron goes one way rather than another. There is an additional problem, however, in that as we shall soon see, quantum mechanics involves correlations that do not appear to have a causal explanation (Pruss 2007, 161)."[312] There is no reason or causal explanation for why electrons go one way over another. One solution for salvaging a reasonable causal explanation is to suggest, as Alex Pruss does, that electrons have "dispositional" properties (i.e., properties of substances that depend on specific necessary conditions being met for their actualization) that cause them to go one way or another. David Bohm promises a solution that incorporates the notion that electrons have intrinsic "dispositional" properties (Pruss 2007, 162).[313] Naturally, the challenge for such an account is that these properties are invisible to us.

The simplest explanation for the electron moving one direction over another is occasionalism. Assuming that at some event at time x where y is produced, it could be that in accordance with regular physical laws, a supernatural being simply creates directly at event time x. These offer us ways out of the problem and they supply us with sufficient causal explanations for an event at time x that produces y.

But, if the emergentist assumes a dispositionalist account, we are left with an insufficient explanation. The emergent-mind depends on these regular laws and chance serves as the proximate cause of a mind. In addition to supplying a rationale for why electrons move one direction rather than another direction, the defender of emergent dualism must supply a sufficient explanation for how it is that the underlying physical stuff could come to produce the mind, or *a* mind. The supposition could be to posit, once again, additional invisible "dispositional" properties that actually give rise to minds or mind-stuffs. Somehow, the underlying material properties have dispositional mind-stuff and at some level of complex arrangement of a neural network, a mind comes into being. On this account, material creation ex-nihilo follows. Minds are products of something they are not, namely, the underlying material.

a. Creation Ex-Nihilo

There is a unique creational concern when we consider the 'perfect duplicate' objection, which will become clear in due course. Many have raised the charge of physical creation ex-nihilo to emergent views of the substantial mind (Farris 2018a; Farris 2018b).[314] It is not hard to see why. Emergent dualism of mind and body is the view that the mind emerges from a sufficiently complex neural structure, and, further, is functionally dependent on that neural structure.[315] In other words, mental substances are produced by the underlying neural structure, and come to exist as functionally dependent but ontologically nonidentical. In this case, if the defender denies that the mind is created by an agent (i.e., the view that an entity is caused to exist directly and immediately), it is either the case that the mind is a creational product of the physical or the product of a mediating process.

What that mediating process is, is unclear, but there is one option, namely, some version of panpsychism (i.e., the view that fundamental material is not non-experiencing, purely mechanistic stuff that is governed by regular lawful mechanisms). At the fundamental level, then, particles are experiences, experiencings, or disposed to become subjects of experience. All of reality is intrinsically experiential or disposed in that direction, i.e., there is something of what it is like in particles and all higher-order products that come from them. In fact, one prominent defender of emergent dualism has recently leaned in this direction. William Hasker, in his underappreciated book *The Emergent Self*, defends emergent dualism and takes it that the underlying material has built-in mechanisms or dispositional properties that give rise to minds at a sufficient level of neural complexity. Recently he has leaned in the direction of panpsychism as a way out of physical creation ex-nihilo. Panpsychism, it is argued, gives us the resources to account for the physical and mental duality as substantial (and not simply qualities) by re-conceiving the underlying physical parts as partly mechanistic (i.e., non-experiencing) and partly experiencing or disposed to an experiencing subject. By doing this, emergent dualists are able to reject Divine creation of minds and material creation ex-nihilo (Hasker 2018b).[316] The advantage of the present form of emergentism is that it avoids the gappy relation of origins between minds and bodies.

These discussions raise a more important issue, however, about the origin of minds in general on mere emergent dualism (without panpsychism or divine creation) because of the radically distinct natures of minds and physical things. The question is: how do these minds originate? If substantial minds, with a novel thisness *that* unites all the parts, originate from something from which they are substantially distinct—namely, matter, then it seems we have an instance of physical creation ex-nihilo because rather than emergence this amounts to magic of a novel thisness (that does the work of unifying) (O'Connor and Jacobs 2003, 540-55; Hasker 2012, 108-99).[317] But as I argued earlier, this comes at a cost. There is no ground for the existence of mental substances that sufficiently explains individual mental existence. Physicality, as such, is an insufficient condition for the emergent-soul (Hasker 2018b, 58-9).[318] It seems to me quite clearly from the models of laws on offer that physicality is an insufficient condition for the emergent-soul, and panpsychism does nothing to alleviate the 'perfect duplicate' problem, as laid out earlier. Hence, we do not have material creation ex-nihilo of minds. While Hasker and others see this as a mediating solution that avoids creation ex-nihilo (see Hasker 2018a and 2018b), it does not avoid the 'perfect duplicate' objection precisely because it relies on a regular generalizable process similar to materialism and other emergentisms (see Hasker 2018b, 58-9; Chalmers 2018).[319]

The problem is that there would exist no causal condition that makes it determinate that an *individual* mind is produced rather than another *individual* mind apart from the parts that come to comprise the individual in question. Relatedly, there is nothing to prevent the emergence of perfect duplicates or the indistinguishability of two empirically verified duplicates.[320,321]

The emergent dualist, on this account, faces the same problem as a physicalist, which itself is based on a qualitative understanding of individual mental particularity.[322] How one would individuate one mind from another mind is utterly mysterious, and, ultimately minds exist without any explanatory reason for their existence. There is, then, no difference between duplicates and identical objects because, as with physicalism, there is no fact of the matter to make the distinction between two objects with all the same properties. Because there lacks a distinguishing and particularizing fact, it also follows that a chance explanation may provide us with some of the necessary conditions for mental emergence, but it lacks a sufficient condition for the existence of *particular* minds. Hence, there exists no sufficient reason for believing that two duplicates are nonidentical.[323]

So, then, what are we left with? We are left with either emergent dualism or creationism.[324] On emergent dualism, we are left with material creation ex-nihilo as one option. Material creation ex-nihilo, however, lacks any sufficient reason for *my* existence and how *I* came to exist—even assuming panpsychism as a part of the solution. Panpsychism only helps avert the problem of creation ex-nihilo if we reject the view that supplies us with a sufficient reason for its existence. Assuming emergent dualism, with its lawful regularity, if we want to avert material creation ex-nihilo and supply an explanation for the origination of one's existence, then we must take up Divine creation ex-nihilo. One way to do this is to adopt the solution listed earlier regarding the indeterminist physical view, via quantum mechanics, which is to situate physical ontology in a broader ontology where God is the direct cause of the *particular* mind at the moment that the brain reaches a specified level of neural complexity, but this appears to yield occasionalism of the Divine acting in such a way that the natural cause (in this case) just is the Divine cause. And, it is clear that some are not willing to accept what is perceived by many as an exotic metaphysical position. In which case, there is good ol' Divine creationism of souls.[325]

What has been shown here is that if we are going to supply a sufficient content that makes determinate who I am and who you are, then we need something like a haecceity (i.e., a primitive thisness of subjects, and not simply a thisness of minds that serves as the unity of consciousness). Without this, we run into the problem of being unable to make determinate the individual nature of persons, and as I have laid it out above the problem from perfect duplicates. Beyond the need for a metaphysical individuator of souls as supplying sufficient content to those souls, we are not only in need of some particularizing feature that is ostensible to our consciousness upon analysis of our phenomenal experience, but given the principle of sufficient reason, we necessarily have it if we exist as individualized things. Guided by the principle of sufficient reason, we necessarily have a particularizing feature (haecceity) that individuates individual souls and we have an explanation that is not rooted in natural events but something like a personal cause. Before addressing these issues in more detail and with additional scrutiny, the next chapter will consider the prospects that we are sophisticated animals along the lines of what Aristotle might have conceived.

Chapter 10

Why we are Not Animals: Where Aristotle and Thomas went Wrong

(Modified, adapted, and updated from my: "Thomist Survivalism? And the Cartesian Alternative," *Chicago Studies*, vol. 58.2, Winter/Spring, 2019-2020)

The following chapter addresses a unique set of views motivated by Aristotle and Thomas that retain considerable attraction today amongst theologians and scientifically-engaged thinkers. However, it retains a similar problem to its materialist contenders in its commitment to persons as fundamentally animals—a problem that begins with personal identity but comes into focus when trying to account for personal survival (a dogmatic piece of furniture in most corners of the Christian Church). This is not to say that all who follow Thomas affirm that the body or the material is the source of the individuation, which causes not an inconsiderable amount of confusion in the Thomist literature and, worse, a problem with personal identity.

Contemporary Christian theology presents something of a challenge concerning the hope of survival after somatic death. The contemporary tension of disembodied hope and re-embodied hope raises a question about what is central to a Christian theology of hope. In the present chapter, I will focus on the first part, namely, the hope of disembodied survival because it crystallizes the problem of personal survival for naturalistic solutions as well as other theistic solutions found in Aristotle and Thomas. Aristotelianism and Thomism would be considered non-natural mind-body options. Contemporary Aristotelianism and Thomism are, to be honest, harder cases to make conceptually clear rendering their status as naturalist or non-naturalist difficult, at times, to pin down. Yet, these options find significant footing historically and growing support in contemporary discussions about persons. Whether or not we categorize them as naturalist or non-naturalist, they satisfy the conditions as forms of emergentism.

The Christian tradition teaches that humans will persist in the disembodied state. Accounting for disembodied persistence is difficult. There are two commonly proposed views that account for the intermediate state, Thomism (i.e., a shorthand referencing what some call neo-Aristotelianism and neo-Thomism) and Cartesianism. I will show that there are significant doubts regarding the merits of Thomism, and that Cartesianism (or the minimal Cartesian thesis that it is my soul that makes me *me*) is likely true. In order to accommodate the challenges from human embodiment to Cartesianism, below I will put forward an updated Cartesianism that takes seriously the structural properties of the brain as common or normative to the proper functioning of the mind. In order to account for the intermediate state, the following desiderata will need to be accommodated: 1. Souls survive somatic death. 2. Persons are their souls. 3. Persons can persist disembodied (and not simply souls or informing principles). 4. Persons anticipate being re-embodied. Central to my survival is that the individuator consists in the type of soul I have. If I am to persist disembodied, then it is my soul (as the carrier of the individuator) that would make me who I am. Hence, I would not be wholly material or partly material. On all or most Thomist accounts of personal survival, I am either wholly material or partly material. Thus, my soul is probably not a Thomist soul because I would not survive but the part that previously composed me would survive in a disembodied state. The main claim: my persistence as a soul requires that I be essentially identical to my soul or that the essential part of me that carries my personal identity is *my* soul. The basic logic is as follows: If I'm not identical with my soul, I don't persist if only my soul does. Further, I show that persistence of personal identity x (the soul) requires z feature (primitive thisness). Y (Thomist soul) almost certainly does not have z feature. Thus, x is probably not y.

Souls Survive

All of traditional Christianity affirms the doctrine of the soul (i.e., at a minimum as an immaterial ingredient), which underlies and explains the persistence from this life to the next life.[326] The Roman Catholic Catechism explicitly states that humans will survive physical death in virtue of the soul.[327] Yet, this is not simply a dogma of Roman Catholicism, it is a dogma of all the Reformed, albeit catholic, tradition. Recognizable authority in Reformed theology and Princetonian theologian Charles Hodge reflects this, when he comments on Christianity generally: "As all Christians believe in the resurrection of the body and future judgment, they all believe in an intermediate state. It is not, therefore, as to the fact of an intermediate state, but as to its nature that diversity of opinion exists among Christians."[328] The famous Leiden Synopsis offers a summary of confessional Reformed theological opinion across numerous symbols (hence, there was a conciliar consensus reflected in the confessions, which furnish much of the doctrinal foundations of Reformed churches) of the Reformed theological tradition and it affirms in more than one place that persons survive physical death and persist into an intermediate state.[329] One important symbol of the Reformed theological tradition the Westminster Confession reflects this normative conciliar teaching in all of Reformed theology, when it helpfully articulates the disembodied intermediate state of personal existence as a soulish existence:

> The bodies of men, after death, return to dust, and see corruption: but their souls, which neither die nor sleep, having an immortal subsistence, immediately return to God

who gave them: the souls of the righteous, being then made perfect of holiness, are received into the highest heavens, where they behold the face of God, in light and glory, waiting for the full redemption of their bodies. And the souls of the wicked are cast into hell, where they remain in torments and utter darkness, reserved to the judgment of the great day. Beside these two places, for souls separated from their bodies, the Scripture acknowledges none.[330]

In other words, the souls of those who die survive the death of their bodies. The souls of saints will go to be with God and the souls of the wicked will go to eternal torment. Central to this claim is the idea that souls survive somatic death, and this is commonly understood to be the immediate hope of the Christian, though not the final hope (i.e., physical resurrection).[331]

The modal fact of our survival is rooted in an actual fact about the nature of our constitution. Charles Taliaferro has proposed a modal argument, which begins with our intuition about the nature and constitution of humans, for what he takes to be a common-sense substance dualism. He argues: "1. If I am the very same thing as my body, then whatever is true of me, is true of my body. 2. But my body may survive without me (it may, for example, become a corpse), and I may survive without my body (I might have a new body or exist in a disembodied state). 3. Therefore, I am not the very same thing as my body."[332] The modal intuition that I am not identical to my body, or the parts of my body, underlies the logic of Taliaferro's argument — as the possibilities are grounded in what is actual. We could further motivate the conclusion that I am not identical to my body, or the parts of my body, by advancing the argument from mereological replacement. Consider the following mereological replacement argument.[333]

Take any garden variety material part of my body, and you will intuitively take it as fact that you are not that part. When I reflect on the parts of my body, I instinctively believe that I am not the parts of my body. While I reflect on the hands typing in front of me, I realize that it is not I that am identical with those hands. I could conceive of my hands being lopped off and me continuing without my hands. I could apply the same thought experiment with all the other parts of my body and come to the same conclusion. I could conceive of the possibility of losing the lower half of my body, yet the *I* that "I" identifies remains. We could even speed up the process and the fact of my continuing would presumably remain a possibility. What is under consideration is whether I could exist without any part of my body. In other words, it might be the case that I am nonidentical to any parts of my body, yet I still might depend for my ongoing existence on some part of my body (say, for example, my brain and central nervous system). This is where other sources factor into the discussion of the fact that I will survive bodily death or the fact that I will cease to exist. The probability that I will exist will depend on the data from revelation and any potential empirical evidence (i.e., out of body experiences and near-death experiences).

Yet, the fact that I could exist from p1 (i.e., point 1 in time) to p2 (point 2 in time) is somehow grounded in the fact that I am not identical to my body or the parts of my body—like my brain or central nervous system. In fact, if it is possible that I could exist from p1 to p2 and on into the afterlife beyond somatic death, then this seems to presume something about *me* that is not identical to my body. It presumes a fact about me that is essentially something other than *my* body and the various parts that comprise my body. Based on the reasons given here, it seems that what survives is something other than my body or the parts of it, but, instead, it appears to be something that is metaphysically distinct and unlike the body. That which makes me *me* is a metaphysical simple, i.e., that which lacks any composition, or so I will argue below. By arguing this, my goal is to distinguish personal identity as something that is not necessarily dependent on the body or any part of a body, but rather is explained by particularized soul. In this way, we are back to the tradition's reasoning for why we are souls or minds. But, there is something distinctive about the soul that makes me *me* and not just any ol' soul.

Persons just are their Souls

I have given reasons that we are not, strictly speaking, identical to our bodies or the parts of our bodies, which means that there is some*thing* else that persists. Historically, this something else has been called a soul or a mind because it is a substance that gives rise to and sustains thoughts, emotions, desires and other properties that are, strictly speaking, nonidentical or non-reducible to the parts of the body. With that said, in keeping with our modal argument above, there is a further notion or intuition that must be true in order to develop a coherent theory of persistence beyond somatic death. It is not simply that my soul-part persists, which makes coherent the survival of me, but it is that *I* actually survive. In order for that to be the case, it would follow that I would need to be identical with my soul (or mind) and not the parts that are separated from my soul at death. In other words, and keeping with good Cartesian intuitions, I just am my soul (where a soul is understood to be a substance that instantiates thoughts, desires, and mental experiences).

The Cartesian notion that I just am my soul is the intuitive or common-sense assumption implicit in the possibility that I could survive my bodily demise. Roman Catholic theologian Stephen Yates in his work, *Between Death and Resurrection*, reflects this initial sentiment that if souls survive their bodies, then Cartesianism or Platonism—the historical name for what is often later conflated with Cartesianism—is the most likely candidate for this being the case. For if the soul persists and it has operations independent from the body, then it appears to be a substance in its own right that can exist, experience, and live without the body.[334]

There is a further fact that makes Cartesianism the most likely accounting of survival. The fact that humans carry a primitive thisness *via* their souls. Cartesianism provides us with an account of personal identity at a time and across time. Descartes' most important contribution was likely his insight into the nature of personhood as simple and strictly identical to the soul. It is important to note that Descartes saw the person as persisting because of the soul as that which is separable from the body. Descartes famously represents this intuition, when he says: "We can't conceive of half a soul."[335] For Descartes, he not only was his soul, but that soul cannot be split so as to give off a new soul nor can the soul become something else. As it stands, the person as substantial soul is absolute, simple, and enduring.

We can develop Descartes' basic intuition about personhood. If we can grant for the sake of the argument that what is most distinctive about persons is that they are psychological beings, then Descartes' basic insight becomes quite apparent upon reflection. For Descartes, humans are fundamentally 'thinking things' (and by that we can safely include the fact that we are agents, experiencing things, and desiring things). In fact, we are not fundamentally animals for the simple fact that there is no garden variety physical object that we can point to and say—'hey that's me' (consider the thing I see in the mirror). Upon reflecting on our common-sense assumptions, our faculties rub against the notion that we are animals or parts of animals. When I survey various parts of my body, I make the implicit assumption that I am not identical to that part of the body. When I conceive of my hand, I can also conceive of my existing quite apart from my hand. And, in fact, we have cases where individuals continue existing as the self-same individuals quite apart from their hands. The same applies to every part of the body (e.g., from the foot, to the leg, to the arms). While that seems intuitively the case that we are 'thinking things' or psychological beings, some have attempted to combine the insight of Descartes with the view that I am an animal (see Olson). By animal, Olson is intending a semi-technical understanding. He is not seeking to convey that we are brute beasts, instead he intends to identify 'animal' with that physiological part of which we point to when we point to *that* person.[336] For the argument goes something like the following:

- (P1) Presently sitting in your chair is a human animal.
- (P2) The human animal sitting in your chair is thinking.
- (P3) You are the thinking being sitting in your chair.
- (C) Therefore, the human animal sitting in your chair is you.[337]

There are common responses to the 'thinking animal' argument, which attempts to unify the fact that we are animals and 'thinking things.' There are two problems. The first, and most obvious, is the problem from the one and the many. As physics seems to suggest, there is no reason to think that there are physical wholes because physical things are potentially infinitely divisible all the way down. In fact, what is there in the mirror just is an aggregate of physical parts. If we follow the physicalist animalist, Peter van Inwagen, that physical animals are just events then we are left wondering if there is a substantial whole that is present in the mirror that I am looking at when I look at myself or that I am just an aggregate of physical events swirling around in such a way as to appear Joshua-wise.[338] A second problem is that we intuitively, and readily, make a distinction between the thing thinking and the animal constituting the thinking, i.e., the whole is the kind of thing that is distinct from the animal.[339] Further, it is not clear at all why we should assume P2—namely that the thing thinking is identical to the human animal in a strict sense. There is nothing obvious about the animal's properties that epistemically support the notion that those properties are psychological properties. And, further, there is nothing about the psychological continuity of the thinking thing in the chair across time that is accounted for by the properties of the animal sitting in the chair. So the first concern questions whether there is a 'thing,' as a whole, at all that is sitting in the chair or looking at self in the mirror. The second concern questions whether the whole that is thinking is identical to the thing that is sitting in the chair and in the mirror. In order to arrive at a sufficient criterion of the thinking thing, namely the 'I' that thinks, we must look elsewhere beyond the animal sitting in the chair or the thing in the mirror.

I suggest that I, and you do as well (assuming your cognitive operations are similar to mine), have a sufficient criterion for my being me, but it will not be found in the physical parts or the physical whole (namely, the animal). Instead, it is something I have access to as a thinking thing. A psychological substance (i.e., what I here assume just is mentalism—is sufficiently similar to a mental substance) is aware upon reflection that s/he is the type of thing that has one property that is presupposed in all discrete acts of thinking at a time and across time.[340] That property presumed in what some have called self-presenting properties.[341] Self-presenting properties are those properties that are properties of thinking about some property. If I have a thought about such and such a property, then there is also a property of thinking about that property. But, there is a further property that needs distinguishing. This property is the kind of property that is necessarily present while I am thinking. The fact that I have thoughts about my hands or my animal presupposes that *I* am thinking those thoughts— and unless or until we can demonstrate that those properties are reducible to the properties of physical things, physicalism of all kinds is necessarily excluded as an explanation for this data. Instead, I am a primitive characterized by the thoughts I

194

have. I am neither the whole animal, the parts of the animal, nor the thoughts that I have—but, I am a substance that makes my thoughts *my* thoughts, which I show is a feature (or property of distinct souls as mental substances).[342] There are other thought experiments that support the fact that I am a primitive mind or psychological being.

Consider the fact that certain qualitative experiences are potentially dependent on my particular substance (something like a trope), but not on any properties that universally explain those qualitative experiences. All we need to show is that my cognitive operations support this modal fact in order to demonstrate that some explanation is missing when it comes to qualitative experiences. Let's take the qualitative experience of peanut butter. Why is it that some individuals like peanut butter and others do not? It is true that, in some cases, this can be partially explained by the properties of one's own biology. There are cases that make the tasting of various items different from person to person, but it is not clear that all cases are explicable in terms of said genetic and biological properties. In fact, in all of these cases part of the explanation depends on the reports of the experiences that individuals have, for example of peanut butter.

Testimonial reports depend in some way on the fact that there is a mind that has powers of access to one's own experiential states that are quite invisible to other minds. In other words, the public-private distinction plays an important role in determining what it is that distinguishes one mind from another mind. In this way, there is either a sufficient explanation for my being me or there is not. The apparent distinction I have of my own mind that is quite distinct from other minds or other objects and furnishes a sufficient ground for *my* being me.

Coming back around to the question of Thomistic variations of personhood, Thomist understandings of the soul, or the person as soul substance, appear to provide an insufficient ground for understanding identity at a time and across time without this fundamental Cartesian principle. Hence, as some would say, the Cartesian principle regarding the person as a primitive mind is unavoidable.[343] With this in principle in view, let us consider some of the most sophisticated Thomist options.

For Aristotle and Thomas, a complete human being cannot exist *via* the soul alone. Instead, for Thomas (and this goes for Aristotle as well), the disembodied (or unembodied soul, if there is such a thing like God) soul is not a complete human being. Aquinas's understanding requires that humans are animals because they "can be grasped by the senses and occur in nature."[344] "Since the soul is a part of the human body, it is not the whole human being, and my soul is not me."[345] If this is Thomas's understanding, then, intuitively, it appears that we do not survive our deaths. Yet, on a Platonic or Cartesian conception we can and do, in fact, persist as complete in some sense.

There are two models in Thomism that attempt to account for survival beyond somatic death. The first is extinctionism or corruptionism.[346] The second is survivalism. In the next section, I will put forward these Thomist views and advance defeaters (reasons to reject these views) to them.

Defeaters to Thomist Survivalism

While I am most interested in versions of Thomist Survivalism, let me say a bit about Thomist Extinctionism. Extinctionism is the view that I will not survive. The human animal with which I am identical does not survive, but, at most, only my soul as a partial substance (or an ingredient to a complete human being) survives later to be reclaimed when it conjoins with the material to comprise the human composite once again. I will touch on this a bit more below.

In the dialectic, Thomists struggle to assert the essentiality of the body and the centrality of the soul as a microcosm. They either, like Thomas, tend toward Platonism when they conceive of the soul or, as of late, they do one of two things. First, they try to make sense of an Aristotelian ontology that allows for disembodied persistence.[347] Second, they tend to reconceive of the intermediate state.[348]

In an attempt to make sense of a kind of surviving in Thomism, we must consider two types of souls. There are two apparent ways to understand how the soul is individuated on Thomism.

(1) One way, the soul is simply individuated by the body.
(2) Alternatively, the soul is impressed by the bodily particularity.

Both of these understandings yield versions of Thomist extinctionism. Aristotle likely agrees with the first, and some Thomist interpreters take that route while others assume the second option. While the first option is the most likely way to interpret Aristotle, it is not without a significant problem. There is an immediate challenge. Upon somatic death, the body becomes something else and the soul as form persists without individuality or particularity. The second option is more promising as an accounting for the soul's particularity.

Thomas likely takes the second option, according to Pasnau. Thomas describes substantial forms that inform matter as "shaped at the very start in accord with the matter to which they are united."[349] But, according to this view, we have a qualitative difference in the soul, i.e., a nonessential property instantiated in the soul, but not an essential property of the soul. This, of course, raises a significant doubt as to the possibility that the soul would lose the distinguishing property (i.e., individuator) of the soul during the disembodied intermediate state.

Two problems are apparent for these options. First, both

views of particularity form a general problem of being able to account for the persistence of personal identity. For on such a view persons would persist in virtue of their souls. While this is the case, the soul only carries with it personal identity as a contingent property of the soul. Yet, if on Thomism, we are strictly or essentially identified with a composite of soul and body, then when the body dies so does the composite. That is the *prima facie* concern.[350]

Second, the traditional view presumes a person that experiences the beatific vision (either initially during the disembodied state or only after somatic resurrection). Roman Catholic theologian Stephen Yates in his excellent work, *Between Death and Resurrection*, reflects on the worry over a soul surviving bodily demise, given that the soul would appear to be inactive during the disembodied state, but if this is true then it is tantamount to nonexistence. For Thomas, keeping pace with Aristotle, it is quite severe to think of a substance that is inactive. For a substance to be inactive is for that substance to not be. The most obvious alternative is Platonism where the soul is active and participating in a higher reality, but most Thomist interpreters, Yates included, wish to dismiss Platonism.

Upon dismissing a Platonized reading of Thomas where the separated soul is now free to partake of a "higher source," Yates states: "Appealing alternatives to this are, however, difficult to find. It is tempting to hypothesize instead that because the soul has operations independent of any bodily organ, it would still be able to cognize in the interim state by making use, through reflection and reasoning, of just that knowledge acquired while it was in the body." For on Thomism, the human intellect (i.e., rational soul) requires phantasms (i.e., representations of reality). Yates concludes that there are three apparent options: Thomas's preferred option, the ad hoc option or the Platonic option. He states:

Given such difficulties, it is worth examining further the view that separation from the body enables the soul to receive divinely impressed species (a view toward which Aquinas seems consistently inclined in his writings on the separated soul) in order to ascertain whether this can be couched in a manner which would preserve it from charges of being either ad hoc or Platonic.[351]

The fear, according to Yates, is that Thomas's option will become ad hoc or slide very quickly into Platonism. Yates argues, however, that there is a way to make sense of the Thomist view without Platonism, which in characterizing his interpretation of Thomism he writes, "constituting as it does, an impoverished and unnatural mode of existence, rather than an ontological and epistemic liberation."[352]

Yates, in distancing himself from Platonism, instead elects to follow Pasnau. There are, however, two unpalatable consequences. First, he must accept that persons are complex entities, and when one of the essential parts is lost the person effectively becomes half of a person or the part that is lost simply is not essential to that part that survives. Second, he must accept that the identity of persons is a contingent property of the soul during the disembodied state of interim existence.[353]

There are alternative Thomist options, which reject Thomist extinctionism and attempt to salvage Thomism as a version of personal survivalism. I will look at two sophisticated Thomist options.

Edward Feser on Thomist Soul Survivalism
Edward Feser advances one version of Thomist Soul Survivalism. On Feser's interpretation of Thomas, there are eight ingredients in a Thomist view of human nature. First, all substances, including human substances, have form and matter. Second, human beings, like all other beings, are composites of

form and matter. Third, forms are universals. Fourth, there are two types of forms, i.e., substantial and accidental. Fifth, matter is potentiality and form is the actuality. Sixth, forms are tied to specific individual things. Seventh, powers exist where substantial form/matter composites are present. Eighth, powers are non-reducible to their constituent parts.

On the surface, there are some odd consequences following from Feser's interpretation of Thomas's survivalism. One odd consequence is that accidental forms can exist on their own and apart from substantial forms.[354] Further, there exist different kinds of matter rather than a generic kind of matter that is the stuff of all bodies. This results in the fact that composite substances are described by their powers rather than essential and accidental properties. This raises a question about Thomist substances on Feser's interpretation. How far can we whittle a substance down to constituent parts before it becomes something else? The answer to this last question is not clear.

For on Feser's view, humans are beings with a rational nature composed of matter and intellectual form. The intellectual form is distinguished from other kinds of species, namely vegetative forms and sensory forms. In order to illustrate the view and the intuitive nature of survival on it, Feser draws an example from *Guardians of the Galaxy*. In the story, there is a figure by the name of Groot. Groot is a tree-like figure with some low-form of agency, but what is important is what happens to Groot in part of the story. At one point in the story, Groot is blown apart and the parts that previously composed him are disconnected bits. Yet, somehow Groot survives as a twig-like figure that after some time and watering is able to grow again into a matured Groot. Unfortunately, this leaves us with several questions about Feser's Thomism.[355]

The most important question that needs to be answered is: when does a twig become just another twig? Or would the twig survive as the form that could develop into another Groot? In other words, with enough time and watering, why would it not be possible for two different twigs that previously composed original Groot to become Groot again? If that were possible, then we could take twig 1 and twig 2, and after a sufficient amount of watering and time, twig 1 could emerge into Groot (what we will call Groot 1) and twig 2 could emerge into Groot (what we will call Groot 2). At some point, it becomes a bit absurd that there would be two Groots. But, this raises specific ontological questions about Feser's Thomism, e.g.: What are the generables that factor into matter-form composites? What are the nonessential parts that could be lost, and yet, Groot remain the self-same Groot (which violates the x and y principle listed earlier)?

What was intended to supply us with an intuitive or common-sense solution to survival, then, actually turns out to be quite silly. Instead, there are far too many questions that remain unanswered. More importantly, the problem of duplicates emerges, namely that there could be two Groots rather than one (and when applied to humans, there could be two persons that were originally one person). And, yet, there is another problem for Feser's Thomism. Charles Taliaferro raises the problem quite clearly when he discusses hylomorphism and the problem from the 'corpse objection.' Discussing Patrick Toner's version of hylomorphism, which is not significantly distinct from Feser's Thomism, Taliaferro argues that when separated from the body—the body substantially changes and becomes a corpse and the soul is something other than the body it once formed. Taliaferro explains,

Toner rightly notes that what many of us see as death is a substantial change. The difference between a substantial and accidental change is that in a substantial change, you lose a substance or substantive individual, whereas individuals persist through accidental change, as when I cease to be a philosopher and become a circus clown. I think there is an admirable plausibility in Toner's depiction of the integration of embodiment. When healthy, we identify our bodily parts as forming a functioning, whole organism, whereas after we have died, our hearts, lungs, and so on, no longer function as hearts and lungs... While I believe Toner's position is ingenious and, if the overall case for hylomorphism is plausible, the preferred solution to the Corpse Objection, I still think it does not outweigh the positive case for dualism and its more common-sense approach to the corpse, which is to claim that it is the very same thing as one's body, only it is dead.[356]

In a similar way, Feser's Thomism confronts a problem of being able to account for what is most intuitive about what it is that makes an individual human being *this* individual and not *that* individual, which is distinguished from his or her body upon somatic separation.

Jeffrey Brower on Thomist Survivalism
Jeffrey Brower offers an alternative in Thomist survivalism. Brower offers a nuanced distinction in two types of Thomist survivalism. On extinctionism, as we have seen, it is the fact that souls persist upon biological death, but humans do not. On survivalism, humans persist beyond the grave. However, Brower is convinced that personal identity persists and humans essentially but not actually persist. In this way, he distinguishes his position from Thomist human survivalism. He argues that the problem is as follows: "1. Human beings are essentially human. 2. Human beings cease to be human at death. 3. Human beings do not cease to exist at death, but rather survive." He states that this forms an inconsistent triad. He begins with one solution: "The Naïve Conception of Natures: (4) If x is essentially F, then x is non-contingently F (and hence such that x cannot

cease to be F without ceasing to exist)." He further modifies this in the following by claiming that Thomist human survivalism has it that one cannot survive essentially without the primary nature being intact. So he offers his modified solution in the following: (4″) satisfies: "If x is essentially F, and F-ness is x's primary nature, then x is non-contingently disposed to be F (and hence such that x cannot permanently cease to be F without ceasing to exist)."[357] On Brower's hybrid, the person survives as "essentially" human but not "actually" human, i.e., survival as a human person but not a human being.

Apart from Brower's hybrid being perplexing, his view has the appearance of being *ad hoc*. Distinguishing essentially human from actually human gives the appearance of being *ad hoc* precisely because Thomism has it that substances just are matter-form composites. For a matter-form composite to lose matter would effectively make it something else. For on a substrata account of substance, substances are matter-form composites all the way down. While there might exist a kind of substance dualism, where the matter-form arrangement is concerned—the matter-form of the embryo might be distinct from the matter-form arrangement that gives rise to a human being at some point in the process of maturation, the notion of the soul existing independently of the substance is foreign to a matter-form ontology and begs the question with respect to the soul's nature. And this leads to the specific problem of Brower being unable to account for the fact that an essentially human person persists beyond somatic death without an 'independence' thesis of substance. Granted, Brower is working with a distinct understanding of essential as those properties that flow from the form of a thing in question, but not that the thing actually exemplifies those properties to exist. So a human is bipedal by essence but not all humans are actually bipedal for we could conceive of some humans losing parts that render their not being bipedal. However, this being the case, the property of being bipedal would seem to be a normal or 'common' property of humans, but that seems to fail as a helpful parallel when it comes to humans existing as actual humans without their bodies—instead, if Brower were consistent then he would need to say something like to exist as an actual human one would need to take on a distinct matter-form arrangement during the intermediate state. Such a view, though, defies a common-sense understanding of the body in the grave, as discussed earlier.

Conclusions

The further problem is that these Thomist models fail to give an explanatory accounting for the particularity of personhood during disembodiment that is sufficient for my having thoughts and experiencing God in the immediate post-mortem state. Not so on a Cartesian account where the mental substance (as an immaterial thing) is a bare particular that exists independently of material parts. Further, if there is a feature that makes one mental substance this mental substance and not *that* mental substance, then there is a sufficiency to my being the person that I am. On this understanding of Cartesianism, I just am my soul and I have an essential property of thinking my thoughts, which becomes a ground for experiencing God and the world (the unavoidable Cartesian thesis). If I do exist during the intermediate state, then I exist as a substance (hence the independence thesis). If I exist, then it follows that I exist wholly and not partly. If I were partly material, then I would not wholly exist during the intermediate state (following Pasnau). Granted you might take it as a fact that a substantial whole is either presently existing or it is not presently existing. Instead, the whole might be less than it was before upon losing parts, but the important question is, what it is that is essentially a whole that persists? I suggest that I do exist wholly in the intermediate state so I am not partly material nor is it the case that I would essentially be a matter-form compound, but, instead, I would essentially be that part that persists (even if my form has the essence of being material or being embodied).

But why think that a Cartesian soul would be reunited with a body, as the dogmatic teaching of the physical resurrection demands? This is the challenge for Cartesianism. As I have explained elsewhere, this need not lead us to accept hylomorphism or a version of Thomism.[358] Instead, if the soul is functionally dependent on the brain, then we can grant that the powers and properties of the soul normatively function properly in relation to a brain. On my view, the soul depends on a functionally suitable brain, central nervous system, and body for fully functioning. The generables or determinables of the mind's cognitive power are functionally dependent on the brain in a fine-grained way—similar to the way that an emergent mind is dependent on a properly functioning brain. While there is a substance or fact of the matter concerning personhood in the soul, the functional properties are products of the mind or soul-body compound. A view along the lines of divine creationism mediated through a functional body/brain would supply a story that accounts for the fact of personhood that has a robust functionally integrated dependence relation on a body/brain, thus uniting the virtues of what some might call pure substance dualism (i.e., the view that souls are the carriers of personal identity and are, at least modally, distinct from their bodies) and compound substance dualism (i.e., the view that humans are structured entities with essential properties and teleo-functional, albeit, contingent properties of embodiment). In this way, for full intellectual functioning, one would anticipate being reunited to a body upon somatic death. Guided by a theological reason, we might take it that the beatific vision (or the final end of the saints, which is the elevation of human intellectual capacity) occurs in the physical resurrection and not in the intermediate state of disembodied existence, which lends further credence to the notion that the resurrected body is necessary, but this is deserving attention elsewhere.[359]

What this chapter has helped us to see is the viability of the neo-Cartesianism over and against its non-naturalistic competitors that have several benefits over their naturalistic competitors and are garnering significant support amongst theists. The present chapter shows that something further beyond a soul is needed to sufficiently explain personhood that is not adequately or apparently accommodated in neo-Aristotelianism or neo-Thomism.

Part IV

Creationist-Selves

Chapter 11

Why Creation of the Self is a Better Solution?

If you once thought that creationism was an anti-scientific view that disregards clear teachings on the age of the universe, then hopefully you have been disabused of that use of the term. Throughout *The Creation of Self*, I have argued quite forcefully for two claims. First, I have argued that materialism, emergentism, panpsychism, and neo-Aristotelianism all fail to provide a solution to what is not only apparent to that which is strictly speaking true of persons—i.e., that they are metaphysical simples that bear a feature or fact that makes them what they are. In fact, some of the views appear, on the surface, to fall into a category mistake regarding that which is most apparent to what makes selves. Others run into the problem of complexity. And, others, still, create (no-pun intended) a problem for themselves that fails to furnish a sufficient reason that *I* actually exist or worse that I could exist as two persons or a plurality of persons, which is clearly absurd. This seems to point to the fact that there is a primitive feature that is neither found in the body or a set of properties, but something that stands below the properties. This primitive fact about persons seems to be what is needed to preserve personal identity, something you and I know to be true upon honest reflection of our selves. Yet, I would take it even further and argue that this fact is necessarily true, based upon the principle of sufficient reason. In what follows, I will spell this out more clearly in an argument and canvass options that might be construed as versions of creationist-dualism—something I have gestured toward in several places earlier. I will also lay out a version of what I construe as a version of idealist-immaterialism, which will force me to leave behind the common-sense position that I have been committed to thus far in many of the arguments made above and revise my understanding of the physical. But, it is important to point out that this position, even moving beyond common sense, does not negate or contradict common sense. Rather, it would seem that it is simply not the product of common sense. Instead, after following the common-sense road as far as it goes, upon further analysis it may be that through the lens of science and recognizing the limitations of physical explanations one may have to say that common sense can take us no further.[360]

Second, I have argued that creationism is likely the best explanation for these types of individuals. They are not complex configurations, at least not essentially. They are not event-products of some such complex process in biological evolution. Instead, they are likely sufficiently explained by a personal cause that brings them about directly (and, probably, immediately). This view is the product of a personal paradigm where God (or some such supernatural being that we call God) makes sense of the fact of persons that is foreign to either naturalism or atheistic Platonism (i.e., the term that philosophers use to refer to a view, or set of views, that affirm immaterial agents and abstract objects that exist eternally without invoking a God-like agent). Herein, I will canvass different creationist options. Finally, I will consider an alternative option that makes better sense of the world and persons, but it requires that we give up a global pluralism in favor of a global monist position. Making determinate the truth of either global pluralism or global monism takes us more deeply into metaphysics and how it is that we conceive of the structure of the world. It is here that I gesture toward reasons favoring pluralism over monism, but such a definitive case will be difficult to make here and would require additional work elsewhere.

An Argument for Creationism

I have shown that 'obscure' dualisms have a problem because they lack a sufficient designation that individuates selves. Further, the naturalist (or pseudo-naturalist) posits mechanisms that are only versions of creation ex-nihilo or are simple cases of magic. This creates insuperable problems that are parasitic on them, including, and most important, the problem from perfect duplicates. But the view I advanced depends on a conception of the world that employs the principle of sufficient reason (or the principle of causal sufficiency), which is one novelty in the literature.

In order to defend such a view, I will lay out a defense of the principle of sufficient reason and a formal syllogism for divine creationism of souls, given the principle of sufficient reason. I advance an argument for a strong principle of sufficient reason (hereafter PSR).

PSR can be defined in the following: every state of affairs has an explanation, a reason for its being that state of affairs. All contingencies have some explanation. The possibility of there existing no explanation, would itself be an explanation. We have no reason to suppose that something existing has no reason for its existence. There is no objective probability that can be assigned if there is no explanation to be given. If this is the case and our perceptions have no connection to reality, then we have no reason for thinking that anything has a reason for existing and we are left with universal skepticism. PSR is known a priori and is a condition for knowing anything at all (i.e., a precondition for the intelligibility of the world).

PSR is a necessary truth. Following Bruce Gordon, we can defend PSR in what follows.

(1) For all p, if p is a contingently true proposition, then it's *possible* there's a proposition q such that q completely explains p.

(2) (1) is uncontroversial: given any contingently true proposition, it is merely *possible* that there exists an explanation for its being true.

(3) The fact that q explains p entails both p and q, since q cannot explain p if q is not true, and p must be true if it is explained.

(4) For a contradiction, assume that p, in fact, has no explanation.

(5) Let p^* be the following proposition: p is true and there is no explanation for p.

(6) Since p is contingently true, so is p^*.

(7) By (1), there is some possible world W at which p^* has a complete explanation, q.

(8) If a conjunction has been completely explained, so has each conjunct.

(9) Since p is a conjunct of p^* and q completely explains p^* at W, q explains p at W.

(10) But q also explains p^* at W, so p^* is true at W, in which case there is no explanation for p at W.

(11) Hence, p both has and lacks an explanation at W, which is contradictory.

For a contradiction, assume that p, in fact, has no explanation. Let p^* be the following proposition: p is true and there is no explanation for p. Since p is contingently true, so is p^*.

By (1), there is some possible world W at which p^* has a complete explanation, q. If a conjunction has been completely explained, so has each conjunct. Since p is a conjunct of p^* and q completely explains p^* at W, q explains p at W.

(12) The supposition that p has no explanation leads to a contradiction and therefore is false.

(13) Thus, for any contingently true proposition p, p has an explanation.[361]

In applying the strong version of PSR to the origination of the self, the argument is quite simple. If PSR is necessarily true where every contingent event of S (for a primitive mind) exists, there is a sufficient reason for its existence and a sufficient reason for the fact of its existence. Either agent creationism is true or some naturalistic solution is true. Naturalistic solutions supply no sufficient reason for the existence of S's. As I have described naturalism above, it is broad enough to include emergentism and panpsychism with their regular law-like (i.e., where biological neo-Darwinian mechanisms of genetic adaptation, survival mechanisms, and genetic drift explain humans) mechanism for the generation of persons. These mechanisms do not supply an explanation to furnish a ground for making it so that *this* self is not *that* self. Hence, a personal or agent explanation is the explanation with the resources to provide a sufficient reason for the existence of selves. Presumably this person or agent is a Divine agent that has supernatural powers of the sort to create something like persons out of nothing.

Variations of Creationist-Selves (i.e., Creationist Dualism)

Property-emergence
(Drawn from a portion of, "Creational Problems for Soul-Emergence from Matter: Philosophical and Theological Concerns," *Neue Zeitschrift fur Systematische Theologie und Religionsphilosophie*, volume 60, (2018), 406-427)

An Alternative Proposal: Creationist-Souls
In what remains, I sketch a plausible creationist, even Cartesian, theory of the soul's origin by utilizing the doctrine of emergence. But, it is important to distinguish the kind of emergence here from the kind of emergence found in Hasker and in O'Connor.[362] It seems plausible to suggest that bodies contribute powers to

souls and causally activate powers in souls.

Creationism is the view, minimally, that God creates human souls directly. Hasker's story is that material processes are *somehow* endowed with powers and potentiality, but it is, arguably, problematic, given some of the concerns offered above, that the material would ever give rise to a mind. My claim finds additional support when one reflects more deeply on Hasker's response to O'Connor's worry. Some might consider Hasker's response to O'Connor's creation ex-nihilo concern (given above) *ad hoc*, and agree that it amounts to a variant of creationism (either Divine or material). It is true that Hasker is challenging our understanding of the powers of the material world, but either the material has some power (given by God) that causes minds or it does not. If it is not the case that the material has these powers, then it is divine agency that brings about the existence of the mind. In what follows, I propose a different option to the one advanced by Hasker and O'Connor that maintains important Divine creational assumptions.

What if we were to approach the soul as a creation of God that comes into existence with its body—where the body is physically generated in biological evolution and through biological reproduction? It is not the case that the brain/body produces the soul. Rather, the soul depends on the brain as a part of the human compound. And, as a part, God creates *that* part directly. God simply creates souls alongside or with his creation of the world, where the world and human bodies unfold in time, and souls come in to existence when the bodies prepared for them come to exist.

I recommend a property emergence view of human personhood, which remains creationist. On this view, both the soul and the body have respective properties and powers fitting for the other substance. This means that the soul is not a generic or relational soul, but souls are kinds of souls. Relational souls do not bear a biological relationship or kind relationship to the respective biological organism, but, conceivably, can assume different kinds of bodies. So, one soul could assume a human body as well as some other body, e.g., a cat's body. They are kinds of souls in virtue of their respective relationships to bodies. As kinds, souls come into existence in union with their bodies, which is the instance of creation or the effect of the soul following from creation. While souls are *contingently disembodied* souls, they are not *unembodied* souls because they have a kind relationship to their bodies. Disembodiment requires that the soul *can* be de-coupled from its body, even if it is an unnatural state. The term "unembodied" seems to yield the idea that souls just are bodiless, not bearing an essential aptness relation to bodies. Human kind-souls have an aptness for bodies. Souls disembodied are diminished souls that lack the power to function properly in virtue of the fact that these souls have an aptness for the bodies or a designed relationship for those bodies.

By property emergence, I mean that human nature itself is abstract. Souls and bodies are fitted for one another. Souls are kind souls, so in this case they are human souls not relational souls. Those souls exist in a compound relationship with their bodies, bodies contribute powers to souls, become causally necessary for souls to function, and bring about a novel emergent property—allowing for new powers. One way to understand this causal necessity is according to dispositionalism. If souls and bodies have dispositional properties appropriate to their natural functioning, then the interactive relationship between the two becomes normative. For example, the body becomes the vehicle by which the soul understands and experiences the world (e.g., pain). I suggest that souls come into existence as embodied souls, which makes some sense of the idea that bodies contribute to souls, bodies are causally necessary for soul-functioning, and that souls necessarily depend in some deep ways on their bodies.

Souls are created as embodied souls (by embodied, I mean that a soul exists as one functional unit with the body it owns). And, souls are embodied when the body is prepped to receive souls. By understanding souls in this way, one can stave off the idea that souls are *totally* disconnected from biological evolution. In what follows, I develop specific features of the view I am proposing, which I am not arguing necessarily or definitively rules out Hasker's emergent dualism view.

Bodies contribute operational controls to souls. Souls, in themselves, are thinking and volitional beings, but they lack certain abilities in the physical world. In and through their bodies they are capable of experiencing spatial extension, being causally present where their body is present, while they themselves are not spatially extended. They also gain additional controls and powers contributed by their bodies. This would include the ability to see, to touch, to hear, to vocalize, and to taste. It also contributes to the soul the ability to walk and to extend oneself to do things in the world (e.g., from picking up apples, to climbing, to opening doors). Swinburne discusses something like this state of affairs, when he discusses the goodness of the body: "All of this requires us to have bodies in the sense of public regions of basic control and perception, and a machine room necessary for our actions and perceptions and the source of our desires. To have a choice at all I need some power over and knowledge of a region."[363] Accordingly, we gain knowledge by acquaintance in and through our bodies.

Bodies are causally necessary for the soul's fully functioning in the material world. This much seems true when we assume that souls are kinds rather than relational souls. For a thing to have kindedness would amount to the soul's existing in a complex arrangement to a larger biological grouping. A natural kind is comprised of a set of properties that are internal to individual things. For example, individual dogs are classified into canine groups that bear a set of properties that unite to other dogs. In the case of humans, individual humans bear a set of necessary and/or essential properties internally common to other humans—hence a kind essence not to be confused with a personal or subjective essence. When we understand the soul in this way as a part of a larger structure, it is natural to conclude that souls come into existence in this way.

Souls depend on brains for operating in several ways. In order for souls to function properly, they do so dependent on brains. Hasker rightly points this out when he argues for the intimate relationship between souls and brains. When there is a knock to the physical head, it necessarily affects the soul.[364] Such a state of affairs reflects the natural kind relationship between souls and their bodies.

The interaction of the body and soul brings about novel emergent properties. Some examples include sensation. We might say sensation is a property of the soul, but it is partly physical in that the soul depends on the brain during the process and requires the body to experience the physical world sensually. Or it may be that souls are dependent upon brains for specified properties, but those properties are not instantiated by brains. Take for example the case of "pain." Pain is a sensation that is arguably partly physical and partly immaterial. It is only souls that experience pain, but they experience that pain as embodied souls dependent upon brains. A useful illustration may clarify the situation. Consider the following state of affairs. Such a state is novel in that it is unique to the interaction of soul and body and would be otherwise unexpected apart from their union. In other words, I bear properties, as a mental subject, that are partly physical.

Two kinds of properties deserve disambiguation. First, there are structural and derivative properties that ensue as a result of the soul's union with the body, which would be totally predictable from say a non-embodied soul that later unites to a body. They are emergent, but not novel in the hierarchy of emergent features or properties. Structural properties would include the additional controls and space given to the soul when embodied, as mentioned above. When the soul walks in virtue of the body or when the soul uses the hand to open a door, we have an example of a structural property. These actions are not novel, but they are a structural consequence of the soul's embodiment. Second, there are novel emergent properties that are *sui generis* and unpredictable, e.g., pain. Pain requires first-person consciousness but is not predictable of the soul alone. It is also not predictable from the body alone. Imagine the following, a part of the body receives a hard blow from an iron wrench and the blood rushes to that part of the body creating a new color, but this in itself would not suggest pain. Pain is a state that an agent, with a first-person perspective, experiences in virtue of the body.

One *natural* and *intuitive* assumption is that souls "tend" toward their bodies or have a kind of aptness, given all that is said above about the contribution of the complex configured body to the soul.[365] Rather than a 'tendency' existing in the material substance that somehow produces the soul/person, seen in emergent-monism and emergent dualism, the creationist soul has a tendency toward the body, assuming souls have teleo-functional properties. Teleo-functional properties are dispositional in nature. The soul's functioning necessarily depends, in some strong sense, on its body and the operations of the soul require the body for fulfilling its purpose.[366]

A common objection or worry to dualism is that it downplays the significance of the body. As I discussed above, the soul, as a kind soul not a relational soul, comes to exist as an embodied soul. Furthermore, the body provides the soul with additional powers and it provides a causal context for the soul's functioning. In fact, for souls to have a robust full experience of other persons they would seem to require bodies, so it would be mistaken to view the body as insignificant to the soul.

The nature of the emergence is different from those advanced by Hasker and O'Connor. The present view respects the *distinctness* of substances similar to Hasker's view, and in contrast to O'Connor's view. The present view is that the material has a 'tendency' not in terms of a *productive relation*, but in terms of a union relation that fulfils the respective human nature. The brain is causally necessary for the soul, and it is in this context that the soul gains structural properties as well as novel properties.

Summary:

a) Bodies are 'prepped,' as a logical priority, to receive souls.
b) Bodies contribute operational controls to souls.
c) Bodies are causally necessary for the souls' functioning.
d) Souls functionally depend on brains.
e) The interaction of body and soul brings about novel emergent properties (e.g., pain, sensation).
f) Souls, while kind in nature and potentially disembodied, exist as a part of a bodily arrangement.
g) Souls tend toward their bodies or have aptness.
h) Souls originate with their respective bodies.

What is not entirely clear is the answer to the *how* and *when* the soul comes to exist in a body. But, these questions are to be expected given the radically different natures of the substances. One might motivate a conceivable story or several different stories that make coherent the possibility that God creates a soul directly that is somehow mediated by the neural arrangement.[367] In the end, this challenge does not somehow detract from the plausibility of soul creation with emergent properties, but that challenge is a topic for another paper.

Another way of articulating both emergence and creation that might fit the broad category of property emergence (from two discrete basis) or a transcendent account (which is discussed below) is found in Patrick Lee and Robert George's understanding of Thomistic emergence. They state:

> As Aquinas points out, an entity can come to be only in the manner in which it exists; if it exists through itself (not dependent on the whole of which it is a part), then it can only come to be through itself (though caused by another), that is, directly, not through the coming to be of another. Hence, the human soul must be directly caused to be, not produced through the coming to be of the whole (the human being) of which it is a part.[368]

Again, this could describe a unique situation in which property emergence occurs where souls that require the direct and immediate agency of the Divine also originate in the manner in which they function, flourish as embodied beings.

Transcendent Thomism (secondary causation) is the view that there is one primary cause and secondary created causes of which both are present in reality. According to Kathryn Tanner, and other Thomist inspired theologies, all of the natural world is caused by God and secondary causes. And, these causes are not competing one with the other but respecting of each in a compatible system. Unlike the picture of a person who fashions a piece of metal and adapts it as a piece of hardware to fit into a central processing unit, the picture of God and creaturely causation on this account is different. Unlike what some call personal theism or theistic personalism, others call this view a version of 'alterity' theism (the state of being distinct from normal perceptions—in this way common-sense causation does not quite capture what is going on). Tanner defines it, here:

> The end exists only in virtue of efficient causality and exerts an influence as final cause only because of the act of an efficient cause tending towards it. Similarly, a formal cause

achieves actuality, in determining matter to be a particular kind, only through efficient causality. All other order of causality as Thomas understands them are in potency, therefore, vis-à-vis the founding acts of efficient causes.[369]

The picture here might suggest that soul-creation is just one of many normal actions in which God generally acts (where all secondary causes are discrete events of Divine action), but that would be mistaken given the unusual nature of soul origination. However, a different picture of soul-origination is on offer.

Dualist-occasionalism is that view that what we experience as something we produce or are interactively involved in is actually the product of direct and immediate Divine action. In the special case of the generation of persons at their origination, the story may be something like this. What we perceive to be the direct product of sexual intercourse between male and female where the semen implants in the egg, which appears to be the direct cause of physical emergence of persons, is, instead, the direct bringing about of Divine creation of the soul of what otherwise appears to be an emergent-individual. William Hasker and Brian Leftow have criticized the creationist views of Thomas and other historical Thomists by arguing that their understanding of the soul appears to be a special case of emergence, but is really a version of occasionalism. Leftow states,

By a continuous rearranging of live matter (we'd now say: by the brain's development), the human fetus becomes able to host the human soul, i.e. develops the full material base for the capacity to think in (what Thomas thinks is) the soul-requiring way. At that point, the capacity becomes present, and with it the individual(s) it requires. So if we leave God out of the picture, the Thomist soul is an "emergent individual." … The law-like way brain-development leads to [the] soul's appearance may make it look like the brain's development causally accounts for the soul's appearance, but in this one case, Thomas is (as it were) an occasionalist.[370]

This is not the view that all natural events are Divinely caused or that the physical world has not independent substantial existence, but that this one event is such that God causes it to be. It is not clear that Hasker and Leftow have rightly interpreted what Thomists are doing when they define causation. However, as shown above this may not be an accurate picture of how Thomists construe primary and secondary causation where God is present causally in the whole of the natural world, even uniquely so at the 'emergence' of the self.

Idealist-occasionalism is similar to dualist occasionalism, but in this respect all natural events are direct actions of the Divine being, and this unique event of soul-emergence would amount simply to God acting in a unique way to bring about an unusual, albeit common, event. This view would cohere well with Berkeley's view of the physical world as non-substantial material and as ideas that are communicated by the Divine mind to creaturely minds.

All of these ways of working out the soul-body relationship are consistent with the core claim that very few philosophers, theologians, and, especially, science-engaged theologians are willing to take seriously, namely, the unavoidable Cartesian core of persons—that fundamental, primitive essence that is not grounded in properties or the body. The feature, that is non-multiply exemplifiable, is a necessary truth of persons that is missing or eschewed by its naturalist alternatives along with theistic alternatives that have failed to consider the uniqueness of persons.

Chapter 12

Constructive Creationist Solutions

I have advanced a variety of ways to parse out Cartesian dualism that have the resources to preserve the same central or core idea about selves that are either eliminated, eschewed, lack a sufficiency condition or the position is unarticulated on other naturalist and theistic accounts. All of these presume a broader paradigm of theism where God is a personal God of which we, as minds or souls, resemble and are like. All of these views presume a sort of idealist view of the world in that all of reality is dependent on the mind of God, and it is this mind that provides, at a minimum, an explanation for the world in which we live (i.e., an epistemic idealism of which mind is central). The idealist notion is not that there are a plurality of minds that explain reality (although there are a plurality of minds), but one mind that unifies the phenomenal experiences or provides the explanation and reasons for the existence of things in the world.

Theistic Dualism is a version of idealism in that minds, in this case Cartesian minds, and, particularly, one mind explains the natural world. What this means is that ultimately natural laws are explained by theistic intentions. God's mind is what explains the world, and its laws, and shapes how it is that we understand the meaning of that world beyond its machinery. Charles Taliaferro has championed this view of the world as a scientifically compatible view of the world that preserves the Cartesian intuition and offers an aesthetically pleasing picture of the world beyond that of naturalism. Taliaferro explains:

On the other hand consider theistic idealism: From the position of a God's eye point of view (omniscience), if something matters now, X, (for example, the birth of a healthy child who will be nurtured and become a philosopher at the University of California, Riverside) then its value is preserved and not dissipated by any other, conceivable point of view. Of course a God's eye point of view may include other matters that impact the value of the present X (it turns out that the professor becomes a moral monster), but all that is a matter of an expanded view of the values at stake not a distant, "zoom-out" point of view that utterly calls our values into question (e.g., why should we care now about X when a million years from now, X will not matter). In brief, theistic idealism is a more sturdy framework in which to recognize enduring, meaningful values.[371] (Taliaferro, 2020)

He explains theistic idealism (or dualism) in terms of values, but elsewhere he explains it in terms of natural laws. But, this says nothing about the nature of the physical objects in the natural world. On this view, it is within its purview that the material world is substantial, but if it turns out that science (particularly quantum science) leans us in the direction of an idealist conception of the physical world, given the open space at the level of particles demonstrated in the wave/particle revelation through quantum experiments, then there is another option that preserves the Cartesian conception of the self.[372]

Theistic Idealism is the view that moves beyond an epistemic idealism to metaphysical idealism. On this view of the world, physical objects are not only dependent for meaning and value on a plurality of minds or one mind, but their ontological constitution is dependent on minds, or a mind. Following the Bishop Berkeley, physical objects are phenomenal sensations that are ontologically non-substantial, hence material substance is a fiction. He explains such a view, here:

224

Anaxagoras, wisest of men, was the first to grasp the great difference between thinking things and extended things, and he asserted that the mind has nothing in common with bodies... Of the moderns Descartes has put the same point most forcibly. What was left clear by him others have rendered involved and difficult by their obscure terms. (DM, 30, vol. 4: p. 106)

Physical objects are products of the mind that are constituted by ideas of which God communicates to creaturely minds, souls, or selves. In this way, the physical world is a set of phenomenal sensations projected by a mind. Hence, what we have is a version of what philosophers call occasionalism where the Divine mind communicates and what appears to be an action that created minds bring about in the natural world is actually the action of a creator.

Natural Dualism might be another option that could make sense of souls or selves depending on how we understand the nature of emergent-minds. Such a view requires theism as the final explanation of creaturely minds, but would grant some independence to the natural world, its mechanisms, and the product of mental reality. Yet, at its base, theism supplies the explanation for how it is that natural laws could give rise to minds. Such a view leaves mysterious the mechanisms of natural emergence from a highly specified neural arrangement to a mind.

In this section, I have opened up the nature of consciousness to its implied theistic options as ways of understanding the structure of the world. While naturalistic solutions are unsatisfying options concerning consciousness in relation to ultimate reality, there is, at least one, alternative idealist understanding of consciousness in relation to ultimate reality that serves as a promising competitor.

Bernardo Kastrup on Reality and Persons: A Monist alternative to what I have proposed

Bernardo Kastrup provides a picture of the world and persons that is a coherent and provocative alternative. What it entails? The loss of persons that I have been advancing throughout the course of *The Creation of Self*. In other words, there is no stable self, which some might see as a benefit because of the instability with personality—so common in psychological studies. I for one am not ready to go there. Are you? It means trading in pluralism for a monistic alternative, although compelling, and it means giving up a common-sense core that is at the heart of Christian theism.[373] Here's his proposal.

Bernardo Kastrup offers a compelling metaphysical narrative that explains or is the product of several lines of reasoning coming from quantum mechanics with the duality of wave/particle reality that demonstrates for us that reality is, arguably, fundamentally reducible not to material substance in the world, but to the mind or a set of minds and its/their ideas. It is here that perspective becomes fundamental to neural activity and physical events. With the growing interest in dualism and idealism, Kastrup offers a fascinating proposal that is refreshing. However, rather than defend a form of ontological pluralism with respect to the fundamental furniture of the universe, he advances reasons that favor some form of ontological monism.

Kastrup recognizes and forcefully shows in a number of contexts that materialism has an intractable problem making sense of qualitative experience of subjects of consciousness. This is called the hard problem of consciousness and it is a problem that persistently confronts the materialist. Despite the fact that materialism is the mainstream view within science, this does nothing to resource the problem of qualitative conscious experience.

Kastrup is also clear about the problems of panpsychism. Constitutive panpsychism, which says that consciousness is fundamental to the metaphysical furniture of the universe and that what is underlying subjects of experience are bits of consciousness, or conscious potential entities similar to the physical particles that underly all larger metaphysical objects. The problem that Kastrup points to is the combination problem. There is no "coherent, non-magical way in which lower-level" consciousnesses could come to comprise "higher-level subjective points of view." There must be another explanation.

Kastrup advances a version of global monism that is similar to Absolute monistic idealism where there exists literally one mind of which our conscious perspectives are parts. This might legitimately fall under a version of panpsychism (also called Cosmopsychism) in that Kastrup affirms the fundamentality of mind, but mind is not affirmed as bits that comprise the universe in the same way that physical particles (i.e., quarks or atoms) comprise all other material objects—in fact even these are ideas or projections of the one mind. Instead, drawing from the psychological phenomena called 'dissociative identity disorder' (previously called multiple personality disorders) explains how it is that there exists literally one mind that is spread in a plurality of subjective perspectives. In brief, the disorder identifies a subject of experience that has multiple personalities. During which one of the personalities is active the other personalities are often quiet or inaccessible to the personality that is active. In a similar way, one can provide an explanation of how it is that there exists one mind that has discrete perspectives that appear to exist as discrete subjects or substances of consciousness.

Up to the point that Kastrup advances his monist thesis that subjective consciousnesses are alter identities or folds in the *one* consciousness, I find myself compelled to agree with him. As I have argued to this point, materialism is a dead end. Emergentisms's building on a materialism basis, too, are dead ends and amount to little more than magic or material *creation ex-nihilo*. Panpsychism, on the surface, is better off than materialism insofar as it takes seriously consciousness and places consciousness as fundamental to reality; however, it too fails to capture what it means to be a self or a subject of conscious experience. However, it is at the point that Kastrup advances the notion of dissociative identities, alter egos, of the one Ego that I must bow out, and this for several reasons.[374]

First, his departure from common sense seems to go too far in that he not only advances a view that is not a product of common sense, but actually contradicts common sense at one level. This is a step too far. The fact of a haecceity, as that feature which makes me *me*, would be eliminated on this view.

Second, the ontological pluralism that I advance is the product of a deep set of reflections that come out of Western intellectual history. This intellectual history is the product of great minds that continue to pour over the best of the Western world. It is a product, ultimately, of Christianity—with the intellectual forces of Christianity like Augustine, Anselm, and Aquinas. At one level, I see no reason for rejecting their authoritative voice in favor of a metaphysical worldview that effectively eliminates what is deeply entrenched in Western history and has produced some of the most important minds in global history.

Third, and related, I am a Christian. As a Christian, my experience of the world is a product of my phenomenal experience of conversion, presuming a plurality of minds that have independent powers to intend and act. This experience takes epistemic priority over the need for unifying reality under one consciousness.

Fourth, and this is a philosophical reason that is the product of the argument throughout *The Creation of Self*: I have access to the haecceity (again a technical term used by philosophers to refer to that individual nature of persons) that makes me *me*. This haecceity is something that I am aware of upon honest reflection and it is a feature that sufficiently explains who I am and makes me distinct from other selves. Richard Swinburne has referred to the notion of self-reference to the 'I' as an informative designation when the person refers to the self. I have called it a sufficient designator based on the *a priori* principle of sufficient reason. Much, obviously, hangs on this understanding of Selves.

Taken together, these reasons provide fairly strong grounds for affirming an ontological plurality rather than Kastrup's ontological monism. However, like all worldviews, there will be some weighing of sources of authority and how they fit into one's epistemology (i.e., the term philosophers use to talk about how one arrives at knowledge and is justified for believing those items). Furthermore, one might take it that the view I advanced regarding the self's primitive particularity can be rejected. That said, for those who are Cartesian and Christian, these ideas mutually support one another. But, delving more deeply into consciousness and how it is that we account for the meta-structure of the world in which the 'I,' selves, or the mind situate would take us more deeply into the realm of metaphysics. What Kastrup lays out is a fascinating, provocative, and coherent proposal that takes mind as fundamental to the world. Concerning the fundamentality of the mind as an immaterial substance we are in agreement, and we share similar motivations that materialism is not only a dead end, but a distraction from reality. With all that has been said concerning his view, Kastrup's proposal deserves more substantive critique in a different context.

Conclusions: The Anti-Scientific Worry

Your final worry, and certainly the worry of many academics, is that what I have proposed is anti-scientific. But is it? If we take it that science just is, assumed by many scientists, methodological naturalism (i.e., the view that science is methodologically the study of that which is empirically detectible through observing and hypothesizing about natural events of causes and effects, triggers and pulleys), then there may be a challenge here that is worth considering.

But, it's not clear to me that we should take it that science just is methodological naturalism. For methodological naturalism itself isn't partitioned off from the social constructions which include our basic assumptions about the world, the proclivities or virtues that we come to develop over time in our communities, and the standards set by those communities have an ongoing and deep impact on the manner in which a member of that community interprets scientific findings. Methodological naturalism with its appeal of utter and complete objectivity is an illusion. The idea that once I have investigated an item, using the scientific method, in the material world I have arrived at a purported mastery is just that, an illusion. Methodological naturalism with its purported neutrality to arriving at demonstrable certainty concerning a subject matter is not immune from the real values governing the scientific community or the virtues for which that community is habitually aimed. The deception incipient in some scientific circles that practice what they call 'methodological naturalism' is what some have called 'scientism' — i.e., the view that all of reality is subject to the scientific method (i.e., methodological naturalism) and this is the surest way to arrive at a knowledge of the world, or it's the only way really. Our intuitions, common sense, and traditional knowledge are all suspect and subject to the control and determinations of scientific investigation.

Then there are those 'new atheists' that think this is precisely what should be done because philosophy left to itself is subject to misguided notions of the world, and religion... well... that's just bad. Hence, there's need for a new magisterium to set itself up as the hierarchy of knowledge under the guidance of a select few who are its guardians.

The nonchalance of Sam Harris (among his new atheist cohorts) that there is no hard problem of consciousness or that the emergence of mind from matter is normal, and to be expected, is little more than blind faith and wishful thinking in his mystical world that science is the highest and best way of knowing the world. According to him, we need to just get over that idea that some things seem "magical," like emergent-consciousness, and get on with science because of its purported accomplishments. Harris's advice just is to give up on distinct disciplines like philosophy and theology and embrace science as the highest form of knowledge. He states: "We must abandon the idea that science is distinct from the rest of rationality. When you are adhering to the highest standards of logic and evidence, you are thinking scientifically. And when you're not, you're not."[375] It sounds simple, right? But it's a bit of simplicity clouded by his stubborn denial of the actual nature of consciousness as phenomenal consciousness that comes with it the ability to access the contents of one's own mind and discriminate by the sheer power of the intellect. The fact that he has ongoing access to his own thoughts and that metaphysical ideas are actually guiding his interpretive work of science, and conditioning him to deny those persistent realities constantly confronts him with an enigma. But, that is a common problem with scientism. Those like Harris who dig their heels in and believe it despite the daily confrontations with their own consciousness will be met with ongoing perplexity, and anything that poses a challenge, they will simply chalk up to "magic" or offer up a promissory note that science just hasn't yet figured it out.

We need to give up on this idea of scientism. But, methodological naturalism need not be taken so narrowly, necessarily, so as to exclude the legitimate data coming to us from philosophy, theology, history or common sense.

We might take it that these are just distinct, independent, sources of knowledge that while they are not "science" are, nonetheless, legitimate sources of knowledge that inform, and should inform the way in which we interpret empirical data.

Alternatively, we might take it that all these disciplines comfortably sit in a broad paradigm of cognitive reliabilism— the belief that our mental faculties lead us to truth (something that is not reducible to the scientific process, but works with it) when our faculties are functioning properly, in a conducive environment and they are properly aimed at truth. Such a framework, though, is not so rigid as to leave all the work to what some in a bygone era called the "hard sciences" (e.g., biology, physics, chemistry) as the legitimate means by which to arrive at the surest truth claims about the world. No, instead, a reliabilist framework takes seriously the ideas that belief in God, souls, morality, and the afterlife can be known and can inform our beliefs about science or, even, be the product of scientific investigations, but this presumes that other disciplines are reliably consulted like psychology, philosophy, and the neurosciences, which consider testable patterns and markers that are accessed through the use of cognitive science where we can arrive at probabilistic knowledge when considering how it is that our cognitive faculties are functioning in specified environments. But all of this is set within a broad framework that the natural world is non-reducible to triggers and pulleys and recognizes the telos within the natural world and its operations.

But, we might also expand the definition of science beyond what some consider artificial boundary markers contained within 'methodological naturalism' to a pluralism of sources that are useable, or testable (albeit indirectly). This would certainly chip away at the exalted view of science that has conditioned us to take only the claims of 'science' seriously when we know deep down that there are some things in the world that are, and will always be, outside the purview of empirical access. For some examples include the facts about the nature of truth, the principles of logic, the fact that all contingent events have a cause or sufficient reason for their existence, the value of love, goodness, and beauty. It is these things that powerfully reassert themselves in our daily experience, and it is these things that we cherish most deeply. We can ignore them. We can stubbornly persist in the belief that they do not need explaining, but, as a practical contradiction, continue living as if they really do matter.

These beliefs about the empirical process include or are guided by beliefs about values and virtues. The belief that there is a moral system of beliefs, a code, that we ought to live by. And, despite the persistent confrontation with reality, even naturalists who affirm scientism, consistently have this problem. Ecologist Jerry Coyne at the University of Chicago demonstrates this when he ironically claims, "The illusion of agency is so powerful that even strong incompatibilists like myself will always act as if we had choices even though we know we don't. We have no choice in the matter."[376] Maybe his attempt to believe that which his view of the world tells him can't be true isn't science, but his own metaphysical assumptions about the world guiding his science. The argument that science gives us no evidence for free will is really an argument from silence, if, in fact, we take it that science is insufficient as a source of knowledge for all aspects of the world.

What is behind this belief about morality and free will is something more persistent still and that is the recalcitrant reality that 'selves' actually exist. Selves are real and they think, have thoughts, have dispositions, make choices, and live as if there is a moral world out there. Even though psychologist Bruce Hood asserts that we should dispel ourselves of the belief of selves by putting the "free willing self" in "retirement," he follows up by concluding that once we've "abandoned" this bad belief, "we're forced to reexamine the factors that are truly behind our thoughts and behavior and the way they interact, balance, override, and cancel out."[377] Ironically, Hood suggests that once *we* realize that there is no "free willing self" *we* will need to reexamine what stands "behind *our* thoughts and behavior" (emphasis added). Yet, he provides no evidence for the claim that the free willing self doesn't exist, and his persistent self continues to reappear despite his efforts to deny it. This isn't a mere linguistic convention that needs excising from Hood's language; instead, it is basic to his operating in the world and with other selves.

These persistently and deeply held beliefs about freedom of choice, consciousness, morality, virtue, and, underneath it all, the enduring self are not anti-science. Science may tell us little about them. No matter how much science can tell us about selves through these helpful means, science (construed as methodological naturalism) will always have its limitations. In the same way that there is a sense in which the self's essence will always be privately accessible by the self, so will its ideas, intentions, and desires be hidden, in one important sense, from empirical observation. That doesn't mean that we can't have knowledge about a person's makeup through a study of genetics, psychological study of his or her upbringing, or through second-personal encounters, but that aspects of the person's ideas, and especially his/her essence, is only directly available and privately accessible by the self. And, this should be expected when we are discussing that which is most cherished and central to the world in which we live. This doesn't mean that the self is beyond explaining. If we have a view of the world that accepts transcendence and a personal paradigm where the highest reality is a personal God of which we are similar reflections, then we have reason not only to believe that we are selves but we have a reason for living beyond our*selves*.

Afterword

By Stephen C. Meyer

What is primary: mind or matter? The question is an ancient one. Does our world—and ourselves—ultimately trace their origins to atoms in the void? Or are we the creations of a Mind? In *The Creation of Self*, Joshua Farris has combined philosophical precision, common sense, and mastery of the field to argue for the latter. Each human is not a mere body, but rather has a substantive soul. And our souls are at the center of personhood, including what it is to be an individual, a self with a unique consciousness and experience of the world. We are *persons*, not things.

Notable in Farris's defense of neo-Cartesian dualism is his careful critique of rival theories. Among these are not simply the usual suspects of secular reductive and non-reductive physicalism, but also religious rivals as well, including prominent versions of emergence. Farris repeatedly shows that these rivals, whether secular or religious, are incapable of capturing the self—in particular, the singularity and *thisness* of each individual's experience.

Moreover, Farris has also answered another age-old question: whence the soul? He convincingly argues that souls do not emerge from any 'bottom up' material process but rather originate from the 'top down.' Our souls are special creations of God. We are not merely of earth, but of heaven as well.

As Farris himself notes, humans have intuitively recognized for millennia that they are not mere matter and that consciousness is not the kind of thing that can arise from any known material process. Moreover, in the historical sweep of human experience, our collective and reflexive instinct has been to conclude that our souls come from a transcendent source.

After all, if matter cannot produce us, then the explanation must lie beyond anything physical. Such has been a default belief for the majority of humans in our history.

So why this book? Why is this book so *necessary* when common sense and collective wisdom suggest the matter has been long settled? One would think that the answer might be something like the following: a defense of the soul (and of its creation by God) is necessary because in the twentieth and twenty-first centuries new developments in philosophy, cognitive science, physics, and elsewhere have produced powerful new evidence that personhood is explained by bottom-up material causes. New rivals, complete with broad explanatory power and amassed evidence, now threaten traditional views. The old fortress must be buttressed.

According to this line of thinking, advances in science and philosophy now threaten traditional views of the soul. As such, thinkers like Farris must marshal a defense against an unstoppable tide of opposition. Such is the standard narrative among many elite academicians. More fully, the narrative tells a story of the increasing merit of materialistic causes. All of this allegedly occurs in a series of inevitable stages. When unadorned, The Great Advance narrative (as we might call it) runs something like this:

Stage 1

For a very great while in human history, the naïve default of the vast majority of human beings was to repeatedly and instinctively identify the self as a substantive soul. They also believed, largely by intuition, that the origin of the soul was from a divine source. Unfortunately, this view persists to the present day, especially in lay circles. Various attempts to articulate and defend this folk view—notably by Plato, Aristotle, Aquinas, and Descartes—have been invariably unsuccessful. Of course, more enlightened thinkers suspected all along that these theories had intractable problems. How could Descartes solve the interaction problem, for example? But for centuries, no naturalistic alternative had been suitably articulated and defended.

Stage 2

Then came the second movement in The Great Advance. Charles Darwin showed in the *Origin of Species* that human beings arose from earlier, primitive primates; and those primates themselves arose from still simpler mammals, and back down the line. As such, the human 'soul' came about by material processes in a long and unbroken line of cause and effect. We are creatures of the soil, not the sky. Of course, at this moment in history, enlightened thinkers still lacked a robust naturalized account of the soul. Their theories did not yet have the imprimatur of strong empirical justification and broad explanatory power. Some accounts showed promise, but data gathering in particular was nascent and unrefined. Solid empirical evidence remained elusive.

Stage 3

Then came the next wave of The Great Advance. Starting in the mid-to-late twentieth century (or thereabouts) the deliverances of cognitive science and other fields joined forces with rigorous analytic precision to produce a unique melding of naturalistic theory and scientific evidence. At last, credible material alternatives to the traditional view were on offer. As research progressed, some of these alternatives required revision or rejection, of course. And yet, despite strong differences of opinion between some practitioners, the naturalistic research program produced an embarrassment of riches: new theories, both reductive and non-reductive, were articulated, defended, and refined. Although some thinkers viewed the enterprise with suspicion, it was widely held that one of these naturalistic theories, nor something near enough, was surely correct.

Such is the story of The Great Advance—material causes and their inevitable ascendency in light of growing evidence. But as Joshua Farris has cogently argued, contemporary naturalized theories are in fact inadequate. Among other things, their merit came about in part ignoring or downplaying the very lifeblood of any inquiry: first-person experience and the singularity of personhood. And even non-reductive accounts, which take first-person experience more seriously, do not at all *explain* how mere matter brought about conscious experience. Not remotely. None of the proponents of these theories have *any* defensible idea of how mind could arise from matter. Non-reductive accounts are little more than materialism with qualifications and apologies.

Yet all along, the official narrative among such thinkers was that *some* bottom-up account had to be correct. Even a number of religious thinkers accepted this idea, pausing to reassure lay believers that God was hidden behind material causes. Yet on this view, the Great Advance was inevitable. Why? The answer, at least in part, had to do with Charles Darwin. He was said to have settled the matter, at least in basic outline. (Of course, a broad range of other thinkers and forces were also influential—Marx, Freud, Dewey, and others, not to mention the complex machinations of politics, economics, and the like.) Yet whether tacitly or explicitly, a number of thinkers today believe that the *Origin* was the pivotal beachhead. Of all the causes and characters in play, Darwin is first among equals. And on Darwin's theory material causes are the driving force behind evolution, including the evolution of human beings. Matter gives rise to mind. On this view, some naturalized theory *has* to be correct. The faith of today's elites in the efficacy of material causation finds a great deal of its deep justification in the *Origin of Species*. Doxastic inertia follows as a matter of course. In effect, Stage 1 of The Great Advance decided the matter.

Moving Onward

Of course, the deeper question is whether Darwin is in fact correct, and whether faith in his research program was (and is) well considered. Two brief points can be made on this score. The first is simply to point out the increasing power of cumulative case for intelligent design across the sciences — from cosmology to astrophysics to biology to paleontology. Again and again, scientific evidence points to the activity (and detectability) of a Mind rather than purely material causes. Science itself shows that materialistic explanations are not making a Great Advance but in fact are in clear retreat.

And a second point. Let us suppose for the sake of argument that, *if* Darwinism is correct, *then* some bottom-up theory of mind must be correct. (As we have seen, this is a core tenet of The Great Advance.) Supposing that this is so, then Joshua Farris's argument has provided a neat and devastating modus tollens to this line of thinking. Among other things, he has shown that bottom-up theories are untenable. They cannot account for persons. And, if he is right, then by the internal logic of The Great Advance itself, Darwinism itself is incorrect. Farris has demonstrated that Stage 1 of this advance is mistaken. Today's elite academicians, whether secular or religious, should have never placed their trust in the *Origin* and its commitment to the inevitable triumph of material causation.

That is why, in the end, *The Creation of Self* is so important. Among other things, it promises to liberate readers from soulless naturalistic theories of the self. It promises to restore personhood as it was intended and as we experience it every day. Still further, *The Creation of Self* promises to free readers from a moribund 19th century biological theory and its failing quest for dominion. And beyond even those important contributions, Farris's book points all readers to the transcendent God who is, in the deepest sense, the Creator of each and every person.

Endnotes

1. I have adapted this analogy from a symposia. Joshua R. Farris, "An Unwelcome Guest: A Response to My Critics," *The Philosophy of Theological Anthropology, EPS Web Project.* http://epsociety.org/userfiles/art_Farris%20(Response%20to%20my%20Critics%20on%20The%20Soul%20of%20TA--EPS,%20AAR-083121)(1).pdf [accessed on September 20, 2021].

2. *Novum Organum*, Aphorism XXXVIII, LIX, XLIII. Aphorism LXV discusses the notion of bridging the gap between science and the Divine. In a helpful article, Mostyn Jones and Eric LaRock show how Murphy's non-reductive physicalism does something like what is described by Bacon. They signal some of the implications toward secularism on non-reductive physicalism in their: "From Murphy's Christian Physicalism to Lowe's Dualism," *TheoLogica: An International Journal of Philosophy of Religion and Philosophical Theology*, vol. 5, no. 2 (2021), 100-28. Unfortunately, they defend E.J. Lowe's emergent or non-Cartesian version of substance dualism.

3. In the same way that we do not ultimately want to have an encounter with an illusion brought about psychedelics. In the show, *Nine Perfect Strangers* on Hulu, this scenario is raised as a possibility, even an actuality that through the use of psychedelics one, or a group of persons, could have an encounter with a dead family member. The question is raised if the person is real, but quickly dismissed as irrelevant if the phenomenal conditions are met. But, is that really satisfying or sufficient? The present thought experiment reminds me of the thought experiment raised by another thought experiment called "the pleasure machine" by Robert Nozick, *Anarchy, State, and Utopia* (New York:

Basic, 1974), 42-45. Nozick raises this thought experiment against a utilitarian view of ethics (that what brings the most pleasure to the most people is ethical) is insufficient to account for ethical motivations, and that most people would find it insufficient because it is not real. There are two recent mainstream works that advance imaginative scenarios in which this is the case regarding consciousness and personal identity. See Meghan O'Gieblyn, *God, Human, Animal, Machine: Technology, Metaphor, and the Search for Meaning* (New York: Doubleday, 2021). O'Gieblyn imaginatively advances the possibility that an AI dog of hers actually is conscious and has an identity. A part of her struggles with identifying the machine in this way and another part, at times, imagines it as a live possibility. By the end of her engaging work, O'Gieblyn takes what I will call the agnostic position on AI, machines as conscious individual persons. The other takes a more firm stance in favor of AI as being possibly conscious. See Michael S. A. Graziano, *Rethinking Consciousness: A Scientific Theory of Subjective Experience* (New York: W.W. Norton and Company, 2019). However, both fail to provide a theory or an explanatory worldview that furnishes a theory about the nature of consciousness as phenomenal, qualitative or how that could be reducible to brain states or neurons firing that could be reduplicated or modeled in AI. This is a significant problem. There is a growing set of literature suggestive of the fact that AI might be or could someday be conscious motivated in large measure by Ray Kurzweil's *The Age of Spiritual Machines* (New York: Penguin Books, 1999). Also see: Martine RothBlatt, *Virtually Human* (New York: St. Martin's Press, 2014).

4. I explore this notion in the context of the tradition and modernity in more detail, here: "The Unsuitability of 'Unsubstitutability' in Theological Anthropology: Bridging

the Christian Tradition, Modernity, and the Soul," *Theology Today*, vol. 77, issue 1 (April 2020), 54-62.

5. Mark Baker and Stewart Goetz, *The Soul Hypothesis* (New York: Bloomsbury, 2011), 1.

6. Francis Crick, *The Astonishing Hypothesis* (New York: Scribner, 1995), 3. There were several other works in the 90s and early 2000s that took a similar stance that purported that science itself gives no room for the soul or that given what science shows us, we have no need of a soul anymore. See Daniel C. Dennett, *Consciousness Explained* (New York: Back Bay Books, 1992). One of the earliest books advancing a similar position is Patricia S. Churchland, *Neurophilosophy: Toward A Unified Science of the Mind-Brain* (New York: Bradford Book, 1989). A more recent by the same author, *Touching a Nerve: The Self as Brain* (New York: Norton & Company, 2013).

7. Owen Flanagan, *The Problem of the Soul: Two Visions of Mind and How to Reconcile Them* (New York: Basic Books, 2003), 3.

8. Cognitive Scientist Julien Musolino makes this case in, "You don't have a Soul: The Real Science that debunks Superstitious charlatans," *Salon* (January 25, 2015). https://www.salon.com/2015/01/25/you_dont_have_a_soul_the_real_science_that_debunks_superstitious_charlatans/ [accessed on September 16, 2021].

9. Nancey Murphy, *Bodies and Souls or Spirited Bodies?* (Cambridge: Cambridge University Press, 2006). Murphy certainly does not hold the staunch naturalistic views of the authors cited earlier, given that she affirms some conception of a God and that she affirms that humans have some transcendent relationship to that being. However, there are methodological assumptions, principles, and trends that have shaped her project to grant too much weight to 'science' or certain scientific conventions that are strongly held by some in the scientific community.

10. Joel Green (ed.), *What About the Soul?* (Nashville: Abingdon Press, 2004). Also see, Joel Green, "Why the *Imago Dei* Should not be Identified with the Soul," *The Ashgate Research Companion to Theological Anthropology* (New York: Routledge, 2017).

11. Paul Bloom, *Descartes' Baby* (New York: Basic Books, 2005).

12. Mario Beauregard and Denyse O'Leary, *The Spiritual Brain* (New York: HarperOne, 2009).

13. Charles Taliaferro, *Consciousness and the Mind of God* (Cambridge: Cambridge University Press, 2005). Richard Swinburne, *The Evolution of the Soul* (Oxford: Oxford University Press, 1998).

14. For what is regarded now as a classic criticism of the Cartesian view, see: Gilbert Ryle, *The Concept of Mind, 60th anniversary edition* (New York: Routledge, 2009; first publication 1949).

15. And a definition of substance held by Descartes is that a substance could exist, persist, and act (in some capacity) without depending on another substance or part. See René Descartes, "Replies to the Fourth Set of Objections," ed. by John Cottingham, R. Stoothoff and D. Murdoch (trans.), *The Philosophical Writings of Descartes* (Cambridge: Cambridge University Press, 1984), 159. "The notion of a substance is just this—that it can exist by itself without the aid of any other substance." And it is this notion that Descartes sees as avoiding the possibility of souls/persons being split into two or a multiplicity of smaller parts.

16. How one works out the relation of the two substances will vary. One might advance that the two comprise a larger substance of which the body is contingent to a human person (not a contingent identity). This core Cartesian notion, however, is compatible with versions of idealism where there is strictly speaking no material substance. Matter is, in one sense, a fiction.

17. The concept of the soul has had currency throughout all of Ecclesiastical history, has been a common-sense belief and has tradition. Presently, there is a renaissance in studies on the soul that deserve the attention of philosophers, theologians, scientists and anthropologists. See the following examples. *Soul, Body, and Survival*, ed. by Kevin Corcoran; *Persons: Human and Divine*, ed. by Dean Zimmerman and Peter van Inwagen; *Body & Soul* by J.P. Moreland and Scott B. Rae; *The Evolution of the Soul* by Richard Swinburne; *The Emergent Self* by William Hasker; *The Soul Hypothesis*, ed. by Mark C. Baker and Stewart C. Goetz.

18. Substance Dualism, in reference to persons, is the notion that persons are somehow comprised of two concrete-parts—body and soul.

19. Keith Frankish, "What if your consciousness is an illusion created by your brain," *Aeon*. https://aeon.co/essays/what-if-your-consciousness-is-an-illusion-created-by-your-brain [accessed on September 15, 2021].

20. Christopher S. Hill, *Meaning, Mind, and Knowledge* (Oxford: Oxford University Press, 2014), see especially "Ow! The Paradox of Pain," chapter 9.

21. John Foster, *The Immaterial Self* (New York: Routledge, 1991), chapter 6. For recent neuroscientific research reflecting the zombie thought experiment, and, thereby, buttressing Foster's arguments, see: C. Willyard, "Rise of the Organoids: Biologists are building banks of mini-organs, and learning a lot about human development on the way," *Nature* 523 (7562), 520-23.

22. For examples of this position see: John Foster, *The Immaterial Self: A Defence of the Cartesian Dualist Conception of the Mind*; W.D. Hart, *The Engines of the Soul*; K.R. Popper and J.C. Eccles, *The Self and Its Brain*; Charles Taliaferro, *Consciousness and the Mind of God*; Roderick Chisholm,

Person and Object (Illinois: Open Court, 1976), 104.

23. For this debate see Gulick, Robert Van, "Understanding the phenomenal mind: Are we all just Armadillos? Part I: Phenomenal knowledge and explanatory gaps," in *Consciousness: A Mind and Language Reader*, ed. by Martin Davies and Glynn Humphries (Oxford: Blackwell, 1992). Physicalists, if honest, must eliminate *qualia* from their ontology. See Kim, Jaegwon, *Physicalism, or Something Near Enough* (Princeton and Oxford: Princeton University Press, 2005).

24. For a brief discussion, see Howard Robinson, "Dualism," in *The Stanford Encyclopedia of Philosophy*. <http://plato.stanford.edu/entries/dualism>. See specifically 5.2.1.

25. These reasons could comprise a case against a nihilist 'I.' For a contemporary argument for a nihilistic 'I' see Mark Johnston, *Surviving Death* (Princeton and Oxford: Princeton University Press, 2010). See especially chapter 2.

26. The reality is that scientific knowledge requires and presupposes a first-person knower.

27. See Frank Jackson, *From Metaphysics to Ethics* (Oxford: Clarendon Press, 1998).

28. See Roderick Chisholm, *Theory of Knowledge* (Englewood Cliff: Prentice-Hall, 3rd edition, 1989), 18-25; *The First Person* (Minneapolis: University of Minnesota Press, 1981), 79-83.

29. This is a kind of Knowledge by Acquaintance that is a brute given without it nothing else really makes sense.

30. For a useful defense of endurantism see Ned Markosian, "A Defense of Presentism" in *Persistence: Contemporary Readings* (Cambridge, Massachusetts and London: The MIT Press, 2006), chapter 17.

31. One could argue in favor of stage theory and say that these memories are 'apparent' memories. This seems to defy common sense.

32. Richard Swinburne, "From mental/physical identity to substance dualism." See especially pages 151-165.
33. Qualia are a universal property for things that are experienceable. These require an experiencing subject.
34. This is famously called the "unity of consciousness" argument for the soul. See Charles Taliaferro and Stewart Goetz in *A Brief History of the Soul* (Oxford: Wiley-Blackwell, 2011).
35. On a traditional realist understanding, propositions really exist as mind-independent.
36. See Eric T. Olson's Animalism in *The Human Animal: Personal Identity Without Psychology* (New York: Oxford University Press, 1997). Also see Trenton Merricks, *Objects and Persons* (New York: Oxford University Press, 2001); Kevin J. Corcoran, *Rethinking Human Nature: A Christian Materialist Alternative to the Soul* (Grand Rapids, Michigan: Baker Academic Publishing, 2006); Lynne Rudder Baker, *Persons and Bodies* (New York: Cambridge University Press, 2000).
37. See David Shoemaker's *Personal Identity and Ethics* (Ontario, Canada: Broadview Press, 2009), chapter 2. Also see David DeGrazia, *Human Identity and Bioethics* (Cambridge: Cambridge University Press, 2005).
38. This is not a foolproof case.
39. Peter van Inwagen makes a persuasive case for the person following the brain in his *Material Beings* (Ithaca and London: Cornell University Press, 1990), chapter 15—he holds a non-reductive view.
40. See Foster's *The Immaterial Self: A Defence of the Cartesian Dualist Conception of the Mind* (London and New York: Routledge Publishing, 1991).
41. Locke, John, *An Essay Concerning Human Understanding*. Abridged and Edited by Kenneth P. Winkler (Indianapolis and Cambridge: Hackett Publishing, 1689; 1996).

42. Swinburne, Richard, *The Evolution of the Soul: Revised Edition* (Oxford: Clarendon Press, 1997), see chapters 8 and 9. See Swinburne in "Personal Identity: The Dualist Theory" in *Metaphysics: The Big Questions*, ed. by Peter van Inwagen and Dean W. Zimmerman (Oxford, UK: Blackwell Press, 1998). Also see Swinburne in *The Christian God* (Oxford: Clarendon Press, 1994), chapter 2, "Thisness," p. 45.

43. Swinburne, Richard, *The Evolution of the Soul: Revised Edition* (Oxford: Clarendon Press, 1997). A fine argument for the simple view is found in chapters 8 and 9 of Swinburne's *The Evolution of the Soul*. In addition, a fine argument is found in Swinburne's essay entitled "Personal Identity: The Dualist Theory." Also E.J. Lowe's essay entitled "Identity, Composition, and the Simplicity of the Self" in *Soul, Body, and Survival* (Ithaca and London: Cornell University Press, 2001).

44. A materialist could develop a simple view, possibly. A materialist could say 'I' exist somewhere in my brain as a simple self that is not divisible (Roderick Chisholm's view).

45. This can be brought out by distinguishing intrinsic properties and relational properties.

46. With the simple view, one is able to say that persons can be numerically identical through change, yet can change qualitatively.

47. For a more detailed argument showing the dogmatic relevance of the soul to Christian tradition, see: Joshua R. Farris, "Christian Physicalism? Issues in Contemporary Protestantism," *Chicago Studies*, vol. 58.2 (Fall/Winter 2019/2020). Also see a series of critiques of Christian physicalism, here: R. Keith Loftin and Joshua R. Farris, *Christian Physicalism? Philosophical Theological Criticisms* (Lexington: Lexington Press, 2018).

48. Nancey Murphy, *Bodies and Souls, or Spirited Bodies*

(Cambridge: Cambridge University Press, 2006).

49. Green, *Body, Soul, and Human Life* (Grand Rapids, MI: Baker Academic, 2008), 22.

50. Green, *Body, Soul, and Human Life*, 21; Nancey Murphy, *Bodies and Souls, or Spirited Bodies*, chapter 2.

51. Green, *Body, Soul, and Human Life*, 70; see also Green in his recent biblical-theological/exegesis of Genesis 2 in "Why the *Imago Dei* should not be identified with the Soul," in *The Ashgate Research Companion to Theological Anthropology* (Farnham: Ashgate, 2015), chapter 14.

52. John Cooper, *Body, Soul, and Life Everlasting: Biblical Anthropology and the Monism-Dualism Debate* (Grand Rapids, MI: Eerdmans, 2000).

53. Daniel N. Robinson, "Theological Anthropology and the Brain Sciences," *The Ashgate Research Companion to Theological Anthropology*, 79.

54. Thomas Aquinas, *Commentary on the Letters of Saint Paul to the Corinthians*, trans. by F.R. Larcher OP, B. Mortensen, and D. Keating and ed. by J. Mortensen and E. Alarcon (Lander, Wyoming: The Aquinas Institute for the Study of Sacred Doctrine, 2012), 472.

55. Nancey Murphy, "Reductionism and Emergence: A Critical Perspective," in *Human Identity at the Intersection of Science, Technology and Religion*, ed. by Nancey Murphy and Christopher C. Knight (New York: Routledge, 2010), p. 79. If you think that Nancey Murphy goes on to defend these rather bold claims, then think again. She doesn't! Not even close. Instead, she discusses the difference between a reductive understanding of the material world and what she proposes, namely a non-reductive or emergentist understanding of the world.

56. <https://www.abc.net.au/news/2018-08-13/sir-john-eccles-the-scientist-who-went-in-search-for-the-soul/10089676>

57. Mario Beauregard and Denyse O'Leary, *The Spiritual Brain:*

A Neuroscientist's Case for the Existence of Soul (HarperOne, 2007).

58. See Paul Bloom, *Descartes' Baby* (New York: Basic Books, 2004).
59. Paul Bloom, "Religion is Natural" in *Developmental Science*, vol. 10, issue 1 (2007), p. 149.
60. René Descartes, *Discourse on Method and Meditations on First Philosophy*, trans. by Donald A. Cress (Indianapolis: Hackett Publishing, 1980), p. 52.
61. Thomas Nagel, *Mind and Cosmos: Why the Materialist Neo-Darwinian Conception of Nature is Almost Certainly False* (Oxford: Oxford University Press, 2012), p. 35.
62. For other reasons to think souls exist, see Richard Swinburne, *Are We Bodies or Souls?* (Oxford: Oxford University Press, 2019).
63. "Religion is Natural," p. 150.
64. See John Cooper, *Body, Soul and Life Everlasting* (Grand Rapids: Eerdmans, 2000). Joshua Farris builds on Cooper's work and deploys the findings in systematic theology by drawing on the Christian tradition and making a unique argument from 2 Corinthians 5:1-10. See Joshua R. Farris, *The Soul of Theological Anthropology: A Cartesian Exploration* (New York: Routledge, 2016). For a set of criticisms against the growing trend to accept a physicalism or materialism conception of persons, see R. Keith Loftin and Joshua R. Farris (eds.), *Christian Physicalism? Philosophical and Theological Criticisms* (New York: Lexington, 2018).
65. I must thank the Carl F.H. Henry Center, The Creation Project, at Trinity Evangelical Divinity School, which afforded me the time to write which was originally an article that I have re-purposed for purposes here. The views here are my own and should not be taken to reflect the views of either the John Templeton Foundation or the Carl F.H. Henry Center.

66. The reality is that scientific knowledge requires and presupposes a first-person knower. The first six pages are substantially rewritten versions of previously published material. (Drawn, modified and substantially rewritten from portions of *The Soul of Theological Anthropology*, chapter 1 and chapter 2.)

67. See Frank Jackson, *From Metaphysics to Ethics* (Oxford: Clarendon Press, 1998).

68. See Roderick Chisholm, *Theory of Knowledge*, 3rd edition (Englewood Cliff: Prentice-Hall, 1989), pp. 18-25. *The First Person* (Minneapolis: University of Minnesota Press, 1981), pp. 79-83.

69. I do not wish to enter a debate over perdurantism or endurantism. I assume this based on the way that it seems to me. Endurantism is the common-sense position and with respect to my thoughts it seems that I persist and I do not seem to perdure. For a useful defense, see Ned Markosian, "A Defense of Presentism," in *Persistence: Contemporary Readings* (Cambridge, Massachusetts and London: The MIT Press, 2006), chapter 17.

70. One could argue in favor of stage theory and say that these memories are 'apparent' memories. This seems to defy common sense, but, nonetheless it is another way of accounting for the data. However, given common sense, I take it that we do have an obvious reason for affirming the truthfulness that I endure.

71. There is some empirical evidence to buttress this with respect to scientific studies and scientific work is presupposed by it. For one example see Mark C. Baker and Stewart Goetz, eds., *The Soul Hypothesis: Investigations into the Existence of the Soul* (New York: Continuum, 2011), see especially chapters 1, 5, 6 and 7.

72. Hence the problem with mereologically arranged aggregates that have externally related parts cobbled

together.

73. Richard Swinburne, "From Mental/Physical Identity to Substance Dualism," *Persons: Human and Divine* (Oxford: Oxford University Press, 2007), see especially pp. 151-165. Mental events and physical events are distinct according to Swinburne in terms of a thing having access to the mind and a physical thing described according to extension and physics. I am not inclined to see along with Swinburne the idea that mental/soul substances exist only when presently having the property of accessing the internal. I believe the thinking thing/substance still exists and still bears, at minimum, one property.

74. Qualia is a universal property for the experience of physical objects. These require an experiencing subject.

75. On a traditional realist understanding, propositions really exist as mind-independent and as abstract. As such, propositions can be instantiated in concrete individuals as concepts. Yet, while the proposition is still one, a concept takes on a distinct characteristic from the individual subject.

76. See John Foster in *The Immaterial Self: A Defense of the Cartesian Dualist Conception of the Mind.* See Richard Swinburne, *The Evolution of the Soul,* on page 157 for a defense of this. I develop it a bit differently here and explore some of the implications a bit further within the I-concept.

77. René Descartes, *Discourse on the Method,* trans. by E.S. Haldane and G.R.T. Ross in *Collected Works of Descartes, I* (Cambridge: Cambridge University Press, 1972), p. 101.

78. A famous argument used by Aristotle, Descartes and Kant to name a few. Also see William Hasker's useful discussion in *The Emergent Self* (Ithaca: Cornell University Press, 1999), pp. 122-135.

79. I am convinced that there is literally one thing, simple, indivisible and without parts. Interestingly there are two

essays where the authors argue for a unified self, yet one argues in favor of a simple self and the other a unified self yet not a metaphysical simple. See David Barnett, "You are Simple," and William Hasker, "Persons and the Unity of Consciousness," in *The Waning of Materialism* ed. by R.C. Koons and George Bealer (Oxford: Oxford University Press, 2010), see chapters 7 and 8.

80. Lynne Rudder Baker uses the term metaphysical glue in *Persons and Bodies: A Constitution View* (Cambridge: Cambridge University Press, 2000), p. 163. She uses it in reference to the first-person perspective, which is odd because on her view a mind is not properly speaking a pure substance with the persistence conditions necessary for uniting conscious mental states. The first-person perspective is an impure substance, and a higher-order property instantiated in the physical substance. It is better to see the 'what' as an immaterial thing that is doing something uncharacteristic of material things.

81. See David Hume, *A Treatise of Human Nature.* Project Gutenberg, eBook collection. See especially section XVI, "Of the Reason of Animals" [February 13, 2013; accessed on April 21, 2014].

82. Eric T. Olson uses these two terms in "A Compound of Two Substances," in *Soul, Body, and Survival: Essays on the Metaphysics of Human Persons* (Ithaca: Cornell University Press, 2001), p. 73. Olson has argued that if one is going to affirm substance dualism, then s/he should affirm a pure version where there is a mere causal connection between soul and body rather than compound or complex versions of the doctrine. He suggests that he cannot conceive of what else there is or what it is that the dualist might desire. In this portion of the chapter, I suggest that we do in fact have greater variety worthy of our consideration than what Olson is willing to grant.

83. Many holding this view would say you survive bodily death, and some may not have a place for survival. Although, it is ambiguous how a soul survives on certain views given that the body is a part of me and the soul depends on the body in some fashion.

84. Often in the philosophical-theological literature, authors raise the problem of the objective and subjective. The soul substance is a kind of thing objectively speaking, but souls are individualized. The subjective dimension of reality does not contradict objective reality, but instead is a part of a realist objective reality.

85. Joseph Butler and Thomas Reid also held this view. See Charles Taliaferro and Stewart Goetz, *A Brief History of the Soul* (Oxford: Wiley-Blackwell, 2011). This is a recent defense of substance dualism in the tradition of Plato-Augustine-Descartes. While a defense of this tradition is not the primary intent of the authors, it is apparent that they hold this view and are defending such a view when reading their discussion of the soul. Also, see a much older article that helpfully compares Augustine with Descartes in terms of their overall project and the relationship of the Self to God. See Marguerite Witmer Kehr, "The Doctrine of the Self in St. Augustine and in Descartes," *The Philosophical Review*, Vol. 25, No. 4 (1916), 587-615. Also see Paul Helm, *John Calvin's Ideas* (Oxford: Oxford University Press, 2006), chapter 5. Herein, Helm persuasively defends the notion that Calvin affirms substance dualism closely aligned with both Augustine and Plato. Furthermore, see Paul Helm, *Calvin at the Centre* (Oxford: Oxford University Press, 2010), chapter 2. Helm defends the idea that Descartes has an Augustinian view of the soul and its relationship to God. Additionally, Helm argues that Cartesian thought as a philosophical project could provide the underpinnings for Protestant theology.

86. Both of the terms *ens per se* and *ens per accidens* are Latin terms which mean essential unity and accidental unity. This plays a large role in how one parses out the relation of mind and body. For Cartesian substance dualism, this becomes very important for understanding whether and how an interactive relation undergirds union or vice versa.

87. A position holding that a thing can exist on its own in a weak sense would say it is comparable to a hand that is detached from the body for a period. We would say that it is a hand that could exist for a short period. If a strong sense, then one would contend that a thing can exist on its own as normal objects would exist and naturally exist on their own. It has the quality of life necessary for living or persisting in existence.

88. It is debatable whether Descartes held to this, but generally and traditionally, this is attributed to him. He does make statements that can be misleading, as do many substance dualists, but logically much of what he does say about what I am calling the I-concept here logically fits best with pure dualism. For a more compound-esque view see Marleen Rozemond, *Descartes's Dualism* (Boston: Harvard University Press, 2002). For a more composite variation, as I construe these below, see Paul Hoffman, *Essays on Descartes* (Oxford: Oxford University Press, 2009), part one.

89. See Nancey Murphy, "Human Nature: Historical, Scientific and Religious Issues," in *Whatever Happened to the Soul: Scientific and Theological Portraits of Human Nature* (Minneapolis: Fortress Press, 1998), p. 24.

90. See Eric T. Olson, "A Compound of Two Substances," in *Soul, Body, and Survival*, ed. by Kevin Corcoran (Ithaca and London: Cornell University Press, 2002), 73-89. For a representative sampling, see the following: Richard Swinburne, *The Evolution of the Soul* (Oxford: Oxford University Press, 1997), especially chapter 8; Gilbert Ryle,

The Concept of Mind (London: Hutchinson, 1949), p. 18 and p. 189. It is not uncommon to refer to Descartes as a compound dualist, but what this means in terms of union is important and unclear in the literature. If one can make sense of a more fundamental union undergirding causal interaction, then we could say that Descartes holds to a kind of per se union. I have already made a case for substance dualism in general by way of arguing from mereological replacement, simple arguments (even though some do not hold to an indivisibility thesis), persistence, intuition and survival. I do think there are other good reasons to contend for substance dualism, from intentionality, introspection and consciousness. So, I do think there are reasons for holding to compound dualism, but that given the problems I raise here one should accept pure dualism or, possibly, if one is not convinced by pure dualism then consider some variety of non-reductive physicalism and seek to account for the problems it has with consciousness. Alternatively, one might consider emergent substance dualism that does not seem to have the problems attending compound dualism or hylomorphism. Brian Leftow uses this analogy in reference to Platonic dualism in his paper, "The humanity of God," in *The Metaphysics of the Incarnation*, ed. by Anna Marmadoro & Jonathan Hill (Oxford: Oxford University Press, 2011), 28.

91. Richard Swinburne, *The Evolution of the Soul: Revised Edition* (Oxford: Oxford University Press, 1997), pp. 145-146. If one is clear on the distinctions between the positions, then Swinburne makes this clear on page 145. Granted on page 146, Swinburne says something that seems in tension with what he has just stated, "The crucial point that Descartes and others were presumably trying to make is not that (in the case of men) the living body is not part of the person, but that it is not essentially, only contingently, part of the

person. The body is separable from the person and the person can continue even if the body is destroyed." This then seems to be in line with a stricter and pure kind of dualism. To usher in 'compound' or 'composite' just brings with it conceptual confusion. If the body is contingent and accidental, then the proper hypostasis is the soul for the body such that the soul subsists on its own.

92. Ibid. 160. Also, see Gilbert Ryle, *The Concept of Mind* (London: Hutchinson Press, 1949), p. 18.

93. Thanks to Oliver Crisp for suggesting this notion of 'expand.'

94. See Swinburne, "From Mental/Physical Identity to Substance Dualism," in *Persons: Human and Divine*, ed. by Peter van Inwagen and Dean Zimmerman (Oxford: Oxford University Press, 2007).

95. Yet, on his view, consciousness causally requires the brain to activate the mind. I believe this is where the tension resides.

96. Richard Swinburne, "From Mental/Physical Identity to Substance Dualism," in *Persons: Human and Divine*, p. 161.

97. Ibid. 162.

98. Ibid. 163 and ft. 24. Swinburne says this: "I think in virtue of my soul thinking." He says this in response to Eric T. Olson's objection from too-many-thinkers in "A Compound of Two Substances." It seems that Swinburne's saying this does not make things much better. If I think in virtue of my soul thinking, then many questions still arise in virtue of the operations of soul and person. Does the soul think apart from me? Is the soul as a part of me only a faculty of mine that I possess? It would simply be the 'I' that is thinking. You might say that there is a functional unity between the soul and the person, but if there are two things thinking then am I not thinking in addition to my soul? If the soul does not think, then what does it do?

99. Ibid. 162.

100. See William Hasker, *The Emergent Self*.

101. Richard Swinburne, *The Evolution of the Soul*, p. 174. Swinburne states: "The evidence of neurophysiology and psychology suggests most powerfully that the functioning of the soul depends on the operation of the brain." Swinburne seems to assume this throughout the chapter, which is part of the reason for confusion in his talk about the body/brain. It is arguable that if this is true then persons are really composed of bodies because souls necessarily require bodies for functioning. I am not making this stronger claim, but just showing the logic behind Swinburne's talk of bodies and persons and some of the reasoning for the ambiguity. This is also the reason he has difficulty in accounting for survival of persons, a traditional doctrine of Christianity. Yet given he says that the core of the person is his immaterial soul he opens up the door to the possibility for survival.

102. Richard Swinburne, *The Evolution of the Soul*, p. 196. Swinburne states: "Lacking a theory of what it is about the brain which keeps a soul functioning, our ignorance about how and when the soul can function is profound." Prior to this statement, Swinburne develops the ground for his concluding this.

103. Swinburne, "From Mental/Physical Identity to Substance Dualism," p. 163. Swinburne also states human persons that are pure mental substances have occasional identity with their bodies. See p. 163 ft. 24. If the person is a pure mental substance that is identical with the soul + body at specific phase sortals and only a soul at other phase sortals, then this would appear to be a variation of hylomorphic dualism. Of course, matters might not be so simple. This would mean that the soul must be literally in the physical body and provide the form of the physical matter, but it seems

that in virtue of Swinburne's commitment to Cartesian interactionism this is not the case. Thus, it is still difficult to ascertain exactly the ontological relationship between the soul and body other than saying it is a contingent matter. If this is the case, then it seems PSD is the better alternative considering the confusion of language and a lack of an ontological connection to distinguish this version of COSD and PSD.

104. This is similar to those who psychologize about persons, thereby construing and defining persons from a psychological basis. Practical concerns are important and we must develop a metaphysical account, which is able to make sense of these practical concerns. In a sense, we may begin with the practical, functional data within the world as illustrative for developing a metaphysic. This is not the manner in which we construct a proper metaphysic.

105. Yet his view is in tension with this notion.

106. Charles Taliaferro, "The Soul of the Matter," in *The Soul Hypothesis: Investigations into the Existence of the Soul*, ed. by Mark C. Baker and Stewart Goetz (New York: Continuum, 2011), p. 40. Charles Taliaferro responds to a common worry from materialists that the dualist has a conception that the soul is like a little man flying a plane that is located somewhere in the brain. Taliaferro states: "In a healthy, fully functioning human being there need be no bifurcation of person and body." This is true, but this seems to be a contingent, accidental and functional matter. Taliaferro is not saying that the person is ontologically identical to the soul and body, but that during embodiment the person is acting as an embodied being.

107. This is not necessarily the case on variations of hylomorphism that see the two substances as *ens per accidens*, which offers an explication on the necessity of the union.

108. Thanks to Jonathan Chan for pointing out the distinction between a relational soul and a kind soul. Jonathan Chan carefully distinguishes 'relational' and 'kind' views of souls in "A Cartesian Approach to the Incarnation," in *The Ashgate Research Companion to Theological Anthropology*, ed. by Joshua Farris and Charles Taliaferro (Aldershot: Ashgate, 2015). In parsing out distinctions concerning souls, Chan is drawing from Oliver Crisp in *Divinity and Humanity* (Cambridge: Cambridge University Press, 2007), 38-50.

109. Roughly following Dean Zimmerman's definition for substance dualism, in: Dean Zimmerman, "From Property Dualism to Substance Dualism," *Proceedings of the Aristotelian Society*, Supplementary Volume 84 (2010): 119-20. However, the definition is adequate for the version of ontic subjective idealism (or Cartesian idealism as I have called it elsewhere).

110. John Foster, *The Immaterial Self* (London: Routledge, 1991), 221.

111. See Philip Goff, *Consciousness and Fundamental Reality* (New York: Oxford University Press, 2017), 14-17.

112. Kit Fine, "Guide to ground," in *Metaphysical Grounding: Understanding the Structure of Reality*, eds. F. Correia and B. Schnieder (New York: Cambridge University Press, 2012), 37-80.

113. Paul Bloom, *Descartes' Baby: How the Science of Child Development Explains What Makes Us Human* (New York: Basic Books, 2005), see especially 209-29.

114. See Charles Taliaferro and Elliot Knuths, "Thought Experiments in Philosophy of Religion: The Virtues of Phenomenal Realism and Values," *Open Theology*, special issue, *Analytic Perspectives on Method and Authority in Theology*, vol. 3 (2017): 167-73. They build on the work from David Lund, *The Conscious Self* (New York: Humanity

Books, 2005), 264-5.

115. David Chalmers, *The Conscious Mind*, see chapter 1. Nagel, *Moral Questions*. Jackson, "Epiphenomenal Qualia."

116. Quine, "Speaking of Objects," in his *Ontological Relativity and Other Essays* and *Pursuit of Truth* (Cambridge: Harvard University Press, 1990), 52.

117. David Chalmers, *The Conscious Mind: In Search of a Fundamental Theory* (New York: Oxford University Press, 1996), see especially chapter 1, "The sense of self."

118. E.J. Lowe, *The Possibility of Metaphysics* (New York: Oxford University, 2001), 161.

119. Alvin Plantinga, "Materialism and Christian Belief," *Persons: Human and Divine* (Oxford: Oxford University Press, 2007).

120. Geoffrey Madell, *The Essence of the Self: In Defense of the Simple View of Personal Identity* (New York: Routledge, 2014).

121. Joshua R. Farris, "The Simple View and Theological Anthropology," *Philosophy and Theology* (2014). Madell on the Baker FPP constitution view: "There are any number of reasons for concluding that this cannot be right. First of all, in the case of artefacts we can say that whatever an artefact is made of allows that material to be organized in such a way that the function of the artefact is realized, be that indicating the time, or thermostatically controlling the heat, or some other function. But, as I said in chapter 1, I have no idea what it could be for some arrangement of physical elements to be a realization of, for example, a state of indignation at the level of tax avoidance and evasion, and I certainly have no idea at all what it could be for that arrangement to be a realization not simply of indignation but also of my indignation. A psychological state such as that of indignation is an intentional state, involving the here-and-now directedness of thought or consciousness to its object.

It has always been a central objection to materialist views on the nature of mind that it is impossible to understand how any assembly of physical items could possibly realise intentionality in this fundamental way. But there is, of course, a further problem. Not only is it impossible to see how any configuration of physical elements could possibly be seen as a realization of an intentional state such as that of indignation; it is also even more difficult to see how any such state could be seen as a realization, not only of indignation but also as one particular, unique instance of that state, the state which is my indignation. To repeat, it is a contingent truth that some such state or set of states differs from all similar states in being mine." (Madell, 125)

122. Richard Swinburne, *Are We Bodies or Souls?* (Oxford: Oxford University Press, 2019), 86-115. This is consistent with Swinburne's understanding of thisness. His work here builds on his other works: *Mind, Brain, and Free Will* (Oxford: Oxford University Press, 2013), 141-74, and substantially on the notion from his *The Evolution of the Soul* (Oxford: Oxford University Press, 1997), 333-345.

123. For additional exploration on these positions in our contemporary science and religion discussions, see: Joshua R. Farris and Joanna Leidenhag (eds.), *The Origin of the Soul: A Conversation* (New York: Routledge, forthcoming 2022).

124. These two issues are related and have implications for the other.

125. See Daniel von Wachter, "Free Agents as Cause," in *On Human Persons*, ed. by Klaus Petrus (Frankfurt: Ontos Verlag, 2003), pp. 183-194. Von Wachter also calls this an initiating event, which brings about more precision to the libertarian sense of causation than others that root it in some sort of determinism, indeterminism, or no cause. A choice-event is not the notion that the agent intends, which

causes my arm to rise. The arm rising is an event that is not caused by anything else, but my choice that just is an event. The two are co-joined and we have a distinct category for this sort of event than what one normally thinks of as an event-cause. Thus, this sort of event is not caused by another event nor is it random, but is the choice of the agent. Somehow, the agent has the instantaneous power of bringing about an immediate event. This notion of a choice-event splits the dilemma of the two-horns between determinism and indeterminism and roots the control of the event directly in the agent. It does so in that an agent with free will has no preceding cause, either deterministic or indeterministic, but the agent begins the causal chain. This is different from the issue of agent-causation where an event could be rooted, metaphysically, in a deterministic process or an indeterministic process (which both are not directly in the control of the agent). This does not bring precision to the agent him/herself, but gives more precision to the notion of a free-action in terms of events. This also does not mean that the initiating event or choice-event cannot be the cause of other events in a causal chain; it can, but it is distinct from the notion of an event-process whether determined or indetermined.

126. This has been called 'emergentism' by some and essentially means the same thing, but emergentism is a more generic term that can refer to the doctrine of emergence whereby sui generis things, properties or laws emerge from a base. Thus, this term can be used in reference to a physicalist view of the mind. I will use this term later as a kind of shorthand for the doctrine of emergence.

127. Generally, I am speaking in terms of the phenomena of emergence and sui generis entities or natures. Specifically, I am speaking in terms of the growing literature in substance dualism like emergent substance dualism and the literature

on Thomistic hylomorphic substance dualism.

128. For some of the best introductory treatments on the mind-body problem see E.J. Lowe and David Armstrong. David Armstrong in *The Mind-Body Problem: An Opinionated Introduction* (Colorado: Westview Press, 1999). E.J. Lowe in *An Introduction to the Philosophy of Mind* (Cambridge: Cambridge University Press, 2000). Robinson, Howard, "Dualism," *The Stanford Encyclopedia of Philosophy*, Edward N. Zalta (ed.), URL = <http://plato.stanford.edu/archives/win2011/entries/dualism/> [Winter 2011; accessed April 14, 2014].

129. This I discussed in chapters 1 and 2. For a useful article on properties see the following: Swoyer, Chris and Orilia, Francesco, "Properties," *The Stanford Encyclopedia of Philosophy*, Edward N. Zalta (ed.), URL = <http://plato.stanford.edu/archives/win2011/entries/properties/> [Winter 2011; accessed April 14, 2014].

130. This is not an uncommon characterization of these distinct properties of material and immaterial things. See Swinburne, *The Evolution of the Soul*, pp. 6-7.

131. In the literature mental intendings or doings have also been called 'tryings.' See Daniel von Wachter in "Free Agents as a Cause."

132. Robb, David and Heil, John, "Mental Causation," *The Stanford Encyclopedia of Philosophy*, Edward N. Zalta (ed.), URL = <http://plato.stanford.edu/archives/sum2009/entries/mental-causation/> [Summer 2009; accessed on April 21, 2014].

133. See William Hasker in *The Emergent Self* (Ithaca: Cornell University Press, 1999), p. 150.

134. Ibid. 150. Hasker does proceed to raise the question that if we can offer a solution to the mind-body problem that sheds some light on the relational union of the mind-body, then we have reason for accepting it instead. This serves

as a part of the movement toward his case in favor of Emergent substance dualism.

135. The only exception to this general rule is mental and physical occasionalism. On this view, it just is that when I have an intention this provides the occasion for the body to behave in a corresponding manner, but it does not mean that my mental act of 'trying' is the direct cause of the body behaving in the manner that it does. For example, the occasion of my arm raising in conjunction with my intending to raise my arm is rooted in a Theistic causal explanation of the relationship.

136. See Dean Zimmerman, "Dualism in the Philosophy of Mind," in *The Encyclopedia of Philosophy* 2nd edition, ed. by Donald M. Borchert (New York: Macmillan, 2006), pp. 113-122. Here Zimmerman goes some way to highlight the differences in the varieties of substance dualism. He particularly distinguishes pure substance dualism with composite substance dualism, but he holds emergent versions of substance dualism to be sufficiently distinct from the other two. He refers to Descartes as a composite substance dualist, which, as I have stated in a previous chapter, is vague and deserves distinction from say Thomistic hylomorphic varieties of composite substance dualism. The two are not the same, and in fact, a Cartesian variety is similar to pure and composite versions, thus I helpfully refer to it as Person-body substance dualism and compound dualism.

137. See Eric T. Olson, "A Compound of Two Substances," in *Soul, Body, and Survival*, ed. by Kevin Corcoran (Ithaca: Cornell University Press, 2001), pp. 73-88. Olson works through the difficulties of articulating a compound or composite version of substance dualism, and argues that if you are going to be a substance dualist of a Cartesian sort, then you ought to be a pure dualist. I have addressed this

in chapter 1.

138. Ibid. 73.

139. Also, see Descartes in the Third Meditation. See an explanation in Justin Skirry's "Descartes: The Mind-Body Distinction" in the Internet Encyclopedia of Philosophy, section 5, Descartes' Response to the Mind-Body Problem. <http://www.iep.utm.edu/descmind/> [May 3, 2006; accessed on April 14, 2014].

140. See Richard Swinburne for a distinction between event causes and personal causes in *The Existence of God* (Oxford: Oxford University Press, 2004). Also, see Swinburne in *The Evolution of the Soul*. Here he makes a distinction between scientific explanations and personal explanations or physical causes and agent causes. John Foster makes an argument that the interactive relation is directly rooted in Divine causation as a personal explanation in "A Brief Defence of the Cartesian View," in *Soul, Body, and Survival* (Ithaca and London: Cornell University Press, 2001), pp. 28-29. Foster's defence contributes to the discussion by arguing that the Cartesian view requires a 'personal explanation' (although he does not use this term) where God establishes an appropriate functional attachment between the soul and the body. There could be other ways in which God personally establishes this connection. One would be that he creates bodies and brains with suitable structures that host souls whereby the body/brain has a teleological structure that gives rise to a law-like relation (regular patterns of succession) between the body and soul.

141. The proponent of this view can very easily incorporate the previous response.

142. Dean Zimmerman argues that most substance dualists affirm something along these lines in "Dualism in the Philosophy of Mind," p. 116. He also states that most affirm the spatiality of the soul in contemporary times, but

I am skeptical about this claim and do not see how souls are spatial, at least in the manner that we normally think of spatiality as being physical in nature.

143. Swinburne in *The Evolution of the Soul* holds to something like this. Also see John Hawthorne, "Cartesian Dualism," in *Persons: Human and Divine*, ed. by Peter van Inwagen and Dean Zimmerman (Oxford: Oxford University Press, 2006), especially the concluding section. Most Cartesians today would consider themselves to be composite or compound dualists; this lends itself to some confusion and deserves disambiguation from other varieties that are composite in nature.

144. See Hasker in *The Emergent Self*, and "Souls Beastly and Human." Hasker's first article defending what he later calls emergent substance dualism is found in "Souls of Beasts and Men," *Religious Studies* 10, issue 3 (1974), 265-277. Hasker is famous for this novel position in the literature on philosophy of mind. In the past he referred to this position as 'emergentism,' but this did not sufficiently distinguish it from varieties of non-reductive physicalism that are also versions of property dualism. Now, he refers to his position as emergent substance dualism.

145. Hasker, *The Emergent Self*, pp. 188-189.

146. Ibid. 190 and 194.

147. Ibid. I take this from page 192 where Hasker discusses the spatial nature of the mind as encompassing the parts of the brain.

148. Ibid. 192 and 193. Hasker says, "the theory makes intelligible, as Cartesian dualism does not, the intimate dependence of consciousness and mental processes on brain function."

149. See Swinburne on mixed properties in *The Evolution of the Soul* on page 7. The notion of mixed properties is a rather perplexing issue and debatable matter deserving further

attention. Yet, we might be able to make sense of mixed properties in a way that I have suggested earlier in terms of functional properties actualized in terms of the mind and body.

150. Traditionally, Lutherans were traducians barring Philip Melanchthon. Augustus H. Strong, W.G.T. Shedd, Gordon Clark, Lewis Sperry Chafer all support traducianism. Contemporary support includes but is not limited to the following: Millard Erickson, Norman L. Geisler, Robert Culver, and Robert L. Reymond.

151. "Souls Beastly and Human," p. 209. Also see *The Emergent Self*, pp. 170 and 196. This is not a criticism of Hasker, but simply pointing out that there may be other traditional options that are non-creationist construals of souls.

152. Tertullian, *On the Soul*, 100.27.

153. Ibid. 27.5.

154. Augustine, however, never firmly concluded what is true. For further explanation see E. Gilson, *The Christian Philosophy of St. Augustine*, trans. by L.E.M. Lynch (London: Victor Gollancz, 1961), p. 51.

155. See Gen. 1:27; 2:2, 21; 46:27; Ex. 1:5; Ps. 51:5; Heb. 7:9-10; Rom. 5:12-13; I Cor. 15:22; Eph. 2:3. These Scriptures have been used throughout Ecclesiastical history as support for traducianism. I am not arguing that Scripture yields this, or that this position is implied by these Scriptures, but one might argue that these Scriptures fit best with or are accounted for by traducianism.

156. Possibly, this is traditional in the sense that these conceptions of souls have some historical precedence.

157. This seems to be Tertullian's view. See Tertullian, *A Treatise on the Soul* in *The Ante-Nicene Fathers: volume III. The Writing of Tertullian*, translated by Peter Holmes DD, ed. by A. Roberts and J. Donaldson (Grand Rapids, MI: Eerdmans, repr. 1981), chapters 4 and 5. http://www.tertulian.org/anf/

index.htm. Also see Swinburne, Richard, *The Evolution of the Soul: Revised Edition* (Oxford: Clarendon Press, 1997), 199. See also N.P. Williams, *The Ideas of the Fall and of Original Sin* (London: Longmans, 1927), p. 236.

158. A soul might be a simple in a very tenuous sense whereby it has essential parts that are necessary and the person cannot be reducible to those parts.

159. Hylomorphism could be worked out as a fissile variation.

160. J.P. Moreland and Scott B. Rae, *Body & Soul: Human Nature & the Crisis in Ethics* (Downers Grove, Illinois: IVP, 2000), p. 221. Something like this is Moreland's version of Thomist dualism. It might be objected that Aquinas explicitly stated he was a creationist, but his Thomist dualism could be worked out as a kind of emergent-traducian view and Moreland provides an example of this sort that might be a version of traducianism or emergent-creationism.

161. The age old expression: 'more than the sum of its parts,' applies to this position. Hylomorphism contends that there are two parts constituting persons, but persons are not reducible to those parts.

162. A modified Cartesian traducianism could be fissile in nature or parturient in nature.

163. See Oliver D. Crisp, *An American Augustinian: Sin and Salvation in the Dogmatic Theology of William G.T. Shedd* (Milton Keynes: Paternoster Press, 2007), pp. 30-32. Here Oliver Crisp gives a useful discussion of modified Cartesianism and how it might fit with traducianism. He also mentions how souls might not be fissile, but could be parturient wherein souls extrude themselves.

164. This is the default view throughout Church History. Traditionally, Roman Catholics and the Protestant-Reformation generally tended toward accepting a creationist view of souls.

165. See Gen. 2:7; Num. 16:22; Ps. 12:7; 139:13-14; 104:30; Eccl.

12:7; Isa. 42:5; 57:16; Jer. 1:5; Zech. 12:1; Heb. 12:9. These are scriptural passages that have been commonly used throughout Ecclesiastical history in support of creationism whether a simple and/or special creation, but I suppose this support could be used in favor of a more emergentist creationism—as I develop in chapter 5.

166. Or this could apply to platonic souls. Platonic and Cartesian souls are not exactly the same, but for purposes here I simply refer to Cartesian souls. Both views hold that the person is his/her soul. Cartesianism is more recent in the history of philosophy, therefore it is more commonly known. This is not anachronistic; I am simply saying that the two positions are conceptually similar. The two views are not the same. Plato may go further than Descartes to suggest that the material body and realm are less real than the soul, which has implications for his view pertaining to mind-body relations.

167. For a useful resource, see Francis Siegfried, "Creationism," *The Catholic Encyclopedia*, Vol. 4 (New York: Robert Appleton Company, 1908). <http://www.newadvent.org/cathen/04475a.htm> [July 24, 2012; accessed April 14, 2014].

168. Human bodies are only secondarily caused by God unless one is a concurrentist wherein God would be directly involved somehow in the process. This could be in terms of ratifying.

169. The only emergence may come from the unity-relation between the body and soul that ensues new properties that would probably be structural or somehow deducible from the unity-relation of the two substances. Some examples would include sensation, some feelings and knowledge of other bodies.

170. Peter Lombard, Sent. II, d. xviii. Quote taken from Francis Siegfried, "Creationism," *The Catholic Encyclopedia*, Vol. 4 (New York: Robert Appleton Company, 1908). <http://

www.newadvent.org/cathen/04475a.htm> [July 24, 2012; accessed on April 14, 2014].

171. See John Foster, "A Brief Defence of the Cartesian View," in *Soul, Body, and Survival: The Metaphysics of Human Persons,* ed. by Kevin Corcoran (Ithaca: Cornell University Press, 2001), p. 29.

172. I do not see any reason why God could not create souls either way and how this would drastically affect the arguments I am making here.

173. Physical life is continuous to varying degrees. This certainly rubs against modern sensibilities where physical reality is one unified and continuous whole. On some variations of souls it requires a suitable body, which may require God's power within the created structure.

174. A philosophical/theological objection immediately arises when thinking of parents and their relationship to the generation of the child. The objection says something like parents have a deep connection to their children because of the procreative act. If God directly creates the soul that is identified with the person, then the parents are merely engaged in the procreative act of the animal part of humans. David Albert Jones made me aware of this in *The Soul of the Embryo: An enquiry into the status of the human embryo in the Christian tradition* (New York: T&T Clark, 2004), p. 106. An initial response is to say that there is more to the human body than mere physicality and that the soul is fashioned by God to be embodied. So the significance is that the parents are participating in the act of procreating a human person with God. This is no small matter. Furthermore, I think emergent-creationism may be a more halfway house between traducianism and creationism. I explore this position below. I do not think this poses a problem for creationists. It might also be argued that human souls are apt for embodiment and that God designs particular souls

for particular bodies. This may be going beyond some traditional notions of souls, but it is not contradictory with them. Take for example Cartesianism, the idea that I am strictly identified with my soul that contingently interacts with my body; these ideas are commensurate with the notion that bodies and souls are designed one for the other.

175. A proponent of 'special creation' could also affirm a young-earth creation view, progressive creationism or theistic evolution—unless on theistic evolution God is barred from interacting with creation and creating some things after the original act of creation.

176. Michael J. Loux, *Metaphysics: A Contemporary Introduction*, third edition (New York: Routledge, 2007), p. 105.

177. It is not actually propertyless.

178. Michael J. Loux, *Metaphysics: A Contemporary Introduction*, third edition, pp. 101-104.

179. Otherwise how would this kind of thing without parts and without properties that is a simple come about through a traducian mechanism?

180. This is not a God of the gaps fallacy. At times God fills an epistemic role in our explanatory process. It seems that in cases like these there is a warrant for positing God as the explanation. Persons are such, on this construal, that they require an explanation outside the spatiotemporal world.

181. It could be that the soul itself that is apt for and naturally embodied is a human soul. It seems on this view that the human soul has an essential property or set of properties comprising the imago Dei that are then instantiated in the soul and/or soul-body union. This certainly fits with Cartesian dualism or potentially other forms of substance dualism wherein the person is identified with his/her soul. Arguably, the imago Dei is the set of properties or a property (being universal) that must be created by God and cannot come about in the natural order according to

physical processes.

182. PR stands for physical conditions in reproduction and is aptly descriptive using terms of physical science. Moreland, J.P. and Scott B. Rae, *Body & Soul: Human Nature & the Crisis in Ethics* (Downers Grove, Illinois: IVP, 2000), p. 220.

183. Ibid. 220.

184. As stated before, John Foster has posited this solution to the mind-body problem and, I suppose, by extension he would posit something similar with respect to the soul's origin in relation to the body. It is established by Divine fiat.

185. There has been a great deal of buzz in the contemporary discussion over emergent dualisms. W.D. Hart would be one example of an emergent substance dualist. See his *The Engines of the Soul* (Cambridge: Cambridge University Press, 1988). Interestingly, Hart does not endorse dualism in connection with theism, but if he did his might be categorized as similar to the position developed here. I am not sure how Hart accounts for a soul's contingent existence apart from a supernatural entity with causal agency. Dean Zimmerman has also written on the subject of emergent substance dualism. See a useful and recent article of his "From Property Dualism to Substance Dualism," in *Proceedings of the Aristotelian Society*, Supplementary Volume 84 (2010), 119-150.

186. This of course is my attempt to codify the essential elements for the purposes of developing a systematic definition. To my knowledge, no one has offered a definition of this view. As explained elsewhere sui generis literally means deeply foundational. It is a wholly new thing when categorizing entities in ontology. It is not deducible or reducible to its constituent parts.

187. The non-reductive physicalist or a property dualist sort might speak of the soul loosely or in layman's terms that

refer to the thoughts, intentions and emotions of man, but not literally as if there is an immaterial substance. The person on this view is literally a physical substance with new properties of a different sort than other properties exemplified in the physical world. For an example of this view see Nancey Murphy, "Nonreductive Physicalism: Philosophical Challenges," in *Personal Identity in Theological Perspective*, ed. by Lints, Horton, and Talbot (Grand Rapids: William B. Eerdmans Publishing Co., 2006), p. 95.

188. The advantage of emergent dualism is that there is actually a new substance that is distinct from the material substance. With property dualism that holds to substance materialism there is a great deal of ambiguity as to what the person as a material substance is. All of our common-sense objects seem to fall short of being identified with persons. Whereas, with emergent dualism there is a substance that has conscious experience. Zimmerman insightfully develops this in his recent article, "From Property Dualism to Substance Dualism."

189. For a discussion of problems with traditional views of origins and materialist views see John Yates, "The Origin of the Soul: New Light on An Old Question," *Evangelical Quarterly* 61:1 (1989), 135-140. Whilst I do not agree with many of his conclusions concerning traditional views on origins, I do find his discussion interesting and useful.

190. William Hasker, "Souls Beastly and Human," in *The Soul Hypothesis*, ed. by Mark Baker and Stewart Goetz (London: Continuum, 2011), pp. 211-212. While the theological issue of origins is closely and intimately related to the mind-body problem and its solutions due to the relationship between the mind and body, the two are not the same and deserve some clear disambiguation. Hasker's essay, while very good, tends to blur these issues.

191. Creation out of nothing may only be an event at the

moment the world comes into existence. At the moment physical matter comes into existence all of life seems to emerge through physical evolution.

192. Mary Midgley, *The Myths We Live By* (New York: Routledge, 2003), 61-67. Fascinatingly, this opens the door to all sorts of monstrous ideas. Here and in the rest of the book, she criticizes the allures of scientism and the temptation to a kind of simplicity that fails to explain all aspects of the world.

193. For a helpful survey of different options along with some critiques, see: Sarah Lane Ritchie, *Divine Action and the Human Mind* (Cambridge: Cambridge University Press, 2019). Ritchie approaches the subject with the intended goal of ground clearing to explore her preferred approach to God's relation to the natural world, what she and others call 'theistic naturalism.' For a useful idealist critique of which I am sympathetic, see: Bruce L. Gordon, "On the Very Idea of Theological Naturalism," *Sapientia* (July 8, 2020). https://henrycenter.tiu.edu/2020/07/on-the-very-idea-of-theological-naturalism/ [accessed on September 17, 2021].

194. Some take it that this is ill-conceived, if in fact, all natural laws are dependent on Divine action already.

195. This of course is not a problem if we take consciousness as somehow fundamental to the structuring of the natural world, including the origins of consciousness.

196. Keith Frankish, "What if your consciousness is an illusion created by your brain," *Aeon*. https://aeon.co/essays/what-if-your-consciousness-is-an-illusion-created-by-your-brain [accessed on September 15, 2021].

197. For a popular treatment of the notion of 'emergence' see: Steven Johnson, *Emergence* (New York: Scribner, 2001).

198. See Nancey Murphy, "Reductionism and Emergence," *Human Identity at the Intersection of Science, Technology*

and Religion (New York: Routledge, 2010), 82. Also see Robert Van Gulick, "Reduction, Emergence and Other Recent Options in the Mind/Body Problem: A Philosophic Overview," *Journal of Conscious Studies* 8/9-10 (October 2001), 1-34.

199. Terrence Deacon, "Three Levels of Emergent Phenomena," in *Evolution and Emergence,* ed. by Murphy and Stoeger (Oxford: Oxford University Press, 2007).

200. There are obvious cases that have been researched like the bacterial flagellum as exhibiting a system that requires a certain set of informational patterns not found in nature at lower levels. Design theorists have championed this as compelling signs of design in nature that are not only non-reducible to the parts interacting, but actually require the inference to design in nature or information being added to nature that requires something of a mental agent. There is a growing and compelling number of literature supporting something like this idea that undermines a fully neo-Darwinian system where all aspects of nature are explained by mechanisms within biological evolution, i.e., natural selection etc. See Michael Behe, *Darwin's Black Box* (New York: Free Press, 2006). There are various ways in which a scientific criterion is applied that is useable to detect signs of design, what Behe calls irreducible complexity and what Dembski calls specified complexity. I only point the reader to this literature as a compelling set of literature that packs a pretty potent punch when it comes to this tendency among many scientists who are committed to physicalism and the idea that all can be explained by neo-Darwinian mechanisms within nature.

201. Timothy O'Connor, "The Emergence of Personhood," *The Emergence of Personhood,* ed. by Malcolm Jeeves (Grand Rapids: Eerdmans, 2015), see 148-157.

202. Samuel Alexander, *Space, Time, and Deity,* Volume 2

(London: Macmillan & Co. Ltd., 1920), p. 348.

203. See Thomas Nagel, *The View from Nowhere* (New York: Oxford University Press, 1986). Nagel, *The Last Word* (New York: Oxford University Press, 2001). Eventually, Nagel moved in the direction of an alternative bridge perspective—naturalistic panpsychism. He does so in: *Mind and Cosmos* (New York: Oxford University Press, 2012).

204. Philip Clayton, *Mind and Emergence* (Oxford: Oxford University Press, 2005).

205. I explore the models of Divine mind and action in the following: "Emergent-Theism(s), Alternative and Inexplicable: Bringing Cartesian Theism Back into Science and Religion," *European Journal of Science and Theology*, vol. 15, no. 2 (April 2019), 39-53.

206. See Joanna Leidenhag, "A critique of emergent theologies," *Zygon*, vol. 51, issue 4 (2016), pp. 867-882.

207. William Hasker is one specific example of this who we will look at in detail later.

208. See Timothy O'Connor, *Persons and Causes* (Oxford: Oxford University Press, 2000). Also see Timothy O'Connor and Jonathan D. Jacobs in, "Emergent Individuals," *Philosophical Quarterly* 53:540-555. See William Hasker, *The Emergent Self* (Ithaca: Cornell University Press, 1999).

209. Several recent Cartesian views seem to move in the direction of affirming that the soul has some intrinsic relationship to its body. See for example Richard Swinburne, *The Evolution of the Soul* (Oxford: Oxford University Press, 1997), especially chapter 7. It may be clearer that the soul has no essential relationship to its body, but I am not sure that it has no intrinsic relationship.

210. See William Hasker, "Souls Beastly and Human," in *The Soul Hypothesis*, ed. by Mark Baker and Stewart Goetz (New York: T&T Clark, 2011).

211. See William Hasker, "Is Materialism Equivalent to Dualism?" in *After Physicalism* ed. by Benedikt Paul Goecke (Notre Dame: Notre Dame University Press, 2012), 180-199.

212. In the present context, I use the terms "material" and "physical" interchangeably throughout, but one might distinguish the two terms where "material" refers to substantially real entities and "physical" refers to that which may be real but is not substantial.

213. For the most sophisticated defence of reductive physicalism see Jaegwon Kim, *Physicalism, or Something Near Enough* (Princeton: Princeton University Press, 2007). In it, Kim works through Smart's type identity thesis and Davidsonian's token identity thesis. While Behaviorism is largely off the table for consideration, token identity is still present. Kim is convinced that we can have reductive physicalism apart from reducing *qualia*.

214. I use the terms 'mind,' 'soul,' and 'person' interchangeably throughout the article.

215. Richard Swinburne works with a similar definition of souls. See his *Mind, Brain, and Free Will* (Oxford: Oxford University Press, 2013), pp. 100-125.

216. There is a growing body of literature defending mind-body dualism (which might include variants of property dualism) and substance dualism. For a sampling of substance dualism see the following: Charles Taliaferro, *Consciousness and the Mind of God* (Cambridge: Cambridge University Press, 2004); David Lund, *Conscious Self: The Immaterial Center of Subjective States* (New York: Humanity Books, 2005); Richard Swinburne, *Mind, Brain, and Free Will* (Oxford: Oxford University Press, 2013); Andrea Lavazza and Howard Robinson (eds.), *Contemporary Dualism: A Defense* (New York: Routledge, 2014).

217. Again see, "Is Materialism Equivalent to Dualism?"

218. J.P. Moreland supports this view in his, *Consciousness and*

the Existence of God (New York: Routledge, 2008), pp. 77-78. Also see a response by Joshua Johnson, "In Defense of Emergent Individuals," *Faith and Philosophy*, vol. 31, no. 1 (2014): pp. 91-104. Johnson argues for a qualified materialism.

219. William Hasker, *The Emergent Self*, p. 189.
220. Again see O'Connor and Jacobs, "Emergent Individuals."
221. Materialism or physicalism, which I am using interchangeably in this context, is the view that everything is physical in nature or supervenes on the physical, including humans (locally). See Stoljar, Daniel, "Physicalism," *The Stanford Encyclopedia of Philosophy* (Spring 2015 Edition), Edward N. Zalta (ed.), URL = <http://plato.stanford.edu/archives/spr2015/entries/physicalism/> [accessed on January 20, 2016]. Often there is an assumption or an explicit affirmation that to be physical is for things in the world to exist as or supervene on the physical, which exists in a closed system. But, when we begin talking about *novel* emergent properties it is debatable whether we are talking about materialism or something distinct that is something else potentially. Hasker makes a similar point in "Is Materialism Equivalent to Dualism," p. 185.
222. Ibid. 540.
223. Ibid. 540.
224. Ibid. 541-543.
225. See William Hasker, *The Emergent Self*, pp. 145-146. Hasker also states this in "Is Materialism Equivalent to Dualism," p. 191.
226. William Hasker, "Is Materialism Equivalent to Dualism?", see p. 190.
227. Hasker is right to point out that there is another option, namely, "dual-aspect theory." There is a "particulate" aspect, which includes the various parts and their interaction. Then, there is the "holistic" aspect that is able

to perceive. See Hasker on "Is Materialism Equivalent to Dualism?", p. 191.

228. Ibid. 196.

229. William Hasker, *The Emergent Self*, 188.

230. Ibid. 188.

231. Ibid. 189.

232. See specifically William Hasker, "Persons as Emergent Substances," in *Soul, Body, and Survival: Essays on the Metaphysics of Human Persons* (Ithaca: Cornell University Press, 2001), pp. 107-119.

233. Timothy O'Connor, "Causality, Mind, and Free Will," in *Action and Freedom*, ed. by James E. Tomberlin (Oxford: Blackwell Publishing, 2000), 110.

234. He offers three solutions, one of which he uses in his response, in his, *The Emergent Self*, pp. 201-202.

235. William Hasker, "Is Materialism Equivalent to Dualism?", p. 187.

236. For a notable authority, see Thomas Aquinas in his *Summa Theologica* 1a.q45. This is a subject deserving additional attention. In fact, distinguishing between an initial instant of creation, ongoing creation, and conservation (or, more radically, continuous creation) has become a discussion not of insignificant importance for the origin of the soul discussion nor of God's relationship to substances more generally. However, it is not entirely clear how one would distinguish between natural causes (i.e., second causes) and Divine causation in relation to them. So, the supposition that the material could be set up with the conditions for producing a mind is not necessarily controversial to several philosophers and theologians today. For a helpful survey of these sorts of issues, see Vander Laan, David, "Creation and Conservation," *The Stanford Encyclopedia of Philosophy* (Winter 2017 Edition), Edward N. Zalta (ed.), URL = <https://plato.stanford.edu/archives/win2017/entries/

creation-conservation/> [accessed on January 4, 2018].

237. The criticism may be that the creation of souls, in the context of emergence, yields overdetermination. However, this is not true unless we make two claims: 1. That God directly and immediately causes the soul to exist, and 2. The material causes the soul to emerge, i.e., the material produces the soul. The creationist need not commit to the second claim, but, instead, can show that souls depend upon brains and bodies, hence they bear a distinct kind of relation from the emergent relation. Even if one were to grant the two claims, there are, arguably, two options open to the creationist. The first is to accept the doctrine of occasionalism, which suggests that all material causes are manifestations of divine action. The second is to accept some form of transcendent causation, common to Thomists.

238. By things, most theists do not include "evil." According to most theists, "evil" is not a thing or a substance that can exist as a distinct kind of thing; instead it is ontologically dependent upon substance.

239. See Robert Adams, "Primitive Thisness and Primitive Identity," *The Journal of Philosophy* 76(1), p. 6.

240. See Lynne Rudder Baker, *Naturalism and the First-Person Perspective* (Oxford: Oxford University Press, 2013), pp. 180-181.

241. See Richard Swinburne, *Mind, Brain, and Free Will* (Oxford: Oxford University Press, 2013), pp. 33-38, pp. 150-151, pp. 164-165, p. 171 and p. 173.

242. Spelling out an argument for the conclusion that we do have haecceity in the sense described (contrasted with Baker and other monists) is the subject of another paper. Here, again, I am offering an exposition of Hasker's emergentism and surveying concerns with it.

243. Ibid. pp. 13-14, pp. 18-21.

244. Richard Swinburne, in a private conversation, confirmed

what I was thinking about this.

245. Hasker has stated in personal conversation that he does not assume we have the kind of haecceity described above. Instead, he accounts for the unique features of the mind based on the causal contributions (e.g., biological, social, conditioning), which shape each individual.

246. Richard Swinburne helped clarify the original intuition I had about the implication to Divine creationism.

247. This is a problem that Hasker raises in numerous places.

248. I am, once again, using 'soul' and 'mind' interchangeably. The argument here leans into the fact that the natural generation of souls, given the laws we have or as we understand them, would not be logically possible. It may be metaphysically possible if there was distinct kind of law, but these would be singularities, as we understand the laws of nature.

249. John Foster has developed an argument for theism based on this intuition that theology provides some explanatory resources that otherwise are not available from philosophy. See John Foster, "A Brief Defense of the Cartesian View," in *Soul, Body, and Survival: Essays on the Metaphysics of Human Persons* (Ithaca: Cornell University Press, 2001). Foster argues that Divine direct causation is necessary for the creation of the soul and the establishment of the soul with a body.

250. For a set of critiques of emergent materialism as a growing trend in Christian philosophy and theology, see R. Keith Loftin and Joshua R. Farris, *Christian Physicalism? Philosophical Theological Criticisms* (New York: Lexington, 2017). For a helpful exposition of variations of the emergence relation, first see John Searle, *The Rediscovery of the Mind* (Cambridge: MIT Press, 1992), pp. 111-112.

251. For one of the most sophisticated and developed versions of emergent substance dualism see William Hasker, *The*

Emergent Self (Ithaca: Cornell University Press, 2001). For a further, similar example, see E.J. Lowe, "Why My Body Is Not Me: The Unity Argument for Emergentist Self-Body Dualism," in *Contemporary Dualism: A Defense*, ed. by Andrea Lavazza and Howard Robinson (London: Routledge, 2014). There are important distinctions between these versions of emergent substance dualism, but an exposition of these two views would take us beyond the scope of the article.

252. I develop some variants of this view, in the following: Joshua R. Farris, "Emergent creationism: another option in the origin of the soul debate," in *Religious Studies*, vol. 50, issue 3 (September 2014), pp. 221-234. I originally worked it out with transcendent causality more clearly in view or as a version of property and power emergence. It seems to me, however, that this theory can be worked out as a version of emergence that is also creationist without situating it in transcendent causality, or a mere property emergence, and also without divine occasionalism. See also Joshua R. Farris, *The Soul of Theological Anthropology: A Cartesian Exploration* (New York: Routledge, 2017).

253. See Searle, *The Rediscovery of the Mind*, pp. 111-12. Also see Hasker's *The Emergent Self*.

254. Joshua R. Farris, "Considering Souls of the Past for today: Soul Origins, Anthropology, and Contemporary Theology," in *Neue Zeitschrift fur Systematische Theologie und Religionsphilosophie*, vol. 57, issue 3 (September 2015).

255. See Hasker, for one example, in his *The Emergent Self*. For a different view that has some of these benefits see Charles Taliaferro, *Consciousness and the Mind of God* (Cambridge: Cambridge University Press, 1994), pp. 114-122. For Taliaferro, the soul sees with the eyes, feels with fingers, and experiences the body in a way unmediated. However, there is a question as to the natural explanation for such an intimate relationship between mind and body. What is the

reason or law-like relation that establishes this interactive union between this body and this soul?

256. See Hasker, *The Emergent Self*, p. 189.

257. To assume a conventional view of the identity of material things is not necessary for the present argument, even if the present author is inclined in that way.

258. See Hasker, *The Emergent Self*, chapter 6. As stated, it does not seem to me that a defender of a Cartesian/creationist soul view must adopt the picture given by Hasker.

259. Both Swinburne and Lowe agree that persons could bear all the perceptibly same qualities, but remain numerically distinct. See Richard Swinburne, "How to determine which is the true theory of personal identity," in *Personal Identity: Complex or Simple?* edited by Georg Gasser and Matthias Stefan (Cambridge: Cambridge University Press, 2012). In the same collection, also see E.J. Lowe, "The probable simplicity of personal identity," in *Personal Identity: Complex or Simple?*, p. 149. Lowe helpfully states, "[I]t is strongly arguable that the only *adequate* criterion of identity for mental states and events will be one which makes reference to their subjects... [P]art of what makes an experience of *mine* numerically distinct from a qualitatively indistinguishable experience of *yours* is the very fact that it is *mine* as opposed to *yours*."

260. And, this would not be alleviated by relational properties because the fundamental property is what makes a person *that* person. One could run several other thought experiments to make the same point, e.g., the test case of identical twins. Also see Robert Merrihew Adams for similar thought experiments, "Primitive Thisness and Primitive Identity," in *The Journal of Philosophy*, vol. 76, No. 1 (January 1979), pp. 10-11.

261. This is something Hasker and other scientifically informed emergentists are willing to grant.

262. French, Steven, "Identity and Individuality in Quantum Theory," *The Stanford Encyclopedia of Philosophy* (Fall 2015 Edition), Edward N. Zalta (ed.), URL = <https://plato.stanford.edu/archives/fall2015/entries/qt-idind/> [cited on February 22, 2018]. The author makes it quite clear that there are non-haecceitic understandings and haecceitic, but the latter are not like the primitive mental view offered here.

263. For a similar argument see Richard Swinburne, "The argument from souls to God," *Religious Studies*, vol. 51, issue 3 (September 2015), especially pp. 303-05. I arrived at this argument independent from Swinburne, but he has helped me clarify it. Elsewhere, I work with the understanding of thisness, and concerns with rejecting it, advanced in the present article. See Joshua R. Farris, "Bodily-Constituted Persons, Soulish Persons, and the Imago Dei: The Problem from a Definite I," in *Philosophy and Theology*, vol. 28, issue 2 (2016), pp. 455-468. Also see Joshua R. Farris, "Creational Problems for Soul-Emergence from Matter: Philosophical and Theological Concerns."

264. I am not suggesting that we should allow the scientific consensus to constrain our theorizing in all cases, but it seems reasonable in this instance.

265. This gives me reason for thinking that souls are natural-kinds rather than relational souls, which, at least during embodiment, have certain constraints that souls might not have when disembodied.

266. Several other examples like the event-bumping my knee and the communication that occurs between the knee, C fibers in my brain, and the mental feeling of pain yield the same point.

267. Richard Swinburne, *The Evolution of the Soul* (Oxford: Oxford University Press, 1997), see especially chapter 10.

268. Hasker, *The Emergent Self*, p. 161.

269. Swinburne, *The Evolution of the Soul*, p. 177. It is not clear that Swinburne is decisive on this point.

270. Ibid. p. 197. Swinburne does raise this possibility, but, again, he is not definitive on this point. The tension could be resolved if one were, so to speak, to bring God's causal activity back into the physical process.

271. See once again Hasker, *The Emergent Self*, p. 161.

272. As suggested above, it is not necessary that we portray God as somehow adding from the outside. See Hasker, *The Emergent Self*. Hasker makes these and other related points in several places. See especially chapter 6. Also see, "Souls Beastly and Human" in *The Soul Hypothesis: Investigations into the Existence of the Soul*, ed. by Mark C. Baker and Stewart Goetz (New York: Bloomsbury, 2011).

273. I am following Hasker's use of Searle in *The Emergent Self*, pp. 175-77.

274. For an account that expands the emergentist options found in Hasker and Searle, see J.P. Moreland, *Consciousness and the Existence of God: A Theistic Argument* (New York: Routledge, 2008), especially pp. 53-70.
Abstract: I am grateful to William Hasker for his recent response to my work, especially his response to my "Souls, Emergent and Created: Why Mere Emergent Dualism is Insufficient," in his "Emergent Dualism and Emergent Creationism: A Response to Joshua Farris" in a previous volume of *Philosophia Christi* (20.1, 2018). In response to my article in *Philosophia Christi* 20.1, he spends more time on secondary issues rather than the central objection. I respond by showing that he gives no good reasons for denying the primitive particularity view and offers no alternative particularity account.

275. Joshua Farris, "Souls, Emergent and Created: Why Mere Emergent Dualism is Insufficient," *Philosophia Christi*, vol. 20, no. 1 (Summer 2018), pp. 83-93.

Abstract: I am grateful to William Hasker for his recent response to my work, especially his response to my "Souls, Emergent and Created: Why Mere Emergent Dualism is Insufficient," in his "Emergent Dualism and Emergent Creationism: A Response to Joshua Farris" in a previous volume of *Philosophia Christi* (20.1, 2018). In response to my article in *Philosophia Christi* 20.1, he spends more time on secondary issues rather than the central objection. I respond by developing the objection in light of creation ex-nihilo in view of his way out *via* panpsychism, and conclude by responding to his charge from Divine occasionalism.

276. At present, there is a vibrant and strong set of literature defending various traditional positions, or something near them, along with various upgraded contemporary variations of dualism. See for example: Andrea Lavazza and Howard Robinson (eds.), *Contemporary Dualism* (London: Routledge, 2016); Jonathan J. Loose, Angus J.L. Menuge, and J.P. Moreland (eds.), *Blackwell Companion to Substance Dualism* (New York: Blackwell Publishing, 2018); R. Keith Loftin and Joshua R. Farris (eds.), *Christian Physicalism?* (New York: Lexington Press, 2018).

277. See his move from talking about his own position as "emergentism" to "emergent dualism." Hasker, William (1982) "Emergentism," *Religious Studies* 18: 473-88. Hasker, William (1999) *The Emergent Self* (Ithaca: Cornell University Press).

278. Joshua R. Farris, "Creational Problems for Soul-Emergence From Matter: Philosophical and Theological Concerns," *Neue Zeitschrift fur Systematische Theologie und Religionsphilosophie*, vol. 60, issue 3 (Fall 2018), pp. 406-427. Also see, Timothy O'Connor, "Causality, Mind, and Free Will," in *Action and Freedom*, ed. by James E. Tomberlin (Oxford: Blackwell Publishing, 2000), p. 110.

279. Joshua Farris, "Souls, Emergent and Created: Why Mere

Emergent Dualism is Insufficient," *Philosophia Christi*, vol. 20, no. 1 (Summer 2018), pp. 83-93.

280. The objection applies not only to Hasker's version of emergence (i.e., where the mind is a unified phenomenal field), but to many other variations of emergent substance dualism and non-reductive physicalisms.

281. I leave open the possibility that this could come about by chance from laws, but I am not convinced that the biological conditions would ever be sufficient as a proximate cause for the particularity that seems present to mental substances.

282. C. Stephen Evans, "Separable Souls: Dualism, Selfhood, and the Possibility of Life After Death," *Christian Scholar's Review* 34 (2005): 327-40, 333-34.

283. It is unsurprising that there would be these discontinuities from a Christian perspective of humans as created in the image of God. Thomists, like Moreland, can account for this discontinuity quite easily with their belief in three different kinds of souls (e.g., plant souls, animal souls, and rational souls).

284. William Hasker, "What Has CERN to do with Jerusalem?" *Philosophia Christi*, vol. 20, no. 1 (2018), pp. 58-9. For a philosophically sophisticated scientific critique of materialism, generally, see: Angus Menuge, *Agents Under Fire: Materialism and the Rationality of Science* (Lexington: Rowman & Littlefield Publishers, 2004).

285. I point this out in, Joshua R. Farris, "Creational Problems for Soul-Emergence From Matter: Philosophical and Theological Concerns," *Neue Zeitschrift fur Systematische Theologie und Religionsphilosophie*, vol. 60, issue 3 (Fall 2018), pp. 406-427.

286. William Hasker, "What Has CERN to Do with Jerusalem?", pp. 58-9. In passing, it is concerning that Hasker would make this move because panpsychism is confronted with a similar combinatorial problem—similar to the

combinatorial problem for materialism's inability to account for a single, unified consciousness. For a recent exploration of this problem for panpsychism, see: David Chalmers, "The Combination Problem for Panpsychism," *Panpsychism*, ed. by Ludwig Jaskolla and Godehard Brüntrup (Oxford: Oxford University Press, 2018).

287. Hasker, "What Has CERN to Do with Jerusalem?", pp. 58-9.

288. Joshua R. Farris, "Creational Problems for Soul Emergence from Matter."

289. Thanks to Angus Menuge for suggesting this.

290. In the previous article, I lay out some reasons for rejecting hylomorphism. I will not rehearse those here because Hasker does not accept a hylomorphic view of matter. That said, the original argument I raised to emerging subjects in a lawful manner would seem to be excluded because of the fact that minds have primitive particularity. Accepting hylomorphism of individual minds requires that one adopts a view of the material world and laws that problematize the physical sciences.

291. Hasker, "Emergent Dualism and Emergent Creationism: A Response to Joshua Farris," *Philosophia Christi*, vol. 20, no. 1 (Summer 2018), pp. 93-101.

292. E. Callaway, "Soapy taste of coriander linked to genetic variants," *Nature: International weekly journal of science* (September 12, 2012). https://www.nature.com/news/soapy-taste-of-coriander-linked-to-genetic-variants-1.11398 [accessed on July 31, 2018].

293. E.J. Lowe, "The probable simplicity of personal identity." In *Personal Identity: Complex or Simple?* edited by Georg Gasser and Matthias Stefan, 137-155 (Cambridge: Cambridge University Press, 2012), 149.

294. See William Hasker, "The Need for Thisnesses: Swinburne on Souls," *Philosophia Christi*, vol. 23, issue 1 (2021), see

especially 171-172.

295. There are different variants of emergentism that work out the constitution of minds differently, but the originative process is similar. All of them are motivated by an underlying commitment to a physicalist ontology along with its commitment to mental origins precipitated by regular lawful processes. See, for example: Lynne Rudder Baker 2013; Timothy O'Connor and Jonathan Jacobs 2003; E.J. Lowe 2012; William Hasker 1999; Eric LaRock 2013. Hasker's view differs from Lowe in that his articulation of mental substance includes a phenomenal unity rather than an object unity. The present argument moves in the direction of establishing that a naturally emergent soul, without direct agential causation, would be a metaphysical impossibility because even perfect duplicates (with all the same properties) would fail to establish identity. Whether there could be perfect duplicates in distinct possible worlds is an open question on my view, but it would still not establish the fact of identity between two modally distinct individuals with all the same empirical verified properties.

296. These particulars are either material particulars (emergent materialism or emergent individualism) or immaterial/ mental particulars (emergent dualism). Concrete particulars are often construed as impure insofar as it is a thing or substance that enters into a relation, instantiates properties, or enters into the exemplification of a property. See Robert Garcia, "Bare Particulars and Constituent Ontology." According to Robert Garcia, in his interesting paper on bare particulars, he argues that its primary role is individuation. Garcia is working from Michael Loux's definition of substance and J.P. Moreland's modification to Loux when replacing "substance" with "particular." See: Michael Loux 1978; and J.P. Moreland 2000. This may be correct, but it seems that it fails to give an account of

what a bare particular is apart from its properties. In other words, bare particulars according to this account only do something, namely individuation, but this does not tell us what they are. In the case of individual essences, they are either understood in terms of properties (as qualities) and relations or as bare particulars, but without some account of what those bare particulars are we are left with an insufficient account or inexplicable account of those bare particulars apart from their properties. I spell out some of these issues in more analytic detail, in: "Creationist-Dualism," *The Origin of the Soul: A Conversation* ed. by Joshua R. Farris and Joanna Leidenhag (New York: Routledge, forthcoming 2022).

297. Joshua R. Farris, "Creational Problems for Soul-Emergence from Matter: Philosophical and Theological Concerns," *Neue Zeitschrift für Systematische Theologie und Religionsphilosophie*, Volume 60, Issue 3 (2018a), 406-427. This is a fairly novel argument in that very little has been advanced which fleshes out the intuition that emergentism, with its regular lawful pattern, would give rise to particularity rather than a generic consciousness. He raises the important question of how the emergentist grounds the particularity of consciousness. Why not a monopsychism? Nathan Jacobs thoughtfully, yet initially, raises this concern in his defense of a version of hylomorphism. In private correspondence, Jacobs confirmed that our intuitions are similar and that I have significantly developed this important intuition.

298. This is a common way to refer to alternative versions of mind-body dualism in the literature. Both Farris and Hasker refer to them in this way. See Hasker 1999, p. x, p. 171, p. 188, p. 194, pp. 196-7, p. 202, p. 206, p. 208, p. 240. Hasker is one example who uses the term "traditional" to refer to Cartesianism and Aristotelianism or Thomism because these versions do not utilize the resources of novel

emergent properties and substances in contemporary philosophy of mind. One could use the term "classical." Hasker, in these places and others, often refers to traditional substance dualism as creationist. Granted, there are traducianist options that could be considered traditional, but the majority view in Church history is the creationist view. Further, traducianism, as traditionally construed, is creationist in some refined sense. On traditional traducianism, God creates at least one if not two souls (namely, the first human or the first human pair). There is a more obscure view called the pre-existence theory, which would be considered "traditional" but this is a minority report in the history of religious thought and is certainly a minority report today.

299. Thomas Nagel, *Mind and Cosmos: Why the Materialist Neo-Darwinian Conception of Nature is Almost Certainly False* (Oxford: Oxford University Press, 2012).

300. E. Callaway, "Soapy taste of coriander linked to genetic variants," *Nature: International weekly journal of science* (September 12, 2012). https://www.nature.com/news/soapy-taste-of-coriander-linked-to- genetic-variants-1.11398 [accessed on July 31, 2018].

301. E.J. Lowe, "The probable simplicity of personal identity," in *Personal Identity: Complex or Simple?* edited by Georg Gasser and Matthias Stefan (Cambridge: Cambridge University Press, 2012).
    – "Why My Body Is Not Me: The Unity Argument for Emergentist Self-Body Dualism," in *Contemporary Dualism: A Defense*, ed. Andrea Lavazza and Howard Robinson (London: Routledge, 2014).

302. For the sake of the argument, I am not interested in parsing out the principle property that characterizes minds. A Cartesian view, following an intellectualist or rationalist view, says that my mind, i.e., 'I,' just am a 'thinking thing.'

A Berkeleyan view, or an empiricist view, says that my mind, i.e., 'I,' just am an experiencing and acting thing that has phenomenal experiences. But, this should not deter us here. For the argument at present is for the thing in question as a countable mental substance and could fit with either a Cartesian or a Berkeleyan understanding.

303. While emergentists and panpsychists generally reject hylomorphism, there is an argument to be made that lawfully emerging subjects would seem to be excluded because of the fact that minds have primitive particularity and not a complex particularity. Accepting hylomorphism of individual minds requires that one adopts a view of the physical world and its laws that problematize the physical sciences.

304. Steven French, "Identity and Individuality in Quantum Theory" (2019), *Stanford Encyclopedia of Philosophy*, Edward N. Zalta (ed.), https://plato.stanford.edu/archives/fall2015/entries/qt-idind/ [accessed July 4, 2019].

305. Ibid.

306. John W. Carroll, "Laws of Nature" (2016), *The Stanford Encyclopedia of Philosophy*. Edward N. Zalta (ed.), URL = <https://plato.stanford.edu/archives/fall2016/entries/laws-of-nature/> [accessed on January 28, 2019].

307. Ironically, while Hasker rejects an Aristotelian conception of matter and matter-form compounds, he does utilize a similar solution to the problem of what it is that individuates or particularizes the mind. See Hasker 2019. Interestingly, he asserts that he would be the same person in other possible worlds, would be this soul because of this body, yet as we have seen the body too is generated and does not seem to supply a metaphysical explanation as Hasker asserts. This is merely an epistemic individuator not a metaphysical individuator.

308. Richard Swinburne, *Mind, Brain, and Free Will* (Oxford:

Oxford University Press, 2013), 35.

309. Ibid. 31.

310. Lynne Rudder Baker, *Naturalism and the First-Person Perspective* (Cambridge: Cambridge University Press, 2013), pp. 5-15.

—. "Swinburne on Substance Dualism," *European Journal of Philosophy of Religion*, vol. 6, issue 2 (2014), 5-15.

311. Max Black, "The Identity of Indiscernibles," *Mind*, 61 (1952), 153-64.

Godehard Brüntrup, "Emergent Panpsychism," *Panpsychism: Contemporary Perspectives* (Oxford: Oxford University Press, 2016).

312. Alexander Pruss, *The Principle of Sufficient Reason: A Reassessment* (Cambridge: Cambridge University Press, 2007), 161.

313. Ibid. 162.

314. Op Cit. Farris 2018a; Farris 2018b.

315. It is worth pointing out that most philosophically inclined scientists and quantum physicists reject the notion that material particles are fundamentally haecceities, and for good reason. French makes it quite clear that the non-haecceity understanding of physical particles is the dominant position, but even if particles are carriers of haecceity they do not carry the same kind of haecceity described in the present article. Aristotelianism would raise doubts about the way that scientists practice science today because of skepticism about the underlying ontology regarding physical things as generalizable events.

316. William Hasker, "Is Materialism Equivalent to Dualism?" *After Physicalism* ed. by Benedikt Paul Goecke (Notre Dame: Notre Dame University Press, 2012).

317. See O'Connor and Jacobs 2003, 540-55; Hasker 2012, 108-99.

318. William Hasker, "Emergent Dualism and Emergent

Creationism: A Response to Joshua Farris," *Philosophia Christi* 20:1 (2018b), 58-9.

–. Hasker in: "Souls without Thisnesses: A Rejoinder to Joshua Farris," in the *Philosophy of Theological Anthropology* web project for the Evangelical Philosophical Society (2019).

–. *The Emergent Self* (Ithaca: Cornell University Press, 2001).

–. "What Has CERN to do with Jerusalem?" *Philosophia Christi*, vol. 20, no. 1 (2018a).

319. See Hasker (2018b), 58-9; and Chalmers, David, "The Combination Problem for Panpsychism," *Panpsychism*, ed. by Ludwig Jaskolla and Godehard Brüntrup (Oxford: Oxford University Press, 2018).

320. The author makes it quite clear that there is no sense in which the physical particles have a primitive thisness in the way that minds do. And, in fact, most philosophers of science deny thisness to particles. Also see Bruce L. Gordon 2002.

321. This thought experiment certainly raises a deeper metaphysical concern about the relationship between natural laws and haecceities in the literature. In many ways, there has been an underlying assumption that natural laws could bring about thisness of individuals, but it is not clear that there is an explanation for this metaphysical feature on many accounts. However, the fundamental question is whether you can get something from nothing (i.e., a haecceity from a non-haecceity). If you cannot, then we must presume that underlying physical particles are carriers of individual thisness, and can give rise to more complex combinations of those thisnesses.

What counts as a sufficient level of neural complexity is not clear on an emergentist account, but promoting the plausibility of the theory does not absolutely depend on providing a clear account of the 'complex' criterion.

322. For a philosophically sophisticated scientific critique of materialism, generally, see: Angus Menuge 2004.

323. In passing, it is concerning that Hasker would make this move because panpsychism is confronted with a similar combinatorial problem—similar to the combinatorial problem for materialism's inability to account for a single, unified consciousness. See Godehard Brüntrup 2016. It seems that Hasker would likely opt for a "nonconstitutive panpsychism," as "emergent panpsychism" as Brüntrup has defined these views. Such a view assumes the reality of downward causation, which may presume a substance (presumably a substance similar to the kind of substance on emergent monism or emergent materialism). This is distinct from "constitutive panpsychism," which is the view that the higher-order mind comes to exist within a physical framework, assuming naturalism (i.e., causal closure of the universe), and is composed by the lower-level experiencings or mind-lets. The problem for Hasker is that it is not clear that he avoids physical creation ex-nihilo because he affirms that a novel substance emerges from a higher-order physical and neural structure. Panpsychism helps him avoid the consequent of physical creation ex-nihilo if he affirms a constitutive panpsychism, but this would amount to an affirmation of the causal closure, naturalism, and the apparent combinatorial problem. It may even entail that the higher-order mind experiences in light of the lower-level mind-lets and experiences by way of the lower-level mind-lets. By assuming a nonconstitutive panpsychism, Hasker can avoid causal closure and affirm a more robust form of agency, but by doing this it seems that his emergentism might entail a novel substance emerging. If this is the case, then his view parallels the physical creation ex-nihilo emergentism. The only difference is how he is construing the underlying metaphysics of physicality (i.e.,

physicality is experiencing or disposed to an experiencing subject under certain conditions not non-experiencing).

324. On this important point, it is unclear if the emergent dualist is concerned with a metaphysical thesis of individuation or merely an epistemic thesis. There are two routes. One, the emergent dualist can opt for the body as the individuator of the soul, but this seems to amount to an epistemic thesis because what we have available to us are empirical, public properties and not an intrinsic whatness that makes me me. Two, the emergent dualist can opt for the brute particularity view, but it is unclear if s/he is endorsing a metaphysical thesis or epistemic thesis.

325. Thank you to Jim Spiegel, S. Mark Hamilton, and J.J. Snodgrass for helpful comments on an earlier draft of the article version. A special thanks to the blind reviewers for help on several items.

326. Chalcedon provides initial support for this. See Donald Fairbairn and Ryan M. Reeves, *The Story of Creeds and Confessions* (Grand Rapids: Baker Academic, 2019), 80-109. The language is reflected in the statement "reasonable soul and body." Granted the language used reflects Aristotelian language and categories, but I think it would be a stretch to suggest that the language of the framers should be presumed as dogmatic and authoritatively binding.

327. Catholic Church, *Catechism of the Catholic Church: Revised in Accordance with the Official Latin Text Promulgated by Pope John Paul II* (Vatican City: Libreria Editrice Vaticana, 1997), 1021 and 1022. The texts use the following language to refer to the immaterial part: "Each man receives his eternal retribution in his immortal soul at the very moment of his death."

328. Charles Hodge, *Systematic Theology Volume 3* (Hendrickson, 1981).

329. Dolf te Velde (ed.), *Synopsis of a Purer Theology*, vol. 1,

disputations 1-23 (Leiden: Brill, 2015), 407-9, 509, 513. This was the common teaching, even dogmatic teaching of traditional Christian theology, and the Reformed theological tradition did not depart from it. Although, they departed on the particulars of what occurred during the intermediate state.

330. G.I. Williamson (ed.), *Westminster Confession of Faith* (Phillipsburg: P&R Publishing, 2004), 32.1. While Reformed churches (and traditional Anglican churches for that matter) work with a confessional ecclesiology, the Westminster Confession is one important symbol that codifies enduring and binding teachings in many church denominations. Even if it is not binding, as articulated above, it reflects a conciliar consensus of a core of dogma that is binding on all Reformed Christians.

331. And, this is precisely what Thomas Aquinas develops in his commentary on 2 Corinthians 5. See Thomas Aquinas, *Commentary on the Letters of Saint Paul volume 38* (Emmaus Academic, 2012).

332. Charles Taliaferro, "Human Nature, Personal Identity, and Eschatology," *The Oxford Handbook of Eschatology*, see 539.

333. Alvin Plantinga famously develops this argument in his: "Against Materialism," in Michael Rea (ed.), *Oxford Readings in Philosophical Theology Volume II* (Oxford: Oxford University Press, 2009), 387-91.

334. Stephen Yates, *Between Death and Resurrection: A Critical Response to Recent Catholic Debate Concerning the Intermediate State* (London: Bloomsbury, 2018), 189.

335. René Descartes, *Discourse on Method and Meditations in First Philosophy* (Indianapolis: Hackett Publishing Company, 1998), 32 and 54.

336. The above thinking is not intended to convey that other animals are not persons.

337. Olson, *What Are We? A Study in Personal Ontology* (Oxford:

Oxford University Press, 2007), 29-39. Also see: Blatti, Stephan, "Animalism," *The Stanford Encyclopedia of Philosophy* (Fall 2019 Edition), Edward N. Zalta (ed.), URL = <https://plato.stanford.edu/archives/fall2019/entries/animalism/> [accessed on March 17, 2020].

338. See Peter van Inwagen, *Material Beings* (Ithaca: Cornell University Press, 1995), 185.

339. The challenge for a constitutional view of persons is that there is at least one property that makes thinking (and the continuity of thinking) dependent on a particular kind of substance is apparent. When combined with another essential feature of the constitutional view of persons I am not properly speaking a substance yields an unusual view.

340. See Susan Schneider, "Non-Reductive Physicalism and the Mind Problem," *Nous*, vol. 47, issue 1 (2013), 135-53. On non-reductive physicalism, defenders would grant that I am the kind of thing that thinks. Further non-reductive physicalists would not assume that these psychological properties are neither identical to the underlying physical properties nor are they reducible to those parts. Although, they must grant that the psychological being is the whole being that includes the physical (possibly the brain) that includes non-reducible mental properties. The problem as Susan Schneider points out is that on all the contemporary views of substance (i.e., the bundle theory or the substratum theory), the non-reductive view is inconsistent with them and unsupportable by our contemporary views of substance.

341. See J.P. Moreland, *Consciousness and the Existence of God: A Theistic Argument* (New York: Routledge Press, 2009), 39-41. Moreland is drawing from Roderick Chisholm, *Theory of Knowledge* (Englewood Cliff: Prentice-Hall, 1989), 19.

342. Animalists might be able to account for this if they can account for wholes. There are some obvious challenges for

the physicalist animalist that I have already touched on. There are fewer challenges on hylomorphist and Thomist versions of Animalism.

343. Howard Robinson, "Naturalism and the Unavoidability of the Cartesian Perspective," *Contemporary Dualism* ed. by Andrea Lavazza and Howard Robinson (London: Routledge, 2016), 154-71. Robinson argues that the Cartesian cogito perspective is required. While Robinson argues for a distinctive ontology of minds as wholly distinct from naturalistic physicalism, he does not go so far as to define what minds are as individuals—something implicit in Cartesianism. Also see Richard Swinburne, "What Makes Me Me? A Defense of Substance Dualism," in the same volume on pages 139-54.

344. St. Thomas Aquinas, *Summa Contra Gentiles* (Notre Dame: University of Notre Dame, 1976), 2.57.1330.

345. St. Thomas Aquinas, *Commentary on the Letters of Saint Paul: Complete Set* (Emmaus Academic, 2012), *I Cor.* 15.2. 924.

346. I take these two technical terms as nearly synonymous, but one might argue that one could be an extinctionist that suggests that the human nature, and the person, does not survive only to come back into existence when the soul-form informs matter once again at the resurrection. On corruptionism, the view is that a soul persists but the person (or the whole substance) does not persist—i.e., survive.

347. J.T. Turner takes a different approach outside of the parameters of traditional conceptions of human personhood. He rejects the doctrine of the disembodied intermediate state altogether in his provocative work, *On the Resurrection of the Dead: A New Metaphysics of Afterlife for Christian Thought* (New York: Routledge, 2018). He argues for a coherent Thomist alternative by defending a version of immediate resurrection rather accounting for

survival *via* the soul between somatic death and somatic resurrection.

348. I will not address these revisionist exercises in this article.

349. Robert Pasnau, *Thomas Aquinas on Human Nature* (Cambridge: Cambridge University Press, 2001), 383.

350. The second option deserves further explanation as a potential option if we say that the soul carries with it a contingent particularity by way of being impressed by the body during original embodiment. While this does not account for the primitive particularity that I have argued is present as a property (or feature) of soul, it may provide an avenue for thinking that a particular soul in fact persists during disembodiment, but such a soul is subject to the problem that particularity is a contingent feature and not an essential feature of persons and could be otherwise. Additionally, it raises the question as to the possibility of a reduplicatable particularity that is applied to what are otherwise distinct souls distinguished only relatively by their spatial occupations. Undoubtedly, there is another concern that I cannot explore in any detail here and that is that without the body providing the sense perceptual data, how it is that humans will arrive at a knowledge of God.

351. *Between Death and Resurrection*, 189.

352. It is worth noting that nearly all Cartesian accounts today could affirm that the disembodied state is an impoverished state in the sense that Cartesian souls are diminished in their capacity and the controls available to them. If by Platonic, Yates takes it that the disembodied state is essentially a state of "ontological and epistemic liberation" then one could arrive at the conclusion that Platonism is unpalatable, but nothing in Cartesianism yields this unattractive feature.

353. Tim Pawl makes this move in his, *In Defense of Conciliar Christology* (Oxford: Oxford University Press, 2016), 32.

354. This is one way that some have made sense of transubstantiation on hylomorphism. That said, I am not suggesting this is the only way to make sense of transubstantiation.

355. Edward Feser, "Aquinas on the Human Soul," *The Blackwell Companion to Substance Dualism*, ed. by Jonathan J. Loose, Angus J.L. Menuge, and J.P. Moreland (London: Blackwell Publishers, 2018), 88-102.

356. Charles Taliaferro, "Physicalism and the Death of Christ," in *Christian Physicalism?* ed. by R. Keith Loftin and Joshua R. Farris (Lexington: Lexington Press, 2018), 183-4.

357. Jeffrey Brower, *Aquinas's Ontology of the Material World: Change, Hylomorphism, and Material Objects* (Oxford: Oxford University Press, 2014), 297-299.

358. Joshua R. Farris, *The Soul of Theological Anthropology* (New York: Routledge, 2017), 76-96.

359. Thank you to Andrew Hollingsworth, Lloyd Dunaway, Matthew Levering, and J.T. Turner for reading and commenting on a previous draft.

360. See Joshua R. Farris, "Cartesianizing Idealism," *Routledge Handbook to Idealism and Immaterialism* ed. by Joshua R. Farris and Benedikt Paul Goecke (New York: Routledge, 2021). Also see Chad McIntosh, "Idealism and Common Sense" in the same volume.

361. Drawn from Bruce L. Gordon, "How Does the Intelligibility of Nature Point to Design?" in, *The Comprehensive Guide to Science and Faith: Exploring the Ultimate Questions About Life and the Cosmos* (Eugene: Harvest House Publishers, 2021), 253-267.

362. It is important to note that this view does not entail or yield "vitalism," the view that the soul is the life of the body. I have not introduced this term here because it is not directly relevant to my argument, but it is important to point out given that other Creationist views do yield

such a view. See William Hasker, "Souls Beastly and Human," *The Soul Hypothesis* ed. by Mark C. Baker and Stewart Goetz (New York: T&T Clark, 2011), pp. 202-221. Here Hasker raises the problem of vitalism. See Hasker, as well, in, "The Dialectic of Soul and Body," *Contemporary Dualism* ed. by Andrea Lavazza and Howard Robinson (New York: Routledge, 2014), pp. 204-219. He addresses two versions of Thomistic dualism that are creationist and emergentist. They are emergentist in an inverse way compared to Hasker's view. Also, "Why Emergence?", in *The Ashgate Research Companion to Theological Anthropology* ed. by Joshua R. Farris and Charles Taliaferro (Aldershot: Ashgate, 2015), pp. 151-164.

363. Richard Swinburne, "What is so good about having a body?" in *Comparative Theology* (London: SPCK, 2003), p. 137.

364. Swinburne uses this analogy as well. Richard Swinburne, *The Evolution of the Soul* (Oxford: Oxford University Press, 1997), 174-175.

365. This is not the same as claiming that there are two causes for one effect, but, instead, the body activates and provides additional controls for which the soul can act. Similar to Hasker's famous example from the magnet and the magnetic field, it is arguable that there are two substances bearing distinct properties. On a creationist view, the brain does not causally produce the soul, as seems to be the case with the magnet and its field.

366. For a useful piece of literature on this see Robert Koons, *Realism Regained* (Oxford: OUP, 2000), 16.2. The experience we have embodied provides some evidence for our soul's having teleo-functions. For some helpful suggestive reflections see Frank C. Dilley in "Taking consciousness seriously: A defence of Cartesian dualism," *International Journal for Philosophy of Religion*, Vol. 55, No. 3 (June 2004),

149.

367. One response is to say that it is simply by divine design. Alternatively, one might see the brain and soul as tied together. The brain could have the power of activating or attracting the soul to itself.

368. Patrick Lee and Robert P. George, *Body-Self Dualism in Contemporary Ethics and Politics* (New York: Cambridge University Press, 2008), p. 71.

369. Kathryn Tanner, *God and Creation in Christian Theology* (Minneapolis: Fortress Press, 2005), p. 63.

370. See Hasker, *The Emergent Self*, pp. 195-196. Also see Brian Leftow, "Souls Dipped in Dust," in *Soul, Body, and Survival*, ed. by Kevin Corcoran (Ithaca: Cornell University Press, 2001), p. 128.

371. Charles Taliaferro, "Why idealism makes for a better default position than physicalism," *Routledge Handbook of Idealism and Immaterialism*, ed. by Joshua R. Farris and Benedikt Paul Goecke (New York: Routledge, 2021). Also see his treatment of theistic dualism, which is a form of theistic epistemic idealism, here: "Emergentism and Consciousness," *Soul, Body, and Survival*, ed. by Kevin Corcoran (Ithaca: Cornell University Press, 2001).

372. Bruce L. Gordon advances compelling arguments for this sort of Quantum theistic idealism in several places that yield metaphysical idealism. See Bruce L. Gordon, "Idealism and Science: the quantum-theoretic and scientific foundations of reality," *Routledge Handbook of Idealism and Immaterialism* ed. by Joshua R. Farris and Benedikt Paul Goecke (New York: Routledge, 2021); "The Incompatibility of Physicalism with Physics," *Christian Physicalism?* ed. by R. Keith Loftin and Joshua R. Farris (Lexington: Lexington Press, 2017); "Constrained Integration View," *Christianity and Science* ed. by Paul Copan and Christopher L. Reese (Grand Rapids: Zondervan, 2021).

373. I advance an argument from natural theology for the viability of the relation between the Divine mind and the human mind as a datum of common sense that provides a fitting grid for our phenomenological readings of Scripture in: "Discovering God and Soul: A Reappraisal of and Appreciation for Cartesian Natural Theology," *Philosophia Christi*, vol. 16, no. 1 (2014), 37-55. In a distinct, but powerful, way and without arguing for Cartesianism (although his understanding of the core is similar), J.P. Moreland develops the common-sense or natural relationship between souls and God in his, *Consciousness and the Existence of God* (New York: Routledge, 2008), see specifically 32-37, 158. For a deep dive into this as it pertains to the science and theology discussions, see: Scott D.G. Ventureyra, *On the Origin of Consciousness: An Exploration through the Lens of the Christian Conception of God and Creation* (Eugene: Wipf & Stock, 2018).

374. See Bernardo Kastrup, "Could Multiple Personality Disorder Explain Life, the Universe and Everything?" in *Science Ideated* (Washington: Iff Publishers, 2021), 105-106. Also see his fuller treatment and defense of this position in his, *The Idea of the World* (Winchester: Iff Publishers, 2019). For a radical, albeit consistent, alternative naturalist view of the world that is being criticized throughout *The Creation of Self* see Yuval Noah Harari, *Sapiens: A Brief History of Humankind* (New York: Harper, 2015).

375. Sam Harris, "Our Narrow Definition of 'Science,'" in *This Idea Must Die: Scientific Theories that are Blocking Progress* (New York: Harper Perennial, 2015), 138.

376. Jerry Coyne, "Free Will," *This Idea Must Die*, 156.

377. Bruce Hood, "The Self," *This Idea Must Die*, 147-148.

Index

access argument 24, 29, 30, 35-44, 63-7, 75, 77
anti-science 20, 186, 195, 230-36
animalism 38
authority, argument from 45-6, 53-7, 59

Bacon, Francis 7, 105
Baker, Lynne Rudder
Constitution view of Persons 46, 119, 129, 175, 189
Bohm 180
behaviorism 117, 151, 278
Bloom, Paul 12, 57, 59, 250, 260
bundle/binding, problem 30-44, 66, 98

Callaway
Coriander and phenomenal qualia 5, 159, 168-69, 172, 183, 261
Chalmers, David 5, 79, 183, 261
Cognitive science, dualism 2, 12, 26, 238
creatio ex-nihilo 88

Descartes, Renes 65, 67
design 240
designator
Epistemic 163, 165, 166
Metaphysical 129, 131, 133, 137, 163, 165, 166, 173, 184

gap issue 79, 81, 82, 182
informative 130, 160
non-rigid 130
rigid 130
sufficient 18, 129, 130, 132, 163, 172, 182, 184, 174
dualism in science
cognitive science 238
fallacies 15
methodological constraints 107, 230, 243
methodological naturalism 230, 232, 234
neuroscience 11, 26, 54, 56, 60, 143
paradigm action 91, 106, 109, 145, 221, 238
regular process/singularity 91, 105, 109, 236, 239

Eccles, Sir John 54,
eliminativism 26
emergent-individualism
problems
thisness 112, 115
qualia 128-29
binding 121

Foster, John 5, 28, 74, 75, 76, 96
French
Quantum Physics 172

God-world relationship
  cosmopsychism 114, 227
Darwinian 18, 111-2, 213
  deterministic 105, 140-1, 155,
  171, 173, 174
  monism 114, 210, 226, 227,
  naturalism ii, 9, 10, 12, 15,
  87, 210, 213, 230, 234

Hasker, William 22, 90, 121,
  126, 127, 146-58, 154, 161, 183,
  213
hylomorphism 82, 201-2, 256-9

introspective knowledge 75-6
indivisibility, self
  conceptual 58, 256
  metaphysical 58, 256

Jackson, Frank 30, 61

knowledge argument, the
  first-person 36, 74, 109, 114,
  122, 218
  third-person 24, 32, 36, 64, 89,
  116, 164,
Kripke, Saul 28-9

Lowe, E.J. 79, 159, 168
Lund, David 5

Madell, Geoffrey 79-81
Mere emergent dualism 99-101
Midgley, Mary 105, 110

modal argument 37, 189, 191
Murphy, Nancey 15, 45, 54, 107
Musolino, Julien 11

neo-Cartesianism 61-81

'obscure' dualisms 73-4
O'Connor, Timothy 110
origins, souls
  complex creation 221
simple creation 99
emergent 221
  soul-stuff 100
traducian 92-100
panpsychism 82

pain, problem 26-7
particularity
  bare 98-9, 166
brute 98, 172-3, 178
  complex 115, 133-5, 141, 170-3
explanatory 165
primitive 156, 178, 183-4
sufficiency 156
Perfect duplicate argument
  personal identity 168
  biological evolution 172-5
  materialism 170, 183
personal identity
  body 38
  memory 40
  simple 41
principle of sufficient reason

211-2
poetry 1
Pruss, Alexander
   Powers 180
pure dualism
   mixed property 34
   haecceity/primitive mental
   thisness 128-9, 131, 155, 164,
   172
   problem for non-
   Cartesianism 137

reductionism 28, 107-9
religious argument
   monism 47-50
   dualism 47-50
replacement argument 54, 189
Robinson, Howard 5

self-presenting properties 62,
   73, 77
Schwartz, Jeffrey 55
simplicity (i.e., scientific)
   Ockham's razor 155, 174
souls
   relational (i.e., generic) 71,
   218
   kind 72
   hybrid 72
   theology/transcendence 49,
   51, 106, 220, 236, 240

subjective appearances 59, 168
sui-generis 35,36, 65, 100, 120,
   123, 218, 273
Swinburne, Richard 34, 68, 69,
   70, 142, 176, 216, 229

Taliaferro, Charles xiv, 3, 5,
   189, 201, 223, 224
Thomism 187-90, 220
transparency
   Brentano 72
   fundamental feature 72
   tradition 72
   first-person 72-6
   character 74

unity of consciousness
   phenomenality, qualia
   63-6
   subsumptive 64
   items unified 133-4
   'I' 122
unity of agent/subject
   phenomenal subject 64, 66,
   122, 134,
   grounding 121
   ownership 121
   individuation of thought 37,
   42, 129, 156, 166, 170

zombie argument 29

Recent bestsellers from Iff Books are:

Why Materialism Is Baloney
How true skeptics know there is no death and fathom answers
to life, the universe, and everything
Bernardo Kastrup
A hard-nosed, logical, and skeptic non-materialist metaphysics,
according to which the body is in mind, not mind in the body.
Paperback: 978-1-78279-362-5 ebook: 978-1-78279-361-8

The Fall
Steve Taylor
The Fall discusses human achievement versus the issues of war,
patriarchy and social inequality.
Paperback: 978-1-78535-804-3 ebook: 978-1-78535-805-0

Brief Peeks Beyond
Critical essays on metaphysics, neuroscience, free will,
skepticism and culture
Bernardo Kastrup
An incisive, original, compelling alternative to current mainstream
cultural views and assumptions.
Paperback: 978-1-78535-018-4 ebook: 978-1-78535-019-1

Framespotting
Changing how you look at things changes how
you see them
Laurence & Alison Matthews
A punchy, upbeat guide to framespotting. Spot deceptions and
hidden assumptions; swap growth for growing up. See and be free.
Paperback: 978-1-78279-689-3 ebook: 978-1-78279-822-4

The Vagabond Spirit of Poetry
Edward Clarke
Spend time with the wisest poets of the modern age and of the past, and let Edward Clarke remind you of the importance of poetry in our industrialized world.
Paperback: 978-1-78279-370-0 ebook: 978-1-78279-369-4

Readers of ebooks can buy or view any of these bestsellers by clicking on the live link in the title. Most titles are published in paperback and as an ebook. Paperbacks are available in traditional bookshops. Both print and ebook formats are available online. Find more titles and sign up to our readers' newsletter at
http://www.johnhuntpublishing.com/non-fiction
Follow us on Facebook at
https://www.facebook.com/JHPNonFiction
and Twitter at https://twitter.com/JHPNonFiction